An outstanding account of different kinds of hauntings... A young man haunted by the spirit of an old woman... An older writer haunted by the past... A strange story of encouragement, youth and age... An inspiring, inevitably controversial record of a ten-year friendship and the lifelong pursuit of the impossible...

Alexis Lykiard, well known as a poet, novelist and translator, was a friend of Jean Rhys during her last decade. His affection for her and her work illuminates this exceptional book. Lykiard's wide range, proven critical and creative abilities and sympathetic insights, make him a uniquely well-qualified chronicler of the literary life in general and Jean Rhys's life and works in particular. Lykiard accurately and wittily details the highs and lows, the solitude and solidarity of the freelance world – with no punches pulled. There is too an unexpectedly moving conclusion to this original, intimate and beautifully written book.

'The Jean you knew, and describe so vividly, was the Jean *I* knew – our personal experiences of her are almost identical. I also think that you are one of the few critics who really understand her quality and praise her for the right reasons. The book is a fascinating meditation on all kinds of themes, refracted through Jean's sensibility and your own...'
     – Francis Wyndham

Alexis Lykiard was born in Athens, 1940. Having survived the German Occupation, his family fled to Egypt at the start of the Greek Civil War, eventually settling in the UK in 1946. Lykiard learned English at six, and in 1957 won the first Open English Scholarship awarded by King's College, Cambridge. At University he edited *Granta* and published his first poetry collection, graduating with First Class Honours. Since 1962 a freelance writer and editor, he now has over fifty books to his credit. These include novels, poetry, and translations from the French. Based in Devon since 1970, Alexis Lykiard lives with his second wife in Exeter.

Jean Rhys (1890-1979) is now internationally recognized as one of the finest writers of the Twentieth Century. She was the author of *The Left Bank* (1927), *Quartet* (1928), *After Leaving Mr Mackenzie* (1930), *Voyage In The Dark* (1934), *Good Morning Midnight* (1939), *Wide Sargasso Sea* (1966), *Tigers Are Better Looking* (1968), *Sleep It Off Lady* (1976) and *Smile Please* (1979). Her *Letters 1931-1966* were published in 1984.

Jean Rhys Revisited

– Stride –

Also by Alexis Lykiard

Novels
The Summer Ghosts
Zones
A Sleeping Partner
Strange Alphabet
The Stump
Instrument Of Pleasure
The Drive North
Last Throes
Scrubbers

Poetry
Journey Of The Alchemist
Paros Poems
Robe Of Skin
Greek Images
Milesian Fables
Out Of Exile
Cat Kin
Safe Levels
Living Jazz
Beautiful Is Enough
Omnibus Occasions
Selected Poems 1956-96

Translation
Maldoror & Complete Works (Lautréamont)
Days And Nights (Jarry)
Two Novels (Apollinaire)
Surrealist Games (Breton, Eluard, etc)

Editor
Wholly Communion
Best Ghost Stories Of Sheridan LeFanu
The Horror-Horn: Best Stories Of E.F. Benson
New Stories 2 (Arts Council)
Beat Dreams And Plymouth Sounds
Out Of The Wood: Prison Writings
The Cool Eye: Conversations With Lawrence Ferlinghetti

Jean Rhys Revisited

Alexis Lykiard

JEAN RHYS REVISITED
First edition 2000
© Alexis Lykiard
All rights reserved

ISBN 1 900152 68 1

Cover design by Neil Annat

Published by
Stride Publications
11 Sylvan Road, Exeter
Devon EX4 6EW

Contents

I know I'm on my way to old age but that doesn't stop me planning work in the literary field far ahead. Why not? There's plenty I want to work at. I don't mean that I want to hurry up and finish this or that before I croak, not that. I mean only that I want to push on into improved work and make myself a better writer.

> – William Carlos Williams,
> letter to Robert McAlmon, 1943

It is by style we are saved.

> – Henry James, to E.F.Benson

Ends and beginnings

When I began this lengthy, gradual process of invocation – starting to summon up memories with a view to reordering them into the personal mosaic which follows – a title flickered unbidden across my mind. It was not one of her own, but belonged to a marvellous book by the still little read novelist David Lindsay: *The Haunted Woman.* Lindsay was a fitfully poetic, musically resonant writer whose evocative phrase appeared to sum up something of lively importance about Jean Rhys.

Jean herself seemed haunted by her own ghosts, her past, just as everybody must be who is fated to live an unusually long life: there is such loneliness in outliving one's peers. Great age can also be the cruellest curse to an artist who retains her keenest faculties of mind and vision. No one remains to understand; there are so few left with whom to communicate. And yet you go on writing. She went on writing. It was as if she had been spared for that purpose and the act itself might save her. Who, otherwise, would choose to linger on in the cold climate of a world so changed, so physically diminished of late? Yet she went on in the newer, more menacing world in which it was all too easy to feel like an unwanted guest. She believed that there could be some point, if not salvation, in continuance, only (as she put it) through earning one's death.

In 1969 when I met her, Jean Rhys was 79 and I was 29. The half-century that lay between us, that entire bygone age, would vanish when I visited her. As for that vanished world she herself clearly recalled, it used to be mentioned from time to time, but mainly we talked about the present. And about writing. For me as a young author, Jean was an example and an inspiration. I'm sure she'd smile now, to think she still is. However, she has returned, in a sense. I re-encounter her here within the pages that follow, which she's inspired. Thus perhaps I may repay what I've come to realise is a strange sort of spiritual debt owed to her wholly beneficent presence.

•

"Thank you for *The Summer Ghosts,*" Jean wrote in July 1969. "Before I read it I thought what a good title!" This was my first novel, written in my teens. I'd hesitated to send it her: more than a decade had gone by since its writing. The book already seemed to me like juvenilia. I was of course in awe of her own talent. She went on: "For I think the long summer evenings can be ghostly – far more so than winter. Especially if it's hot & one's alone. (This is a very silent place.)"

She added: "I'm reading your book for the second time & liking it." But I needn't have worried about her reactions to this early work. Later on when we met, she generously confirmed that she had indeed enjoyed the book. I think she recognized the novel's desperate sincerity – which by then I tended to dismiss as naive – and its raw account of mental disturbance. Maybe too she liked the love-story-gone-wrong element, its romantic, young man's view of Death-and-the-Maiden. At any rate, she said the book appealed to her and she thought that I'd caught on the page a few of those fleeting illusions, our titular ghosts, which appear so real at the time but fade so fast. Here lie the fugitive phantoms of fleshly pleasure!

Her response was gratifying, for I soon realised that where writing was concerned, Jean was invariably forthright, never diplomatic, and she always told the truth. For this reason I miss her most, perhaps, although her presence remains real to me. She died in 1979, a year when I'd returned to Greece. I'd not seen her for some time, nor had there been an opportunity to say goodbye. In one sense or another, she has haunted me ever since.

She and I both knew, however, that the day would come when I should write about her. We'd even discussed the possibility and she seemed happy with that prospect. This book is in a way unfinished business. It has proved, too, a difficult pleasure, not without sadness. I am reminded of her whenever I sit down and start to write.

Just now for instance, I reflect how, living in this city, I can hear nonetheless the sound of a small stream running by the side of our house. There'd also been a river long ago, beside the Irish cottage where I'd escaped to write: that was when I first made contact by letter with Jean. Finally I remember 'The Sound Of The River', her own chilling story about death. There, it seemed she had to exorcise the horror of her husband's sudden death during the night. And so she wrote from herself, out of herself, outside and beyond herself.

There are rivers of living voices that rush past and demand to be heard, and yet this endless flow makes us feel afraid, as if we only lived within the deathly silence of the page. Being a writer, moreover, means one must appear cold and selfish in many ways. But such superficial tactics are often adopted to protect that inmost spark which warms all else – a generosity of the spirit. Most writers may well feel as I do, that there's no end and they themselves are always only just beginning. Where I'm concerned, I've been fortunate, I've managed to keep on and keep going. For me Jean has shown herself (reverting to that wonderful French word) a truly helpful *revenant*. She comes back...*Thus* (in Ford's reminiscing title) *to revisit.*

I look forward in this book to remembering various of my own visits to Jean. I'm also taking time to look back, in loving admiration. Here I shall wave to her once more, in order to make my farewell, so long delayed. Something at last to offer, by way of greeting to that never immaterial, friendly shade.

Identities and names

She was "care of Mrs Hamer", when the young writer first wrote to her in the late Sixties, which were his own late twenties. His agent had passed on the old lady's address as requested, but it was all so beautifully misleading. Ella Gwendoline Rees Williams had been left behind long since, like her distant place of origin. 'Ella Gray' her stage name in the chorus had disappeared with World War One. By her first marriage she became Lenglet, but in the Twenties her lover and mentor Ford Madox Ford (who'd changed his own name from F.H. Hueffer) promptly reinvented hers too. Given that new name, her true name, the writing name she grew into and made shine, she wrote Ford into her first novel *Postures* (itself later called *Quartet*) as "H.J.Heidler". She herself was then rechristened "Lola Porter" in Ford's own version of their relationship, his 1931 novel *When The Wicked Man.* The third participant, spectator and artist involved in this relationship was Stella Bowen, with whom Ford lived. Bowen, however, in *her* book *Drawn From Life* (1941), did not accord the interloper as many pages: a further gift – undue space – would have been an acknowledgement of importance, of continuing significance. The Australian painter and memoirist Bowen, like the others self-exiled and consequently also vulnerable, therefore refused to call her by any name at all. She is referred to with lofty condescension as "a very pretty and gifted young woman" and thereafter as "a really tragic person", "a doomed soul, violent and demoralised".

So what's in a name? For a writer, it bears weight, taking on considerable importance. It seems as if the new name assumed is a very private and particular code or password, its resonance opening the way for some necessary though at first obscure initiation rite. This new name or pseudonym is going to indicate the real you; it will concisely express what you turn yourself into, that which you become. By no means is it simply a convenient brand name, nor one partly belonging to somebody else. Nothing either, to do with legal requirements and matters official or public. At first the half-deliberate, half-accidental acquisition – this magic of a name – may seem alien, ghostly alter ego only. But the chosen talisman has its own knowing way of being worn, and the individual it rightly fits and ever after designates will, through that form of words, inhabit space and populate the blank page. The mysterious cabbalistic combination of letters and sounds which over a lifetime may reveal its hidden pattern – whatever complex Jamesian figure may be discerned in the weave of the carpet – is at once persona, summary and riddle. Or in more banal terms just something whereby you may be reached, addressed.

Hers had a perfect balance, I used to think. Two short groups of four letters each. The paired long '*e*' sounds, written deceptively, of course. The way that, to pronounce her name, you had to shape the lips as if considering a kiss. The name suggested to me then elements of both male and female, Frenchness and Welshness, the everyday and the exotic. Now, writing this, I repeat those two foreign but familiar words aloud, and can fancy that they call up her own very distinctive mewing intonation. For her voice indeed possessed a softly feline sound, ingratiating yet isolate.

Jean Rhys, c/o Mrs Hamer, I had written, therefore. Today it strikes me as odd that the form of address I'd been given, and used in error, correctly implied both her solitary integrity and her abiding need to be looked after, befriended, taken in hand, taken care of. She herself, it later became clear to me, was Mrs Hamer. Hamer had been her third husband's name, and he had died in 1966. So my initial contact seems to have involved someone curiously displaced, at several removes from the person she really was. Someone struggling to take care of herself (after several problem-fraught marriages and widowhood); someone trying to take herself in hand and shed the Mrs-Hamer-domesticity, no longer by mere survival but at last protectively putting the writer-self first.

Origins

What object? The non-poetic statement of a poetic truth.
  – Elizabeth Bowen: *Notes On Writing A Novel*, 1945.

I'd known very few novelists, prior to Jean: a handful of contemporaries, one or two older than myself. Even fewer did I write to or ever become friendly with. We're all too jealous, jealous of our privacy too, and solitary creatures at that. So the mere idea of writing any kind of fan letter to another writer would have induced, on my part, a corrective bout of the dread English disease of hyper-reticence. It never occurred to me that the recipient of an appreciative letter always appreciates its receipt. Nor that writers more than most people are often in certain regards excruciatingly lonely and frequently morose (if not depressed), no matter how successful, preoccupied or self-sufficient they may appear. Such loneliness is inevitable, it's inherent in the nature of the artistic procedure itself. (I except here journalism or other 'sociable' or more collective forms, like screen- or scriptwriting, or the drama.)

Yet what had I myself done, that autumn of 1968, but seek out and explore that same loneliness, making my escape from the metropolis and its manifold attractions that proved distractions? I took the decision to hole out somewhere well away from London, so as to complete a novel-in-progress, and the choice of Irish rural isolation could not, looking back, have been more extreme...

Jean reached me in my solitude, then. The only reading I took with me to my self-imposed exile was several of her books. I'd bought them in a batch, out of curiosity: their author knew her Paris, and men, and drink, all of which was fine with me. Her books belonged, so I thought, to times very far removed from mine. That fact alone ensured that they could provide the escapist reading I required during the interval of my own escape; they were bound to be different enough from anything I was trying to write, and to afford contrast and relaxation. (Following the huge and deserved success of *Wide Sargasso Sea* in the autumn of 1966, André Deutsch had been reissuing these pre-war novels and short stories as hardbacks in handsome, appropriately pictorial jackets.) The contents, to my delight, outdid the fine production: I discovered exquisitely colourful and vividly delineated narratives, sensitive, bold but absolutely precise.

Such honest, unsparing work moved, consoled and gripped me: it opened various possibilities of writing about oneself, or projections of the self, without posturing or sentimentality. The books weren't period pieces, they were admirably economical, daring still. And by a mysterious alchemy, no matter how bleak their subject matter, the final and lingering effect was affirmative, revelatory. Curiously enough a very different, very English author, Gissing, has something of the same feel, a reckless tenderness of spirit opposed to all that is ugly, unjust or mean; he shares, too, the unexpected flashes of grim humour. But of course, this underrated precursor is more hurried, Victorian-verbose, and clumsier than Jean in her own compact, better-balanced prose. I later found she had read, and admired, *New Grub Street* as much as I did.

I felt that just like her, and whether successful or disregarded, I should never find a safe niche or cosy haven within the English way of life. Our respective backgrounds, while utterly dissimilar, ensured a perpetual spiritual displacement, a troublesome sense of unease buried under the surface but liable to assume a host of forms. These presences which might stir themselves to haunt you, could leave you more or less mesmerised, drained and suffering from an extreme enervation, an oddly desperate lassitude. Jean used to refer to such depressive spells as *le cafard*, or 'having the blues'.

What are these moods? Something akin to the apt Ferlinghetti title, *Unfair arguments with existence?* Anyhow it's an angst not at all English; one indeed un-British, at that. The ache of the unsettled ego. The immigrant's inner struggle, reflecting a constant external one, is the writer's also: that disorientation, the sense of not-belonging-anywhere, the nonsensical process whereby words slip away elusively and never quite say what you want them to. Of saying things you doubt will be exactly welcome, and which may be unacceptable: not-at-home truths. Outsiders looking in, yet having to stay outside, out in the cold, unaccepted. Those too proud to accept injustice or condescension from others, but defiant to the end. So: *Let them call it jazz*. As in Jean's story... And her longer story – her life – itself recalled and seemed always distilled in the title of her personal favourite among all her books, *Voyage In The Dark*.

My own life, my writing life, has been illuminated through knowing her.

The fragment that follows represents a fraction of it, half a year living in the mountains, spent trying to write my novel and reading only hers. And when reading her books, for relaxation supposedly, I found myself absorbed, held spellbound. All this was the necessary background, just before I wrote to her, before I came to know her. I don't think I ever showed Jean the

Story behind the story

as I entitled the piece, although I'm sure she'd have appreciated its sentiments. My attempt to recollect in relative tranquillity a gone and genuinely anguished time was, it's clear to me, vital for my survival. I see it now for yet another, albeit voluntary, displacement while struggling to understand – and deliver, the further burden of a book. A poor sort of reward, stolen from procrastination, Young's "thief of time". Still, Jean I think might also have smiled at my fugitive article's opening sentence, which begins once again, and as ever, with *reading*...

– Reading a biography of the much-maligned Ford Madox Ford, it occurred to me that while most people gain from literary biographies insight into the occupational hazards of authorship – those hilarious or tragic quarrels and *contretemps* with a predictable cast including publishers, agents, lovers, admirers and critics – very few of an author's own friends, let alone readers, can ever get to know the day-to-day story behind the story, the unwritten life hovering in the background of every completed book.

Writers often go to understandable lengths to preserve their privacy: unfortunately the desire for hermit-like working conditions is rarely respected and even a Traven is tracked down. But Ford, generous and gregarious almost to a fault, was a compulsive mythologist who reinvented his past until no one knew what to believe. Perhaps he had reflected that telling the literal truth is difficult, dull, not always to one's credit or advantage. The messy incongruity of life – those ironies, loose ends, coincidences, half-finished conversations – is as hard to depict convincingly as the times when little is happening and whole months speed past, swallowed up by the relentless routine of writing a novel. Now and again however, in search of the elusive story behind the story, it's worth a try...

Late in 1967 I returned from a protracted stay in Greece with less than half of an untitled novel (eventually my fourth, *Strange Alphabet*) and a mass of impressions, notes and news clips. Unable to remain in my country of birth any longer because of the deplorable political situation, I needed to breathe freely outside the actual claustrophobic atmosphere I was trying to describe.

For the next six months in London I struggled to shape the material into some sort of coherent form. Concerned about how best to make an urgent moral and political comment, I realised it might be wiser once again to distance myself, both physically and mentally; this would enable me to avoid the novelistic pitfalls of preaching and polemic. London, though, was too turbulent and noisy a place in which to attempt a fiction that could objectively portray the recent distressing realities of life in a country raped by military dictatorship.

In the past I'd been obliged to take temporary jobs unconnected with writing, only to find that far from buying time they merely consumed it, eroding both one's energy and the desire to write. So I decided to gamble. Answering a newspaper advertisement, I calculated on allowing myself exactly six months to finish the book. (Not having received any advance for a novel-in-progress, six frugal months was as long as I guessed my slim resources would last.) Soon I was renting a small cottage in the Wicklow Mountains. I'd never been to the Irish Republic, but had heard it was cheap, peaceful and a century behind the times. Northern Ireland, of course, was just then a dormant volcano, but it was the South's independence and continuing neutrality that appealed to me as a practical and welcome change.

A Dubliner, intending to use the cottage as a summer retreat, had bought it for a few hundred pounds from a local farmer. With its corrugated iron roof, its huddle of old sheds, and a dilapidated stone boundary wall which didn't entirely screen a sizeable rubbish tip at one end of the property, the cottage could hardly be termed attractive. But by English standards it was cheap (£25 per month), it had a sheltered back garden fringed by pines and hawthorns, and the surrounding landscape was breathtaking. Heather- and gorse-covered marshy slopes rising gradually then steeply up the mountainside. A young pine forest. A winding brook splashing past only six foot below one wall. In the distance more mountains and the Wicklow Gap. Some secluded farms, their cattle small as pebbles...

After the landlord drove away down the solitary road – a twisting, rutted cart-track – I began to comprehend how isolated was the motorless tenant at the end of this valley. Eight miles from the nearest village and shops, five from a telephone. I relied absolutely on an all-purpose grocery van calling once a week: its imperturbable owner-driver delivered anything from the *Irish Times* to meat, cakes, cotton-reels or gas cylinders. (These last for the two-ring ovenless cooker: my cuisine was necessarily simple.) Vegetables, milk and bread I obtained from my neighbours at the closest farm half a mile off. Armed with a stick I would walk to the nearest letterbox – a two-mile trek across fields inhabited by frisky bullocks which charged without warning. Correspondence, like ambulation, diminished accordingly. Besides, for the first couple of months I walked and worked little, finding the air at several thousand feet above sea-level deceptive, inducing lethargy and a curious sense of physical and mental dehydration.

Before long the autumnal weather turned colder and the evenings rapidly darkened. Peat burned in the andiron-flanked fireplace. The (summer) cottage had stone floors: I soon discovered it was also full of draughts. Most I managed to eliminate by wadding with newspaper loose window-frames, one disused chimney and various wall interstices. I festooned cracked windowpanes with insulating tape and fixed a blanket across the front door. I hoped that the damp patches on the walls would dry out, but they were to outlast my stay. By February I dreaded sleeping in the narrow bunk bed which remained arctic despite water-bottles and assorted (simultaneous) nightwear of pyjamas, woollen combinations, two pairs of socks, a sweater and gloves.

When the frost made shaving too grim I grew a beard and avoided the shower – there was no bath – leaving it with some relief to the spiders which appeared to thrive there more than I did. Warmth, I decided after a bout of bronchitis, was preferable to cleanliness. The next irritations were, inevitably, fleas caught I imagine from a scavenging sheepdog I sporadically fed, and bites inflicted by angry clouds of hibernating marsh mosquitoes roused by my diurnal visits to the peat-shed.

Rain and wind yielded to snow. I acquired a suitably Hibernian affliction, rheumatism, and typing was only bearable wearing gloves whose ends I'd cut off, and seated in the very alcove of the fire. By way of encouragement I was surrounded by wall-posters optimistically exhorting me to *Smash Fascism in Greece!* or *Visit the Greek Islands*. "Sweat-soaked, he had unbuttoned his shirt,"

I wrote wistfully. "Waves of heat-haze wavered ahead and the limpid water that sucked at his ankles looked welcoming."

For two weeks the valley was snowbound. Gumboot trudges through thick drifts to the farm. The cottage invaded by grateful mice, gnawing any food left uncovered. These mice grew so bold that they would scurry past my chair each evening, hop over my notes, or jump suddenly out of drawers. There were minor domestic disasters: my last batch of coffeebeans got damp and mouldered; a black pudding, when sliced, writhed with maggots. Meanwhile in London some maggot conman had been up to tricks: as a result I received the bill from a Mayfair shop quite unknown to me. And electricity cuts due to storms and collapsed cables meant working by candlelight which in turn and worst of all led to eyestrain.

By way of entertainment there was one of the heaviest, most antiquated radios I have ever seen, a true 'wireless' which sputtered and crackled an obligato to the fire. It was possible to locate late-night jazz programmes on this machine, and between powercuts I would listen to the likes of Willis Conover.

One night during a set of Clifford Brown tracks I found myself dwelling somewhat morbidly on promising musical careers cut short. Two days later I received a telegram. One of my best friends, the outstanding young British bassist John Hart, was dead. The previous week he'd written promising to visit, as he had done when I was in Greece. First, however, there were some sessions to complete with the Albert Mangelsdorff-Philly Joe Jones band, in France... Now, like Brown, and in his mid-twenties also, he too was killed in a car crash.

I didn't have the money or the time to get to the funeral. Shock and cold seemed to have numbed my emotions. The book had reached a crucial stage and I kept going with the momentum I'd so far achieved, doggedly hoping the writing would lead somewhere, out of nothingness, would manage to express just how precarious and precious life was. I learned painfully, as all writers do, that everything one experiences must be absorbed, recycled, imaginatively transformed; that a finished book is both stasis and flux, both fixed 'artificial' pattern and perpetual living flow; and that the writer's own circumstances should never intrude upon or influence the work in progress.

The cold continued ferocious. I became more objective, gradually shaking off the constant images of death, such as the local monument visible on top of a ridge, commemorating an escaped political prisoner who had died nearby during 'the troubles' – of exposure. That I could well believe, but turned my attention instead to a water-pump that kept icing solid. Constant journeys, therefore, to the stream. "A stream, I name not its name" as Clough once lightly wrote of another Celtic tributary, "lest inquisitive tourists/ Hunt it, and make it a lion, and get it at last into guide-books". The stream prompted my own entry in *Milesian Fables*, the poetry-journal I kept of those months (and which I later gave Jean):

Freeze

The river's skin
is ice five inches
thick.
This I hack.
Pail's filled
painfully,
with care
from the cracked
floe.
Water flowing
seems as rare
a thing as sun
or warm air.

Somehow the book's first draft was finished. By then I'd run out of typing paper, and the van-man agreed to drive me to Dublin. Where I encountered, of all things, a paper strike. I replenished my vital coffee supply, and with relief bought a scarce ream of bile-green fibrous material neither foolscap nor quarto. And returned to revise and retype. There was a brief week or so of spring before I was back in London, exhausted and broke.

After two years' work in three countries I discovered that my erstwhile publisher, who knew as they all do that beggars can't be choosers and time is on the publisher's not the author's side, had beaten down my erstwhile agent's modest request for £750. I was offered £500, which I was by then tired and hungry enough to accept. I came to understand why even a Raymond Chandler could write: "One of my few remaining ambitions is to make publishers lose money." These days [my twenties then, my nearing sixties now] I prefer as a professional writer to be consoled by that arch-professional Thomas Nashe. Nashe, who averred in his aptly-named *Pierce Pennilesse*: "'Poverty instructs a man in all arts', it makes a man hardy and venturous, and therefore it is called of the poet *Paupertas audax*, 'valiant poverty'".

Some things don't change in 400 years. Still more appropriate though, since one never can express the inner processes, the truer, hidden stories of the soul, is Rilke's observation: "Remember that we lived for an instant (or a long time, who can say?) in a space quite different from that of reality (properly so-called)..." To me Ireland and Greece alike were full of sadness and joy, the two really indescribable extremes which fiction should try to reconcile and describe.

Dreams and extremes

Jean did achieve that. She knew those extremes, knew also how dreams could be broken and betrayed, or else learned from and used. She knew her Thomas Wolfe, and could herself have told me "You can't go home again"; home for writers is not necessarily where the heart is, but rather in the head.

I returned to that foreign country for the first time at 27, for the first time since my departure aged 5. Being in Greece felt like entering a dream: initial bewilderment, then acceptance of its strangeness, after which a rapid acclimatisation accompanied by the loss of any sense of time... Above all, in that country of dreams and in every dream-world, the dreamer experiences a heady, developing curiosity, as when one is presented with an unexpected gift – this turns into a rare and overwhelming pleasure.

But I should have known that paradise is paradox, it only seems to exist, and any Eden is always taken away. For me it lasted about three weeks. Then came the military coup of 21 April 1967 and Greece was lost, a prison for the next seven years. I lived there anyhow for much of that first year of dictatorship, a depressed and reluctant witness to the changes in what I could and could not recognize as my motherland. *Strange Alphabet*, the novel I'd begun changed along with me, taking on an unforeseen political dimension. Finally I realised I would have to leave Greece once again. For a while. For as long as it took. Most likely for good.

So back to England, then on to Ireland. That novel had to get written somehow, and nothing else mattered. The very words at the start of *this* book, those I recently wrote about Jean, applied also to myself then: my cumbersome original set of names no longer referred to or signified me. They *had been left behind long since, like my distant place of origin.* The only dream of Greece I had left was one I alone could realize. Once again the book weighed me down as it grew; it became an obsession which made me desperate and wretched. It felt as I imagine an unwanted pregnancy must, a frightening obligation, burden rather than fulfilment, but something which needs, in every sense, to be seen through.

When Jean's *Selected Letters* were published in 1984, five years after her death, I was moved to locate and read what was given as the concluding letter in that book. This particular text she'd once mentioned to me. The letter, written just after the death of her third husband, Max Hamer, was addressed to Jean's editor in March 1966:

> I've dreamt several times that I was going to have a baby – then I awoke with relief.
>
> Finally I dreamt that I was looking at the baby in a cradle – such a puny weak thing.
>
> So the book must be finished, and that must be what I think about it really. I don't dream about it any more.

The book was *Wide Sargasso Sea,* and Jean Rhys, aged 76, had thirteen further years to live. She certainly couldn't have dreamed of the success her book was to have. Jean was such a perfectionist that, deep down, she didn't believe a final draft could ever be final; everything, consequently, was subject to doubt, as to improvement. That was why it was always hard to let go of what was brought forth with such struggle and pain.

Yet dreams do help. Dreaming is consolation, advice and itself a creative process, a parallel form of creation. The dream is indeed "one of our roads into the infinite", because "in our dreams the fetters of civilisation are loosened, and we know the fearful joy of freedom". That was how Havelock Ellis described the process, in his 1911 book *The World Of Dreams*. Possibly Jean had read it: I'm sure she would have agreed with Ellis's description. She might even have joked at my own expense – on finding there "that the Greeks, who were such great myth-makers, much occupied themselves in lying in wait for dreams." That particular joke was certainly destined to be on me... But it's another story and one that comes later. As in due course, to borrow the good old omniscient narrator phrases, I shall relate.

Her and not her

Certain North Africans... refuse to allow themselves to be photographed because they believe that in this way a part of their soul is taken from them... Are the North Africans so wrong?
— Simenon: *When I Was Old*, 1970

There is a ten-by-eight inch black and white photograph just beside my desk. I don't know who took this, but it seems to reveal more than it flatters.

She is seated in a flower-patterned armchair. Her head is tilted back and her expression is a mixture of sadness and defiance. This close-up shows her staring off towards the far right of the frame, away from the lens itself, as if the camera does not exist — or rather, as if she is reluctant to acknowledge that initial intrusion and will offer camera and image-maker no easy options.

The left half of her face is in shadow, but the deep vertical lines from the corners of her lips down to her chin are clearly incised, are continued and paralleled by the corded, wrinkled flesh of her neck as it stands out, tense. There are pronounced lines also on her forehead, though these are horizontal.

Smile Please! But its author was not willing to embody her last book's title. Her lips are slightly parted and she remains unsmiling. There in her room, and now here in mine, she stays proud yet distant and wistful. She sits upright, the base of her throat covered by pale (cream?) scarf, her shoulders wrapped in a jacket which appears somewhat too large for her. A sense, then, of awkward vulnerability, enhanced by the wig she is wearing (one I'd not seen before), and that serves to underline the poignancy of the whole composition.

When she first showed me the photo, I perhaps tactlessly exclaimed: "It makes you look like Ivy Compton-Burnett!" My hasty remark had probably been prompted by the shape of the wig: the woman in this close-up portrait didn't immediately resemble Jean. But then, I'd only ever seen one photograph of Compton-Burnett, whose work I find unreadable. Compton-Burnett's arid, aristocratic artifice never appealed to me, nor to anyone I knew, apart from — curiously — one very dear maiden aunt. (That lady could read, too, the novels of Meredith, William Morris and Charles Morgan — all to me continuously impenetrable.) Jean "couldn't be doing with" I.C-B either, it transpired. We laughed at that. Jean was no *grande dame* herself, and her experiences were wider, rawer and very different; neither her upper lip nor her style were ever stiff.

So much for the formal pose – as all too often in her latter days, it was by no means entirely of her own choosing.

Today as ever the photograph brings back a happy memory of my old friend. She sits there aloft, suspended on white wall at one side of my desk, a picture of comfort and inspiration. Whenever I look at Jean, so indomitable if invariably insecure, she makes *me* smile, no matter what. Under this 'unlike' likeness, which she herself liked and wanted me to have, she has written a few words in her familiar and unmistakable script. Black ballpoint laboriously and painfully inscribing its distinctive pattern...

The eye travels down from the monochrome features of her face, is drawn to the blackness on the photo's wide white lower border, to where the writing is. Slow strokes, since twisted knuckles and fingers in the end made even harder work of the hard work of words. Never lose grip, the words say; never give up, say those large, bold-looped letters of hers; find yourself, say the aching, shakingly firm characters. And here can be read what they say with a private smile:

For Alexis. Not Ivy Compton-Burnett. Jean.

CVs and Refs.

Jean Rhys in the last decade of her life was increasingly dependent on, and grateful for, secretarial help. Her publishers did arrange for her to receive such assistance: it was after all in their own interests as well as hers. But I see from a letter she wrote to us – addressed actually to Diane, who'd offered her services as an expert typist – that Jean was then in some disarray. It's the end of July 1970, and Jean has "had rather a crowded time". She must have been relieved to know she could also call on us as friends to help her out, and on a rather more relaxed and informal basis.

"Well here is a potted autobiography. Don't bother to do 100 copies. Twenty will be ample – when you've time & it'll be an enormous help". The short piece Jean enclosed is I think of interest, for in it she herself summarizes the main landmarks in her writing life. I don't recall, nor did Jean tell us, whether she'd been prompted to write it on reaching eighty. It seems most unlikely given her usual reticence about her precise age that she should want to celebrate or give any emphasis to that most recent milestone. So one concludes it was intended as the basis for some publicity blurb and had been compiled at her agent's or publishers' request.

> I was born in Roseau Dominica West Indies & educated at the convent in Roseau till I was sixteen when my father sent me to school in England. But I wrote & asked him if I could go to RADA. He agreed. But when I'd been at the Academy for one term he died suddenly & as I did not wish to go back to the West Indies I got a job in the chorus of a musical comedy on tour.
>
> After the end of the 14-18 war I left England to marry a man I had met in 1917. I stayed in Europe for about ten years mostly in Paris but we also lived in Vienna & Budapest for two years.
>
> Later on in Paris I was encouraged to write short stories by Ford Madox Ford. When I finished my first long novel I was advised to take it to London & try to sell it. I did so though I was very unwilling to go back to England & returned to Paris whenever I could raise the money. I was divorced & married again & wrote four novels during the thirties.

After the second war 39-45 I did not write again for some time then I published several short stories in the *London Voices* etc.

It was after an adaptation of 'Good Morning Midnight', my last work (1939) by Selma Vaz Dias that I wrote *Wide Sargasso Sea*. I am now trying to work on an autobiography.

The reference in the penultimate paragraph baffled me for a while. Then I realised Jean had conflated the *London Magazine* (which had published four of Jean's best stories between 1960 and 1962) with *Voices* (an anthology of stories by different authors, including Jean's 'A Solid House') published in London by Michael Joseph in 1963. I don't remember whether this point was queried or clarified, or that any of Jean's idiosyncratic punctuation was questioned, but she was anyhow pleased with the results, whatever the destination of the copies.

Probably it was more important to her now not to feel lonely, knowing she could count on a wide range of friends for support. Hers was a dogged and difficult achievement, keeping going as she did, writing till the end, and (as she herself intimated) *for* the end – in order to earn that final, most personal release, the ultimate full stop. There would be two more books from Jean Rhys in her last decade, the 1970s: a wonderful story collection *Sleep It Off Lady* (1976) and the unfinished yet fascinating autobiography she mentions "trying to work on", *Smile Please*, published soon after her death in 1979.

Her example was an encouragement to any serious writer. Jean Rhys had outrun and outlasted fashion; she had endured, and would, and does. But like all of us, at times she found life itself hard going. Often her frail health and sense of isolation, both exacerbated by extreme age, depressed her profoundly. Day to day living in "darkest Devon" became hard to bear. Beside me is a letter from January 1970 in which she complains of persisting 'flu and freezing temperatures and worries about the likelihood of burst pipes. At the same time, our recent visit had "prevented Christmas from being rather dismal", and she could write: "I wish your book [my fourth novel, *Strange Alphabet*] much luck & long understanding reviews. I'll think of you on the 15th [publication day]". How sweet-natured Jean could be, Diane and I used to marvel, despite the swarms of real (and sometimes imagined) vexations surrounding her. This letter ends: "A note enclosed for Diane. The road gets rougher, It's lonelier and tougher." Jean here is quoting Ira Gershwin's lyrics to the Harold Arlen song, *The Man*

That Got Away. This, we'd all agreed, was a classic, and the highspot of the film *A Star Is Born.* Judy Garland's delivery of it unforgettably summed up the predicament of the woman as attractive as she is intelligent, and yet her sheer resilience and energy seemed to banish the awful worldweariness engendered in every survivor of the struggle. What wit and sparkle in that few minutes, put across without self-pity! An ideal, exemplary sequence, wherein words, music, images and performance were suddenly and perfectly matched, to become what one best remembers, turning a generally good movie into a genuinely moving picture...

Like Garland, Jean found that fame made few who attained it any happier. In her own case it brought her some material comforts, however belated, and financial stability at last. But she never forgot her early days of hardship, nor indeed how difficult it can be for a young writer confronting jealousy (both sexual and artistic) and obstacles (poverty and shyness). Such confrontations, obvious or not, always exist. Some writers learn to play the system, others evolve a particular formula to which they adhere, or they cultivate the right people and make the right moves: such folk will inevitably be successful. As for myself, I was and have remained an outsider on the British literary scene: this seemed inevitable since, like Jean, I wasn't born and bred here and have generally steered clear of Hampstead. All too often, then, I've had to scuffle along to make even a meagre living.

This meant taking other work, temporary jobs when the need arose. In spring 1974, for instance, I applied for a Writer in Residence post at a northern University. It ran for an academic year or two, and paid more money per term than I had managed to make from my last three or four books. "I do hope that you get the job. It sounds rather good", wrote Jean, who was wonderfully encouraging, as ever. She wrote me a glowing reference, a copy of which she enclosed, adding: "PS. I wanted to say more about your being a poet, then didn't." She began her letter to the professor in charge of the Fellowship: "Alexis Lykiard has been a friend of mine for about six years", called me "a serious writer" (which gladdened me equally) and underlined it with: "I liked his novel 'Strange Alphabet' very much indeed, and think he has a considerable talent and the enthusiasm to inspire anyone who seeks his advice."

I can't even remember now who got the job. Was it someone I had 'heard of'? Or even respected? I think I was shortlisted, but can recall no interview. With hindsight, I think I felt largely relief. I wasn't too disappointed, and certainly never showed any disappointment to Jean. Visits to Jean were always treats, chocolates and smiles and a glass or two of this and that: they were special, cheering occasions. The important thing for us both, old and young, was to carry on somehow. As all authors must – finding the means (let alone the inspiration!) to continue writing. I was glad I didn't need to move up north, even temporarily, and so could continue living in Devon, able to see Jean from time to time.

A couple of years later, when I was offered my first Writing Residency, in London, altogether too much time and money was spent commuting to, and living in, the metropolis. Scarcely any time or energy was left for writing. That lesson I learned to my cost, and it proved more important than money. Singlemindedness is all a writer truly requires, as Jean taught me. To be sure, fame is nicer than obscurity; appreciation, rather than 'praise', is better than being vilified or ignored, and having a modicum of money beats having none.

Looking back over the years, what is it one really values? Here in my own solitude, in Devon still, this moment as I'm writing it, the answer is: good words generously written for me, given to strangers by someone now long gone. She cared and understood, as they did not and could not. For which I remain grateful, thinking kindly in return of my dear departed Referee.

Sensitive plants and uneasy women

> Oh, what ghoulish opportunism are writers prone to!
> – William Styron: *Sophie's Choice*, 1979

At times during the last two or three years of her life, the increasingly shaky and arthritic Jean, her drink problem equally a heart problem, was assisted with the writing of an autobiographical fragment. Her helper was a young American living in London, David Plante. The end-product was *Smile Please* (published promptly after her death in 1979). She'd had secretarial assistance via her publishers for quite a few years prior to that, and friends also helped her out from time to time. (I remember, for instance, Diane doing some typing and photocopying for her on a couple of occasions.) Plante should be congratulated for his efforts as amanuensis: it is better to have even a slight, weary, unfinished book by an octogenarian Jean than none at all.

But while it is naive generally to assume altruism in others, within literary circles in particular purity of motive is as rare a thing as a disinterested observer. No sooner had Jean died than Plante's distinctly peevish, mainly unpleasant reminiscences of her appeared here and there in various newspapers and journals. These were later included in his sneaky, repellent triptych *Difficult Women* (1983). This opportunist opus is not so much a memoir – of an unholy literary trio of Jean, Sonia Orwell and Germaine Greer – but rather a demolition job on former friends. It's a bitchy, misogynist tract that by implication tells readers more than they would probably wish to know about its author's own real or imagined difficulties with women.

The partial view of Jean there exhibited – all drunken decline and self-pity, described without warmth or compassion – would have distressed and probably enraged her. She could see herself well enough as she was and became, usually with detachment and courage. While she did not spare her own weaknesses, she fought also to keep her self-respect, conscious of the inexorable losing battle against time. Trapped in her weakening, ageing body, she tried (in every sense vainly, of course) to write her way out of it, to find some spiritual release or freedom, at least, through which some sense might be made of the whole damnable mess of existence. This process of setting words on a page was painful enough at the best of times, and she had done it the hard way, for so long. Inevitably, as she admitted, she wrote about what she knew best, herself. But she also knew how to transmute that singular vision, imperfections and all, in her art. Whereas Plante is a creeper, he lacks that delicacy and poetic alchemy alike: the result is mean, cruel if clever travesty – a study in disintegration that does not, in the end, lift the spirit.

Jean was a perfectionist; she cared about her own appearance, as she cared about the look and dance and weight of those words on the page. Getting it right made one feel good. Like any serious writer, she could accept useful criticism from whatever source and learn from it in humility. Some things, however, were justified and relevant, others not... And I think she – the Jean I prefer to recall – was a gallant soul, who wouldn't have relished what in her bygone heyday would have been dubbed an 'ungallant' sketch. Maybe her shade shrugged off the very thought of it: alive, she certainly despised hypocrisy more than most. Jean knew, though, that there could be no absolute oblivion for her, not for a while yet. She was quite aware she would continue – both to be read and written about.

It is true enough we all do use each other, writers especially. Everything is material to be used: everybody agrees on that. Fair game. But *fair* game, not unfair game. Accuracy and honesty are always essential, yet there must be, alongside scrupulous loving attention to detail, an innate tact in one's selection. How much, precisely and justly, does even the interested reader need to know? We are all in any case free to caricature those we love, but what vital purpose is served by it? Bile is common, and easy too: style is not... She was an old, exhausted, pain-wracked woman (let alone a rare spirit), who sought the truth in her own way and so deserved respect and rest.

Coincidence and confidence

Tempers like lives are short or long,
yet in this hard, uncertain trade,
discords resound, confound a song
whose rarest air is soon misplayed.

Flashback, further back, to the mid-1970s, when Jean asked me if I'd heard of David Plante. At the time I hadn't. I found out soon afterwards that a pair of his stories had been published in 1969, alongside two of Jean's in the shortlived series, *Penguin Modern Stories 1*. As a young novelist then, I was taking the trouble to read a lot of contemporary prose, but I remained unimpressed by Plante's – inert compared to Jean's or to that of the other less brilliant if skilful contributors, William Sansom and Bernard Malamud. Then, in autumn 1977, I was invited to tutor one of the Arvon Foundation's courses, on Novelwriting. I'd worked there a few times over the previous two or three years. Forty miles from the Devon hamlet where I lived, Arvon invariably proved a congenial and stimulating change.

On this occasion however, I should have known better. Or been leery about some slight misgivings I'd initially felt. I was being asked to deputise at short notice for none other than David Plante. The scheduled co-tutor was a novelist friend of his, a rather humourless and doctrinaire feminist. The little I knew of this woman's work seemed to me shrill and shrewish, and what she lacked in elegance she made up for in pretension. But I took the trouble (and precaution) of meeting 'Una Figgis' while on a brief London trip, in order to discuss the forthcoming course. She admitted that where Arvon courses at Totleigh Barton were concerned she was, so to speak, a virgin, and would be happy to be guided by me. This was as near as she ever got, I later discovered, to being winsome – but for the moment she appeared pleasant and professional enough. I assured her that it was really her course, as advertised, and hence as colleague I would do whatever I could to co-operate and contribute to its success and enjoyment.

That discussion turned out to be the first and last sensible, or even halfway civil, communication into which we entered. For it was clear almost immediately on arrival at that beautiful, isolated old manor house that my co-tutor had meanwhile changed her mind about everything we had discussed and agreed. Her agenda seemed very different from mine: I realised that she now envisaged the course as some form of contest between us, a far from good-natured psychodrama that would enable her to gain control of its participants by polarizing the sexes and setting them in opposition. Attempts at rational literary judgment were promptly sidetracked as pointless, or themselves criticized as hierarchical, before being duly abandoned in favour of point-scoring and confrontation. Tiresome argument (for the most part *ad hominem*, indeed!) was Una's order of the day.

It was an unedifying spectacle to see her wheedling her way round the women and picking off (and on) the men. Una was, to give her her due, an expert games-player, if one appreciated that sort of thing. Most did not, especially when they were the targets for her charmless yet deceptive barbs. She had no favourites, in all fairness, for she affected to sneer at the entire company, staff and students alike. I had received my rap on the knuckles almost at once, when Una informed the assembled group that I was "just a substitute", not her own choice, nor even a deputy for David Plante, but actually only a third choice as tutor. And she then mentioned the name of another, older male writer I'd barely heard of. Such a pity that he, also, had been unable to tutor the course... Her introductory announcement – gratuitously graceless as it was – gave rise to some gasps and giggles, but the warning shots had been fired and I knew where I stood.

Things thereafter veered rapidly out of anyone's control and soon slid downhill: sullen or shy, touchy or hysterical, young or old, every member of the course, regardless of gender, suffered a dig or two from Una's sly stiletto. At least I was being paid to endure this spiteful nonsense: I found ways to escape or parry much of it. How the dozen or so tyro writers felt, or what they absorbed, during what they must have considered – in this instance – an especially expensive five days, I could only imagine. Individually, they compiled a growing anthology of complaints, and I could only attempt to address their manifold problems. But nothing could be done to sweeten Una's disposition. She was, for reasons only she herself could know, an unnecessarily difficult woman.

Writing, as I realised then and reaffirm now, doesn't require prima donnas: the only primacy is that of the page, the page is where it all happens. We all start from there, perfectly equal and pure. And unattractive persons and personalities may well write angelically, managing to create beauty out of utterly wretched or unlikely material: that's surprising yet commendable in itself. To try to *teach* writing is another matter altogether: some practitioners indeed do not acknowledge that it can or should be taught at all. Certainly there are no short-cuts or magical formulae, and the writerly virtues of patience, sensitivity and imagination are anyhow required on both sides. What's unpardonable is to waste everyone's valuable time by misinformation, bullying, dripping boredom or venom into naive but captive ears: all of which represents chronic misuse of one's responsibility and function as writer.

Una doubtless would not agree, unless she has changed greatly, twenty years on. I am, she probably still assumes, inevitably hostile to her, simply via my existence as one of the opposite sex. Opposite: therefore – opposed... But I did have the satisfaction of observing, if not her comeuppance, at least her discomfiture – and by the end of that very week.

The guest author, due to read from and discuss her books on the final evening, was Angela Carter. Angela was a clever and witty person, now very much in vogue among certain spurious feminist critics, largely and unfortunately as a result of her premature death. Over dinner I waited for Ms. Figgis, who was no longer speaking to me directly, to announce to our guest in the spirit of sisterhood that I, like the other males on the course, was of no account, being just a stand-in, a mere proxy for her protégé Mr. Plante. She was not to know, however, that Angela and I were devotees of a sturdier and more rewarding plant (cannabis), and that a couple of years previously I'd spent an amusing weekend of sex, drugs and rock'n'roll with Angela at her house in Bath.

We remained amicable rather than close; I was anyhow pleased enough to see Angela again in a work context. She was I thought a sensible, industrious professional, direct not snide, and she did possess a sense of humour. But Una quickly made sure she herself monopolised Angela, although it was clear from the start that both as women and as writers they were at daggers drawn. Mutual dislike, rivalry rather than sisterly solidarity, prevailed. Their conversational sparring and awkward verbal exchanges grew self-absorbed and sour. A pair of harpies hammering on all evening was not really my idea of fun, while Una's devious prompting seemed to bring out the worst in Angela, who was goaded to show off remorselessly and thus eventually spoil her own reading.

The already demoralised audience – two of whom I'd had to dissuade from leaving the course halfway through – must have wondered what sort of literary fauna these creatures were, so venomously inhabiting their inbred, fashionable London jungle. Baffled, perplexed, embarrassed – and only in the wrong sense disturbed – the longsuffering course members, by now heartily sick of gender warfare, fidgeted and yawned. They took to drifting uncomfortably in and out of the room during the whole wretched show. Some desultory imbibing went on, but there were few questions: no one felt able or willing to interrupt the flighty displays of namedropping gamesmanship until finally the egos had landed. By which time it was too late, everybody seemed numb, exhausted rather than exhilarated. Little generally can be learned from pettiness and disappointment.

Writing surely must lift the spirit somehow. Becoming involved with language shouldn't entail lofty exclusion and false élitism, nor require the wilful undermining of confidence in beginners. I see on finding a carbon copy of my course report a full generation later that I put it down there, in black and white: I expressed the fervent wish never to work with either of "these ladies" again. And I never did... Somewhere along the line, literature had been forgotten. Each of us lost an opportunity that week to communicate, entertain, inform and, incidentally, even to enlighten ourselves.

Life, especially the writing life, is always too short to waste. But one needed to be older and wiser to recognize the fact. We should have heeded Charles Bukowski, that old lush then reviled by all capital-letter London Littérateurs. Buk, still hanging louche and unashamed till his own luck at last turned... By seventy, the acclaimed if never grand old man would put it neatly in a penultimate novel, *Hollywood*. Buk's book let fly at writers who "took more time disparaging each other than they did doing their work. They were fidgets, gossips, old maids; they bitched and knifed and they were full of vanity. Were these our creators? Was it always thus? Probably so. Maybe writing was a form of bitching. Some just bitched better than others."

So what's wrong with writers? Are we a pack of embattled neurotics, wracked with competitive envy, constitutionally unable to get on with one another? Jean Rhys was right enough to be wary of dogmatic feminists enlisting her into their fold. She didn't need them: she was a genuine original, outside all "ism" and pretension, who told her disquieting truth as she had experienced it. Una and Angela were not in her literary league (who is?); their styles were selfconscious and intellectual. Laboriously polemic, they've dated already. Jean, a timeless, exquisite artist, actually improves on rereading, better by the year like the finest brandy. Her work will endure just as she herself endured her long, difficult life – retaining appeal by virtue of a stubborn independence, an isolated originality most painstakingly established, and hence beyond the dicates of mere fashion.

Crossing paths

The self-conquest of the writer who is not a man of action is style.
— W.B. Yeats: *Journal*, 1909

1962 was a significant date for me — my last year at Cambridge and my first reading of anything by Jean Rhys. The introduction to her work, some time of course before Jean's triumphant reappearance on the literary scene with *Wide Sargasso Sea*, came about when I acquired a copy of the three-and-sixpence February edition of the *London Magazine*.

This special poetry issue included writing by the most prestigious names of the decade: Graves, Spender, Hughes, Plath, Gunn, Walcott, Seferis, Durrell, Larkin, Day Lewis, Fuller, Causley and many others. In fact the starry contributors' list was why, as a poetry-obsessed undergraduate, I'd bought the magazine. But it was Jean's superb prose, her story 'Let Them Call It Jazz', which would linger in my mind, haunting me for years afterwards. There was no indication on this, its first appearance, that the author was in her seventies, nor indeed any biographical or contributor's note.

Leafing through the issue again, I find that over the years the pages inside have gradually yellowed. One day they may even match the exterior card cover, which in turn has been fading, shifting infinitesimally to a lighter shade of its own original pale gold. Jean's inscription to me in faint blue ink seems also to have faded somewhat. But to see her handwriting once again, before it became really shaky, makes me smile. I recall her pleasure ten years later when I told her of my student enthusiasm, and remember too my own pleasure as I watched her write those friendly words, knowing that she genuinely wished me well.

Oddly enough, it was most likely the Spanish sun started that fading process. On going down from Cambridge, I'd taken a variety of reading matter with me to Spain. I know I lent that very issue for a while to Gerald Brenan. It was summer 1962, and I'd embarked on my difficult journey towards becoming a writer. There were to be no more essays, supervisions or examinations: I was out of Academe and in the wider world at last, freelancing, yet glad of whatever encouragement or guidance I could find.

Several friends and I were renting a large house on the main square of a small

Andalusian village. This village, Churriana, was in 1962 a delightful and secluded place where Gerald Brenan had lived for many years. The distinguished Hispanophile, at that time in his sixties, was the *doyen* of all expatriate English-language writers on the Iberian peninsula. A couple of my house-sharing friends knew Gerald well, and consequently that summer we all saw a great deal of him and his American wife. Gerald was a most gregarious, hospitable person, as well as being generous and encouraging about my poetic efforts to that date. He was also amused to discover how an Irishman and a Greek, of such different generations, could share similar literary enthusiasms. And this despite incarceration at the same distinctly philistine, if relatively minor, English public school.

Gerald and his wife Gamel Woolsey (herself an excellent writer and translator) did not I think, then know of Jean or her pre-war books. Many books and manuscripts were borrowed, circulated and discussed however, during the few months I knew these kindly yet critically rigorous friends. They're dead now, and the books of course dispersed, but it's probable that the name of Rhys had stuck...

In 1992, while reading Jonathan Gathorne-Hardy's exhaustive Brenan biography, *The Interior Castle,* I was interested to come upon another coincidence. The biographer mentions that Gerald corresponded with Jean from July 1967 until May 1968. Apparently Gerald read and savoured *Wide Sargasso Sea.* (This may partly have been thanks to its prefatory recommendation by Francis Wyndham, who'd also praised one of Gerald's own novels.) At any rate, Gerald was greatly impressed by Jean's other concurrently reissued novels, and he considered her a novelistic innovator. Gerald told his longtime novelist friend David Garnett that in her novels their "elliptical style avoids all explanations and keeps one all the time at the central point of feeling". As always with Gerald, that is nicely and justly put.

Gerald's biographer refers to his "numerous letters" sent to Jean, along with a couple of Brenan classics on Spanish literature and politics. It seems he also extended frequent invitations to Jean to come and stay. Although Gamel herself had been for many years virtually an invalid, Gerald evidently never realised how problematic Jean's own health was, and what an impossible proposition such a visit might be. (Indeed, Gamel's condition worsened and she was to die later in 1968.) Not surprisingly the Brenan-Rhys correspondence came to an end in May that year, albeit with his praise of *Tigers Are Better Looking*. Gerald is quoted, however, as having acknowledged: "If she is at all like her heroines, as I'm sure she is, she must be pretty neurotic."

Gerald himself possessed a considerable, impish sense of mischief, alongside his Irish loquacity and curiosity. He adored congenial conversation and good gossip. But I'm sure he never guessed quite what he'd missed. I sometimes wonder what might have happened if Jean *had* gone out to Churriana. I think they might even have got on. One can only imagine how entertaining and cordially anecdotal that meeting of wise elders might have been. Celtic charm aplenty, witty mutual admiration. Old-style courtesies exchanged over leisurely intake of marijuana and alcohol. Enlightening comparison of revered 1920s authors, especially Gallic ones like Colette. Above all, questions of style. The individual styles both Gerald and Jean worked so hard on and made seem easy do not evolve without keen questioning of oneself and others. Then, after long lifetimes devoted to that craft of literature, such rare writers may bequeath to those younger lucky ones something of their own – the precious personal signatures, the wordgifts they themselves once so clearly possessed.

A touch of the tarbrush

> ... his black hair and something that was not usual in the set of his
> features gave him an exotic, almost an Oriental appearance; hence a
> story... to the effect that Meyrick's mother was a nigger woman in poor
> circumstances and of indifferent morality had struck the school as
> plausible enough.
>
> — Arthur Machen: *The Secret Glory*, 1922

Once upon a time there was an old school phrase, used through ignorance to
place one's race and ancestry in doubt...

Rhys heroines are often marooned somewhere between 'blackness' and
'whiteness': they can't seem to fit into any certainties of race, mood or society.
They're stateless, rootless, profoundly alienated women — more in need of
warmth, whether solar or human — than money. (Although lack of the latter
emphasises their homelessness, slavery and eventual depersonalisation.) Alcohol
often gives them a brief, elusive glow before their frail identities further
dissolve. They seem to submit only to survive, troubled by shadowy recollections
of lost joys. Like ghosts going through the motions of life, their insubstantial
passivity prompts extreme reactions and misinterpretations, yet the spectacle
of their wanderings can touch and inspire. They linger unforgettably in the
mind, for they are always 'real' — human enough to be bruised, but aware when
they are used.

Such characters are utterly at the mercy of others since exiled from their true
selves; they accede to the power, not the love, of others, and those others are
usually men, in so far as that power is male-controlled. Rhys women aren't
calculating: they cannot plan ahead for their independence, nor can they run
with the herd. They're easily singled out as vulnerable. Men find them out, find
them exploitable and hence replaceable. So, like ghosts, these women enjoy
neither strength nor rest. They're spiritual refugees: among the greedy and
successful they pass as phantoms, failed and fallible creatures without real
existence, truly 'displaced' persons.

Yet they yearn to find a place, even to be what they are not. Anna Morgan, the white Dominican of *Voyage In The Dark*, adrift as Jean had been in England, is called by friends 'Hottentot'. She fantasises about having mixed blood, and identifies with a young servant girl prematurely dead, the mulatto Maillotte. Anna feels she has lost out on both her Caribbean heritages and, newly in London, fears she may become the unhappy slave of her first lover. What certainties are there? A fleeting solace in memory, perhaps, as she remembers the black woman who tended her during a childhood illness: "I wanted to be black, I always wanted to be black. I was happy because Francine was there [...] Being black is warm and gay, being white is cold and sad."

References abound in Jean's books to her identification and empathy with black people, but for her part this was not wistful nor wishful thinking, not sentimentality. In *Wide Sargasso Sea*, the young Antoinette reflects: "I never looked at any strange negro. They hated us. They called us white cockroaches. Let sleeping dogs lie. One day a little girl followed me singing, 'Go away white cockroach, go away, go away.' I walked fast, but she walked faster. 'White cockroach, go away, go away. Nobody want you. Go away.'" Jean knew she was in permanent exile, but also that her remembered paradise was not really Paradise either and had never been. There's no home, for black or white, man or woman, so you can't go home again. Jean always realised that, even before her one and only, brief depressing return to Dominica in 1936.

No home means no hope: yet one has to live in hope, and while there's life there's hope, according to Jean's cherished Latin motto. She knew where her real hope lay, however. One of her editors, Judith Burnley (who in 1969 published several of Jean's stories in *Penguin Modern Stories 1*) wrote: "Only in her relationship with her work did she show a cold, hard eye, and a toughness of mind and spirit. The blank page was her mirror of truth..." But in Burnley's own otherwise meretricious novel *Unrepentant Women* (1982), it is the seven pages of 'faction' about Jean Rhys which reflect the most convincing insights. Here in black and white is the Jean I remember: "She had enormous eyes, a pale somewhat watery blue, and there was something about the set of them and the way she rolled them towards heaven sometimes, in what once must have been her 'roguish' look, which made me wonder if she had mixed blood?"

A touch of the tarbrush at that? Jean would not have laughed, but might well have smiled ruefully, being much as Burnley describes, "a victim, who smiled her haunted, camellia-scented smile." "Sometimes," concludes Burnley, "it is the victim who survives." Indeed – and let's hope survivals occur more often than one imagines.

•

Sicut serpentes, sicut columbae

In the 1950s, I was sent to a very religiose public school, a Church of England institution founded as an early-Victorian model of an Oxford College. There I encountered a range of always unprovoked yet constant abuse. The reasons seemed to me either illogical or mysterious, and so I never became accustomed to it. Epithets and insults deployed included: *wop; wog; dago; yid; newboy Jewboy; greaseball,* and *fuckin Ayrab.* All of which struck me as baffling, mistaken or absurdly irrelevant. But the petty war of attrition proved tiring and trying, as intended. I was after all a displaced Greek attempting to become Anglicized or at least assimilated. I dreaded even being noticed, let alone singled out as in any way 'different'.

How could I have guessed that here education was not so much acquired as administered, and that it flourished in ritual guise, using well-tried forms of colonial control? Or that the system was fuelled by an unholy brew of muscular Christianity and routine jingoism. In those days at least, the desired aim of public school was conformity and orthodoxy: pass through this standardisation process (uniformity of thought and ideals) and you take a short-cut to power. Follow the code, don't step out of line. It was thought then and may still be now, that thus one prepared to join the élite, the ruling class. The hierarchy exists, and you're privileged to await your turn to become part of it.

Even to my thirteen year old self, it soon became clear that no matter whether I were to distinguish myself or lie low, I could never be approved of or accepted. Foreigners, in that distant Forties and early Fifties England, weren't really wanted. They'd caused enough trouble in the War, after all. This was well before the first wave of West Indian immigrants, at a time when, for instance, even black hair, an unfamiliar accent, or an unusual name would confirm one's difference. England was freezing cold and unwelcoming and often in my childhood and adolescence felt like an alien nation. Alienation was only fitting therefore, was my preordained fate, with insult its continual reminder.

Nor could I ever fathom what was or perhaps still is the Pure Ideal. The mongrel royal family was itself of dubious antecedents, its racial and national origins more mixed than mine. Its own members were hardly pure Aryan or Anglo-Saxon, whatever these already vague and dilute terms signified. That the Duke of Edinburgh, complete with assumed name and Scottish title, was in fact Greek, helped me not one iota. The new Queen was daily prayed for (almost prayed to) in Chapel.

As for me, I had to recite all such High Church, High Tory gibberish as convincingly as I could, although in the grey postwar context I might as well have been black: I was certainly made to feel conspicuous enough. For me, bullying and abuse weren't just normal routines, part of a greater initiation rite which would magically cease at some agreed point in time. Only by outgrowing or outwitting that detested establishment could I make shift to survive. As it happened, one way did open to me to leave prematurely, and I took it. Books – but that's another story – provided my escape route...

Did I write the miraculous word escape? Is there any? Jean told me in her final years that there was none for her. These days, I think not a single one of us can or does escape. This is no wilful digression: all our paths are linked, and cross over and over again. As I described in the Introduction to my *Selected Poems 1956-96*, when Gerald Brenan and I discovered by chance that we were both Old Radleians, there followed uneasy laughter. Then that distinguished, decorated World War One veteran admitted without his usual humorous diffidence that in many respects it had been easier to cope with life in the trenches. We agreed, drawing comparisons between our respective arrivals there in 1907 and 1953, that such establishments as the old school were sadly slow to change.

I open the copy Gerald gave me of his liberating, carefully written autobiography. At the start of *A Life Of One's Own*, he has penned 'our' school's Latin motto. With Irish irony, however (all that keen-witted humour of the exploited), Gerald has chosen to write down only the first half of the classical tag, since this is what any writer, old or young, should take to heart. The second half of the motto – an injunction to dumb passivity and obedience subtly disguised as cheek-turning mildness – he deliberately omits. This thoughtful subversion sums up how Gerald Brenan himself had lived the best part of his life, as an unconventional even rebellious autodidact. Learn from life's hard knocks, but never let yourself be unfairly ruled: the battle-cry is 'Freedom or Death!'

For the unfortunate Antoinette Cosway of *Wide Sargasso Sea,* there are no options left, freedom *is* death. Incarcerated at Thornfield Hall (in Part 3), she reflects: "I thought that when I saw him and spoke to him I would be as wise as serpents, harmless as doves". But it is as angel of destruction that she finally asserts her desperate self and writes a fiery end.

It may rarely be possible for an individual to acquire enough strength convincingly to beat the system. However, there's always the hope that the system itself by process of attrition will gradually change for the better. At any rate, returning to that tarbrush, and being black as you are painted, you can draw courage from chance meetings and cheerful mentors and crisscrossing paths. The main outcome of my education, I told Jean long afterwards, was that in various respects I ended up as she herself had done. What else was I but a misfit and an underdog? One to whom a classically, terribly British upbringing taught tolerance by default. One whom such an education had failed to fill with either its colonialist leadership qualities or the requisite racist ideology.

Still I go on making black marks on the white page. Trying to come to terms with real or imagined foreignness, learning to make true friends of neutral, even hostile words. Strangely, dead friends too can go on giving the living courage: they in turn encourage you to go on. Somewhere within our linked pasts, our briefly intermingled words and our apparently meaningless fates some truths must reside, black sheep may safely graze.

Once upon a time there was an old school phrase which meant nothing at all, though some thought it did. Boys wishing to turn themselves into gentlemen used it. But they grew careless in its use and fell under its nonsensical spell. So they themselves became enslaved, for it had betrayed and made fools of them in the end.

Some ghosts

Ghosts make sense of life not nonsense.
— Angus Wilson

Questioned by one interviewer in 1970 about influences, Jean Rhys told him: "There was a time when I read nothing but the French – Colette. Something in the air at that time influenced you, if you see what I mean". Jean's own sense of the macabre, and her understanding of the victim mentality puts me in mind of what Colette wrote in *Mes Apprentissages* (1936): "Perhaps the mouse, between one blow and the next, has respite enough to appreciate the softness of a cat's paw". This is no whimsical Gallic fancy, but a notion closer to the Fortean speculation that "we are property", with a terrible yet exquisite perception into the cruelly subtle injustices of life and artistic endeavour. We are prey to influences and hauntings of all kinds which we cannot escape: sometimes – for the most part unaware – we choose them, sometimes they choose us.

Jean, coming as she did from realms of voodoo and obeah, was superstitious enough. In one of her letters from the mid-1970s she writes: "I won't be boring but I can't help feeling that <u>somebody</u>'s doing me wrong! Perhaps not of course. <u>But</u>..." The last small doubt, fading to a very Fordian ellipsis, sums up for me her anxious and hypersensitive spirit. Writers are often accused by others of paranoia: however, if they're any good, their antennae are attuned to the slightest stir of attack, as to anything and everything else. Having a skin too few, authors know about anguish. And that entranced condition required for work – a state of enhanced receptive rawness, even an unwilling attention – lays one open to every sort of 'influence'. These forces in turn must be absorbed or deflected, reordered and freshly directed towards the page. There are, of course, unbidden unwelcome promptings out of the blue (and the dark). How far and in what direction must one explore? Which of these inklings and visitations should one expect or accept? Whether fair, distorted or disturbing, something then waits to be rescued from what Dali called "the limbo of lack of style". Whatever may emerge has been nudging at new life, and is given appropriate, individual form.

One must believe only in the permanence of the work, that alone. Toiling over so-called creative work as best one can is the writer's only relief and release from life's pain. Jean knew that: I don't think she was a convinced believer in much else. People mostly failed you and themselves – we agreed on that. There might be something after death, but it was always the longest odds against. A disappearance absolute as a blank page. Nothing: *that*, at least, was proven! Everybody would have to wait and see. Meanwhile we were all fair game for the cat.

•

During the "abominable" winter of 1969-70, Jean writes: "I haven't done much work alas. The cold makes me so useless". But whether or not her writing went well, she was always reading, and I'd recently lent her a book I was curious to have her opinion on. Her letter starts: "Thank you for sending 'Lilith'. It's a strange book – but I like parts of it & understand why you think so highly of it".

Lilith (1895) is indeed a curious and fantastic novel by George MacDonald (1824-1905). Written in old age, it is the last work of this Victorian clergyman called by Chesterton "a Scot of genius". MacDonald was praised by Dickens and friendly with Lewis Carroll. He was successfully prolific in both literary and familial terms, but his posthumous literary reputation has both swelled and subsided during most of the twentieth century. Quite as bizarre as some of his books is the fact that for the last nine years of his life MacDonald chose, literally, no longer to utter a word.

MacDonald's most recent biographer skims over this, as if she too prefers not to offer any explanation. Perhaps MacDonald felt he had said all there was to say. But if his weird masterpiece had not been properly understood, it was by no means damned or ignored. This silence was apparently not a reaction to the death of his wife, nor attributable to senility. Maybe he considered nothing on earth remained worth expressing. Was this inexplicable decision, amazing for one hitherto gregarious and customarily articulate, taken out of despair? Was it depression, failure of belief in himself, others or God? Or could it have been some sublime form of zen, whereby the old preacher himself became his last sermon, and the man of words extolled through ascetic denial the gift of tongues?

This lacuna of the latter years was more comprehensive, if less comprehensible, than the varying and various hiatuses of women artists, so well recorded by American feminist Tillie Olsen. Jean Rhys is cited as just one example (of a voice lost, recovered, rediscovered) in this fascinating and necessarily provocative work. *Silences* was not published in England until 1978 – just before Jean's own definitive silence. When I lent her *Lilith* though, Jean herself had nine years left; she was destined to live nine years longer than MacDonald had done, yet would continue using words to span that selfsame arc of silence.

I guessed she would enjoy the poetry in MacDonald, for I recalled the sympathetic definition in another of his books: "A poet is one who is glad of something and tries to make others glad too". And W.H.Auden had considered *Lilith* "equal if not superior to the best of Poe". But then I'd forgotten, too, how grimly mythopoeic Auden himself could be, and there is as much terror as consolation in MacDonald's book. A recent critic, Humphrey Carpenter, has seen in "this final fantasy, with its vision of evil-as-good and good-as-evil, its wild, uncontrolled symbolism, and its hotchpotch of gnostic religions and sinister folklore... evidence of a mind in disintegration"! The judgement seems arguably more flawed than MacDonald's artistry, although *Lilith* was not perhaps the cheeriest of choices for Jean, beleaguered as she was by "pouring rain and icy gales".

Carpenter hastens to add: "One is not surprised to learn that, soon after *Lilith* was published, MacDonald withdrew into total silence, not speaking even to members of his family" – as if the post-publication craziness of creators were some sort of occupational hazard. But *Lilith* is indeed a very literary book, and fittingly enough, one which begins and ends in the ancient library of a large country mansion. A young man just down from Oxford next takes up residence as new master of the ancestral house and, through books true and false (including *trompe-l'œil* ones) and dissolving walls, embarks on a series of strange journeys. He finds himself on a singular quest for the insoluble meaning of life and death... The narration is first-person, as in most of Jean's own books, and the work's poignant and beautiful conclusion is a short and mystical chapter entitled "The 'endless ending'".

In one of his celebrated children's stories, MacDonald wrote that "even the wicked themselves may be a link to join together the good". I felt that Jean, so unillusioned about the ways of the world, could have endorsed that mysteriously apt idea, while unlikely to agree with any specific 'religious' message MacDonald might have had in mind. After all, not only the believer C.S.Lewis but also the atheist H.G.Wells rated George MacDonald highly. Nowadays this complex author is often pigeonholed as 'simply' a children's writer; he shouldn't anyhow be too glibly annexed as a conventional Christian apologist. Resurrection of the body in *this* book involves reconstitution and pagan, Protean shape-changing: there is the awesome Lilith of Biblical legend to contend with – leopard, temptress, cat, and vampire. All in all, it's a feast of the dead and the undead. "Dead or Alive?" – as another chapter-title enquires. In *Lilith*, MacDonald suggests: "You will be dead so long as you refuse to die".

Jean believed she had to earn death. Early on, *Lilith*'s unnamed narrator looks into his mirror and, abandoning the self he knows, enters that enticing emptiness, as Jean finally would. When the youthful wanderings are done and the book of old age closes, we read: "I have never again sought the mirror. The hand sent me back: I will not go out again by that door! 'All the days of my appointed time will I wait till my change come'".

•

Years after her death my publishers sought advice on setting up a paperback library of macabre fiction. *Lilith*, out of print yet again, was my first choice, duly resurrected in this country in the 1980s. Alas, the old hardback copy I'd lent Jean vanished, along with some appended notes, into the publishers' private limbo, and they themselves soon followed it, into liquidation.

Jean like most writers was unusually scrupulous about the distinctions between books given, exchanged, and loaned. Being so responsive to words, she was also responsible, appreciative: most visits, I'd take along a book or two and they'd invariably augment the pleasure of our meetings.

As regards further forays into the uncanny and supernatural, I remember giving Jean copies of books I'd edited or introduced for various paperback imprints in the 1960s and '70s. One such gem I'd rediscovered, in an old Norfolk hotel library in 1967. There had followed, early in 1969, the first UK reprint for half a century of William Hope Hodgson's *The House On The Borderland*. Hodgson (1877-1918) had been, *inter alia*, merchant seaman, pioneering photographer and body-builder. He was also a poet, a courageous and eccentric character, as well as an original stylist in the field of British weird fiction. Hodgson's death in action in World War One was a greater loss to literature than anyone at the time acknowledged. By the end of this twentieth century, Hodgson has now resurfaced, with nearly all his *oeuvre* in print, most justly revived. (Natatory images are curiously apt here I realize. The young Hodgson, small of stature but a redoubtable swimmer, was awarded the Royal Humane Society's medal for rescuing a crew member from drowning. Hodgson had dived from his ship to do so, spending the worst part of an hour in shark-infested seas off Port Chalmers, New Zealand.)

I could commend Hodgson's then underrated, visionary novel to Jean as a wonderfully imaginative, if not escapist, read – a work of pure invention of course. It also poetically evoked a rural Irish landscape very reminiscent of Wicklow, whence I'd originally contacted Jean. And the novel was a more stylish and gruesome piece of fantasy than any by the continuingly, if dubiously fashionable H. P. Lovecraft. (At least that reclusive American had shown better than usual taste during the mid-1930s, when praising *The House On The Borderland*).

By a nice coincidence Hodgson like Jean was of Welsh origin (indeed, he was distantly related to the extraordinary Arthur Machen) and, beginning in 1906 with the US publication of the story 'From The Tideless Sea', he created his own Sargasso Sea Mythos. Many of these tales centre upon doomed voyages into that fateful area of legend. In Jean's famous title sixty years later, her wide Sargasso Sea became a potent symbol of the inescapable void, that dreadful nothingness which lay in wait to swallow up a lost soul on its last voyage. For her as well as Hodgson, tropical islands were not always romantic paradisal visions, but dangerously enchanted places to be hastily quitted before they destroyed you, mythical spaces teeming with life either languorous or frenetic, where every species of creature wove its particular spell of fascination and magic...

Perhaps work like William Hope Hodgson's proved not quite to her taste precisely because there *were* such *fin de siècle* or childhood echoes in it: it was not appealingly enough escapist. Although one letter of hers maintained that Cheriton Fitz was "really one of the dullest places under heaven", Jean in darker mood had gone on to confide "there's no escape for me". And yet she didn't especially care for frivolous or knowingly humorous writing. She felt happier, it seemed, with another, equally gruesome book. This was a collection I'd edited by the Irish writer J. Sheridan LeFanu (1814-1873) – in M.R. James's opinion the greatest of all writers on the supernatural. LeFanu's *Carmilla* remains the classic vampire novella; its elegant style perfectly yet mysteriously matches both eroticism and horror. Jean wrote "you can imagine the LeFanu stories will be very welcome. I know one or two not many". As it turned out, she completely agreed about *Carmilla,* and was intrigued, as I thought she would be, by the story I told her of LeFanu's dream. LeFanu, who became a recluse after his wife's death and wrote mostly at night, had a recurrent dream of gazing up at a house that slowly collapsed before his eyes. When his doctor called in one day and found the writer dead, he reportedly said: "It seems the building has fallen at last".

Not of the stature of LeFanu, but nearer to Jean's own generation was E.F.Benson (1867-1940). I sent her my selection of the most effective tales from Benson's four out of print macabre collections. Among these were his chilling story 'The Room In The Tower', which brought me a nightmare or two when I first read it as a schoolboy, while 'The Face' – another story based on a recurrent dream – is in this particular sub-genre hard to beat. It pleased me (as author of only a single ghost story) to think that I was helping to perpetuate a rather specialised, increasingly difficult, but by no means moribund tradition. M.R. James had been Provost of King's College, Cambridge, and Benson had been educated there too. As a Kingsman myself, this too was pleasing, though I don't remember mentioning the Cambridge connections to Jean. She hadn't been happy at the Perse School, even though it must have seemed a lifetime ago; besides, that whole small world vanished with the Great War. Now, beneath the glamour, gloomier aspects of the Cambridge microcosm remain, in essence unchanged. It can be an unfriendly, petty, cold, damp, snobbish, hypercritical place. A more crowded, yet still too narrow and inbred place swirling with fenland mists and ghosts. Such haunts must in time be escaped from, as some spirits neither innately academic nor class-bound discover – as she found, as I found.

•

To write of the inexplicable, attempting to make convincing what is uncanny and thus beyond most readers' ken, requires extreme verbal precision. Nearly all the supernatural 'specialists' discussed above could be, by current standards, too leisurely and slow-paced, if not actually verbose. But that was how life was for educated persons before 1914, the point by which so many of the classic weird stories had already been written. As is often intimated however, the advent of electric light and radio in particular – and of course of Freud – altered the available 'atmosphere', the substance and potential function and focus of the ghost story. The ever-accelerating tempo of twentieth century life must also initially have been bewildering. What with the cataclysmic impact of large-scale war – and the inexorable development of all its associated, horrific technologies of destruction – literary sensibilities became numbed or jaded.

At the more excessive or delirious end of the spectrum, elementals, vampires and the like were grouped with Grimm and co. as fairy stories, albeit for adults. Such sheer grue continued and continues to be written, despite a decline in quality traceable perhaps to poorer verbal, and richer visual, fare. (Literacy dwindles while screens – and screams? – proliferate.) Shock and decadence, hysteria and latterday Gothick, can still be fun: the excruciating experiences of others have always provided us with chills and thrills. I see nothing reprehensible in voyeuristic or vicarious excitements, raw or well-done. All valid enough. It's a matter of taste (or lack of it), skill (ditto), and that elusive mixture of tradition and experiment blended with artistic conviction – into style.

On the subtler side of the 'spectral spectrum', may be located the more scrupulous literary manifestations of dreamlife and the unknown. Here are floated the creative explorations beyond category, but exemplified in those fascinating quieter voices and interiorized narratives. "Inner weather", reflection and reaction rather than action, is what's on offer here, as if to prove the whisper more effective than the shout (or shriek). To express such realities of the unreal, such subtleties of the subconscious, thoughtstreams must not meander: an economical, understated storytelling style needs to be developed, if the author is to convince. As ever, if the reader is asked to suspend disbelief, the writer must first believe his or her own story. That is why such tales are few and hard to tell.

Jean's are also very few, but of rare quality like all she wrote. Of them, the last is best, and I shall come to that in due course. Jean read widely across that spectrum I've suggested, and she would have agreed with how another estimable 'displaced' writer saw the macabre imagination. William Trevor –

the Irish short story specialist, himself a longtime West Country resident – was reviewing a 1987 book of 'ghost stories by women'. (This label Jean would have fought shy of. She'd have been wary too of the feminist press which published the anthology.) Trevor believes "ghosts belong more tellingly in haunted imaginations than in haunted houses, since they are creatures of fear or guilt as often as they are wanderers from unquiet graves". He goes on to lament Jean's own absence from this collection. The omission of a "pure gold" piece of hers is a great pity, since "'I Used To Live Here Once'" is widely regarded as one of the neatest of all ghost stories."

This is the last story of the last book which Jean published in her lifetime, *Sleep It Off Lady* (1976). It's barely a page and a half long, and on the dust jacket it's called "a short prose poem" that "brings the writer back home". That's literally enough correct, as far as it goes… Jean, of course, has gone much further. She (almost always and finally a first-person narrator) is to find how irrevocably things have changed in the house of childhood, that clearly remembered home. She has ignored the Wolfeian warning, "You can't go home again" – and gone back. Only she has also gone forward, passing out of time and through her death and into nothingness. It is an extraordinary imagining (let's hope not a presage) of what it might be like to become a ghost. This admirable and concise story ultimately defies summary, however: it demands to be read, and seems to sum up all that Jean had come to feel about her life and work. Marked by utter conviction and a strangely beautiful calm, 'I Used To Live Here Once', the bleak farewell of Rhys-as-*revenant*, brings – to this reader, this writer, at least – a final note of chilling disquiet and near-tangible sadness.

Early in 1936, almost at the midpoint of Jean's long life, a small legacy had enabled Jean and her second husband to return to Dominica. Her biographer logs what appears to have been a traumatic time generally for Jean, although the visit would prove creatively vital, bearing unique if often bitter fruit years later. Appropriately, their French ship sailed through the Sargasso Sea en route and, most depressingly for Jean, she found the family house and estate burnt out, overgrown. That desolation endured; Jean brought it back, river-deep within her, to England, and it is the word 'nothing' that will be crucial in *Wide Sargasso Sea.*

Yet she was not nihilistic, nor showed herself to be cynical. Nor, while quite aware of the emptiness of so many heads, hearts and lives, was Jean herself void of compassion. "The notion of emptiness engenders compassion", one Buddhist text has it, and out of nothing comes the deceptively tough transparency of the finest art. It's the "glassy look" of the sky in Jean's story, "that she didn't remember". The displaced spirit may linger there, "longing to touch them", but – children, readers – everything has already been left behind.

It seems our author has disappeared and there remains nothing. Nothing exists, except some homeless, disembodied words wandering across time, torn from their context. Look more closely, though, and you may find her again in a text shaped with love. Wherever there is a detached regard, deep concern and care for words. Careful words, words befriended and linked, given their own new life... Something elusive but important survives. The personal 'I' becomes part of the impersonal eye that sees all, and a true and touching creator fixes upon "the only word she could think of. Glassy." *Le mot juste*, full stops on either side of it. So the lost soul may be saved, and the right word found.

Being nothingness

In extreme old age, such as Jean's, we must come to terms – if not live – with our ghosts. The past seems endless and more real than the present, while the future can only be short. When life expectancy is so limited, one expects little else or else nothing. Ghosts come back to inhabit the weary brain, personal phantoms nobody else can see or identify, because younger minds were unborn then and have inevitably grown now to be unreceptive. The young, made of firm flesh and warmer blood, can never recognize these shadowed visions of the unknown in any case.

Who is left alive to recall such visions? They can scarcely be photographed, they blur and lose outline and may easily be blinked away. Perhaps they're released into oblivion only when no one remains to remember. Are they *really* visible and did you *really* see them? Were they real once, to seem so real now? They must have been – but appearances are always deceptive, as all observant authors know. Meanwhile memories among the living become shorter, vaguer, they fade and recede by the day. By night the tricky, restless shades, the wandering ghosts of reminiscence, crowd in stealthily to be readmitted. Welcome or not, they may be exorcised as memories – perceived in whatever shape they are allowed to take on – those apparitions which must surround the very old.

During the last half of the twentieth century, the finest British writer of macabre short stories – consistently and strangely poetic, as well as perceptive, was Robert Aickman (1914-1981). It's baffling that his work is nearly all out of print and that he remains sadly undervalued. Aickman noted in 1966, Jean's triumphant annus mirabilis, that there has been "no people and no culture without ghosts... no land without poltergeist disturbances from earliest times. But England is generally regarded as the metropolis of the supernatural, as of lyric poetry". I think he would have hailed the concise prose – the poetic distillation of a lifetime's melancholy – of 'I Used To Live Here Once'. Aickman (in the same introduction to one of his excellent supernatural anthologies) cites as "the shortest ghost story in the world" the following: "There were two strangers alone in a railway compartment. 'Do you believe in ghosts?' inquired the first, making conversation. 'Yes', replied the second; and vanished." Jean's tale has a similar economy, but it moves one too, as the best art does.

Aickman goes on to suggest how "the present reader" imagines hearing something, opens the door, looks hard, listens... But there's nobody, nothing. Aickman envisages the reader returning slowly, "unreassured" and thus ensuring the inner door-chain is in position. Often since I've been haunted by the thought of Jean, a diminutive figure welcomingly opening the door of her tiny house: you'd have to stoop at the entrance and mind your head. She could often appear unreassured, so inconsolable, beyond all friendly help or comfort. On a bad day (and who knows what the night brought) pale, frail and insubstantial, she seemed like some ghost herself. A presence that has long outlived its time. And yet she is as I remember her, one not lost but somehow magically preserved and saved by her gift.

Many years later, I've still never been able to bring myself to return there. Things will have changed. Of course. Yet she used to live there once, and it's only nine miles away from where I live. What anyhow do I expect to see? There's nothing to see. It's in many ways a frightful place, as she knew, filled with apathy, hostility, cold imaginings. But she coped, she saw out her time. She saw what she saw, and set it down with courage. She set me an example I'm only now starting to understand. "So it is with most phantoms" writes Aickman, himself long-gone too, "nothing about them is so confirmatory as nothing."

Further horrors

In Jean's last collection, *Sleep It Off Lady* (1976), there is a different kind of creepy story, entitled with darkly appropriate humour, 'The Insect World'. Set in London during the Second World War, it presents a heroine (a protagonist rather, for as ever Rhys's women are resolutely anti-heroic) called Audrey, who will soon be turning thirty – a new page for her, and one that fills her with dread. For Audrey's worst, most secret horror, is of old age. Audrey is displaced, dissatisfied, and resentful of the lonely urban existence that her few – all female – friends cannot mitigate. Indeed, these women irritate her quite as much as the overwhelming anonymity of metropolitan life with its busy insect-swarms of strangers drawn day and night down into the tube stations. Life has lost its meaning for Audrey, who seems able to find rest or release only in books and in sleep: "Blissful sleep, lovely sleep, she never got enough of it…" The limpid, precise prose almost lulls the unwary reader before the tale turns nightmarish, as Audrey gradually yet inexorably becomes aware she must face up to her anxiety. She explodes with panic-stricken, fearful rage at the end, since she knows she is on the edge, staring into an abyss far more desolate than any bomb-crater…

There is no escape from herself and her raw, hypersensitive temperament. Audrey tries to explain her schizoid nature ("It's as if I'm twins"), but gives up when she realises that her friend Monica, "an optimist five years younger than Audrey", doesn't want to know or understand how she feels. Everyone is alone, but not everyone is so aware of the fact as Audrey, nor has the capacity to slide helplessly beyond that initial awareness and down towards a pit of existential self-doubt. The downward slide commences, tellingly, with the very simple first sentence: "Audrey began to read."

Audrey, as Jean herself was, is a very *bookish* person. Although she feels trapped, she is able to "give herself up to the written word as naturally as a good dancer to music or a fine swimmer to water." In addition, "Almost any book was better than life, Audrey thought. Or rather, life as she was living it." However, if life can't "soon change, open out, become quite different" Audrey reflects, then "for the time being there was no doubt that it was pleasant to get away from it. And books could take her away." Her trouble is, Audrey imagines, that she can't fool herself, for "she never forgot that books were one thing and that life was another". Yet words on a page can speak to her with hidden power. So much so, indeed, that their influence points this suggestible, susceptible woman along a trail leading indirectly to what she fears most. At the end, she is spiralling out of control towards her own downfall.

The book Audrey has opened bears a hauntingly ambiguous title, *Nothing So Blue*. It seems to her to promise some Edenic return (to the tropics, of course), but in that phrase there lies a catch, a warning and a sinister subtext. Emptiness and anticlimax, for instance, alongside lack of belief, extreme sexual guilt and depression... This particular book has an occult, oddly insidious life of its own; rather like some sinister fetish-object, it seems at first to resist her very accession to it, her ownership of it. The previous owner, furthermore, has inscribed and annotated the book extensively in "his small, neat, precise handwriting". Among other things, the word 'blue' is obsessively underlined throughout. It takes Audrey a long time to erase the marks and comments of this unknown reader-predecessor-familiar, and in doing so she receives an almost physical shock. "Charles Edwin Roofe" (a hint perhaps of "Frederick William Rolfe"?) is or was clearly crazy, a bird of ill-omen, a Corvine cove, some sort of paranoid and misogynist pervert...

By the end, through its malign influence, *Nothing So Blue* affects (or confirms) Audrey's vision of human life itself as an insect world, a restless hellish place devoid of meaning. The act of writing – which always saved Jean – might itself be meaningless she here implies, if accomplished without love. This whole story can be interpreted as a cautionary tale, a haunting parable in which Jean asserts that how and what to read and how and what to write are linked – vital spiritual necessities, essential activities that help restore meaning to life. The writer (as metaphor in the best, broadest sense for any thoughtful, loving, communicating individual) has a responsibility towards the reader (e.g. likeminded individual) whom s/he will probably never directly meet.

But in the course of this unique human act of communication, the creative use of language, there are many risks. Sometimes thus we lay ourselves open to dark forces, to our own destruction. In 1920, two years after William Hope Hodgson's violent and 'voluntary' death (he was far too old, remember, to need to join up), collections of his poetry were published. One of them contained the following lines:

I am dying, and my work is all before me:
As a pencil that doth break beneath the knife
So have I broke before the bitter sharpening
Of the grim blade of thought that shaped my life...

This bears an uncanny parallel to Jean's feeling (also quoted elsewhere), that when she wrote she felt like "a pen in someone else's hand". Such intuitive feelings of mysterious 'possession' link the real and imagined, writers with their creations. And the whole process, the chain of communication, can seem endless and often frightening. Hence Audrey, Jean's character written into 'The Insect World', enters the inner bookworld, the microcosm and psychic jungle of *Nothing So Blue,* only to find clearly inexplicable yet odious traces of the previous owner-reader Roofe, its former 'inhabitant'. This creature frustrated both as man and possibly writer is half-crazed with hostility, writ(h)ing with destructive fury: "He had written 'Women are an unspeakable abomination' with such force that the pencil had driven through the paper."

But it's too late for Audrey: the poisonous legacy of hate has entered her spirit, and now she cannot erase or exorcise Roofe. The shadow of negation (madness, despair, violent aggression) – the spell here cast – hardens into that dark 'roof' which will blot out the sky's blueness. Audrey's angle of vision, her whole horizon narrows: thereafter, nothing so blue can lie ahead. She senses it and, dreading the unknown, mourning her lost youth and bleak future, feels herself alone and doomed. Finally she lashes out at her friend in an access of desperate, frustrated rage. This, with a vengeance, is the hell of the insect world, nor is she out of it! It's a terrifying conclusion to one of Jean's best-written and most profound stories.

The worst aspect of our mindless, cruelly banal world – Jean seems to be saying as if challenging us to disagree – is that it is most dreadful just where it seems most ordinary. And what *is* 'ordinary'? Roofe's "small, neat, precise handwriting" (incidentally quite the opposite of Jean's own bold, generous script) is more than disconcerting, and deceptive, of course. For Audrey, and for Jean, "it was always the most ordinary things that suddenly turned round and showed you another face, a terrifying face. That was the hidden horror, the horror everybody pretended did not exist, the horror that was responsible for all the other horrors." Wartime London and the Blitz, it's true – but Jean was an old woman marooned in Devon when she finally published this earlier story;

moreover, she was neither revising nor recollecting in anything like tranquillity. Her view was always dark and, like the story within this story, like what she says of *Nothing So Blue,* "not so cheering, either".

•

"So if you'd like to cheer me up one December day you'd be welcome", she writes at the end of 1970. "Quite a lot has been happening – mostly sad things & I feel rather battered." Poor Jean! She was cursed with a dark vision and blest with a beautiful talent which was fully capable of exploring and illuminating that interior darkness. All her voyages, turbulent, becalmed or landlocked, led her towards the dark and, well though she knew it, she kept bringing brightness back.

It was always a pleasure visiting Jean, but the cheer was never one-sided. There were laughs on both sides, and Jean with her soft-voiced mewing obliquities – that rueful feline humour of hers – invariably cheered me. As a young writer, I too was finding writing lonely and difficult; my social life was limited and I lived in what Victorian novelists called 'reduced circumstances' in a crumbling old cottage. Isolation in Devon, and lack of funds and friends there meant I had more in common with Jean than an exile's depressive temperament and a taste for drink.

We'd agree that simply to read something truly dismal, something wonderfully 'depressing', could actually cheer you: its overall effect was to lift the spirit. (Books falling into this category, for instance, included Gissing's *New Grub Street* and Hamsun's *Hunger.*) The most appalling or morbid personal experiences, if related without self-pity though with wit, narrative verve and stylistic originality, were not only acceptable but in fact to be welcomed. There but for fortune, perhaps? To travel along on these kinds of journeys, sharing extremes of misfortune and stress, made one feel better before rejoining the fray oneself, no question about that.

I smile to myself on rereading the opening paragraph of another of Jean's letters: "I find Nabokov difficult to read as a rule, but I think I'll like 'Despair'. Thanks for sending it. I'm supposed to be quite well again but still feel very tired (or perhaps it's just a lack of energy). Anyway something to read is a blessing. It's very cold again & the wind howls." How typical of my thirty-year old self, I think now, to have sent this octogenarian a book with such a title! But I don't feel I was being entirely perverse or playful. While Vladimir Nabokov remains for me an admired author, I see better now why Jean could find 'difficult' his lofty and ornate language-games: they must have seemed over-concerned with style, less impersonal than invulnerable. Nabokov was altogether too copious, too fluent, too relentlessly 'inventive' – and so concealed more than he revealed. Jean was an equally exotic exile but a butterfly of very different variety. To Jean, the sparer, nakedly autobiographical writer, style and strength themselves resided in uncertainties: they were dependent, like their possessor, on being placed in constant doubt. She wrote with sureness but from despair and without certainty. So I guess (myself unsure) that Nabokov's appeal was lacking for Jean: sheer wit and literary confidence were not enough. Perhaps as reader she also distrusted, not quite in ways Nabokov intended, the authoritative male tone of his fictions with their elaborate webs, finding there an excessive authorial and verbal contrivance which took up too much time rather than helped her pass it.

I cannot recall, reading Nabokov's letters, that he ever doubted his powers. At least, not on the page. If he had truly experienced the word, the despair of his title, it is nowhere evident, or else he does not choose to share it with us. This arrogant self-possession was something quite alien to Jean. She could therefore write to me in mid-1974: "I'm glad you liked the story. Your criticism is quite right. What happened was that after toiling for a year (off & on) writing & rewriting I despaired of ever getting the atmosphere I wanted. So left it alone".

The work in question was the title-story of her last collection, *Sleep It Off Lady*. It's also the penultimate text in that book, published in 1976, and is followed only by the chillingly final 'I Used To Live Here Once', that strange abstraction of a ghost story distilled into little over a page. The latter, apart from being a fanciful yet cold-eyed postcript to Jean's life, reads like a kind of bemused farewell to the world, both wistful epitaph and premonition of life-after-death. To go so far – reaching this state of quasi-acquiescence, this not-quite-acceptance of fate, whereby the author becomes a ghost, neither resting nor in peace, and visible (or 'living') henceforth only to those who can read her work – she needs first to die. In 'Sleep It Off Lady', Jean therefore imagines the manner of her departure, trying to foresee the worst that might happen, as if the fictional confrontation with her own death could actually help her come to terms with it whenever that time came.

To live something through to the end, in her mind; to imagine it fully and give it a name and a form, fixing it on the page. That way nothing could spring at her unawares from the shadow. She was preparing herself, writing an end to the book of her life, booking a passage as it were, so that the ill-health, the helplessness, isolation and multiple uncertainties of advanced age couldn't conspire to trip her up: she'd had long enough to see them coming! And Jean kept on the look-out for the sly, scurrying approach of death itself...

The very suddenness of the unknown, the fear lying in wait ahead: this was what she tried to face, envisaging the inescapable with blackest humour as Super Rat. This self-teasing rodent image Jean evokes, which lurks to gnaw at the fringes of 'Miss Verney's' consciousness, is appropriately enough evolved via literature – Saki's gruesome Sredni Vashtar – and drink. DTs and the slowly distilled fears of a long lifetime have spawned it, this stealthy yet quick and tricky beast. And the drink-tease doesn't ease the dread of it or of any such creeping crawling creature of delirium...

Jean views her Miss Verney in the third person, but the story loses no immediacy thereby: indeed, it opens "one October afternoon", with two elderly women drinking (only) tea together and discussing death. Miss Verney, older than her friend Mrs Baker, has "been thinking a great deal about death lately". She is unconvinced when Mrs Baker doesn't think it strange, but rather "quite natural. We old people are rather like children, we live in the present as a rule. A merciful dispensation of providence." Miss Verney is right, of course, to be unconvinced: the old aren't like children at all, they've seen too much and aren't consoled by what they still see. The tragedy for Miss Verney is that no one shares her disabused, singular vision; instead, she is disbelieved. The rat she sees is imaginary: it must be, since poison has been put down and no dead rat results. In the sceptical eyes of the villagers, if Tom the handyman's rat poison hasn't killed any rats, ergo there are none, and Miss Verney has been seeing things. "She knew that the bottles in her dustbin were counted and discussed in the village". (Poor Jean, I thought when first reading that sentence, and recalled my initial glimpse of her in the lane with her bag of empties...) She drinks, she gets pills from the doctor, she anxiously cleans the house, does poor Miss Verney: even her name has a paranoid aural affinity with "vermin", we now realise. And she's told that the helpful "Mr Slade" "who cuts the grass" "is a very busy man": he can't clear the shed and thus flush out the rat Miss Verney knows is there. (Mr *Green*slade, a nice villager I remember, predeceased Jean: he was a patient friend and ally and would chauffeur Jean to Exeter or further afield, to Tytherleigh, whenever she wanted to meet us for a meal...) Allies and friends fade away as the rat does not.

Near the end, the story loops back to the opening conversation, as we remember Mrs Baker's false parallel between the old and the young. Miss Verney collapses by her overturned dustbin and, helpless, appeals first to neighbours who ignore her and walk on by. Desperate and cold, with darkness falling, she begs for help from nextdoor's child, "leaning on her gate". This, her last hope, as it turns out, is a twelve year old girl whose "cynical eyes" Miss Verney has avoided in the past and who now treats her with glassy disdain like trash. "Everybody knows that you shut yourself up to get drunk. People can hear you falling about", the "horrible child" lectures her. "Sleep it off lady", she finally exhorts Miss Verney, "skipping away". Miss Verney is left to her fate, and Jean's eye fixed on her is no less cold.

There can be no happy end of course, no nick-of-time arrival of the cavalry, and no rescue from the nightmare rodent no one has seen but Miss Verney. Instead, an inspired coda follows Miss Verney's macabre and awful vigil. There's a mundane yet perfectly judged appearance by the postman (a sort of Chorus-figure), who "had a parcel of books for her". This last lifeline – representing literature and amicable communication with the outside world – has come too late. The man carries her indoors and, again appropriately, tries to revive her with drink, "but her teeth were tightly clenched and the whisky spilled all over her face". That seems to me the ultimate joke by Jean against herself.

Her story could have ended there. Yet the taste left might have been too bitter, its harshness excessive. Grim slapstick, indeed – and echoes of John Webster weren't wanted, nor those of music-hall ("We knew the old girl was dead when she turned down a drink. Only time in living memory she ever did," etc). So in another sense there's a kind of dying fall, and a couple more flat, bleak paragraphs. But that, I felt when reading the story on its first magazine publication, was all that was required. Writing to Jean, I told her how extraordinary I thought her story was. Excusing my presumption, I added: "I felt you could well have cut the last 2, possibly even 3, sentences, which seem unnecessary and soften the impact." She at once wrote back, agreeing with me, as I've described, and her honesty and humility have lingered in my mind ever since.

A letter of Jean's from a year or so later begins:

My dear Alexis,
Delighted to hear from you. Yes, I'm fairly well. & the short stories are done. To my satisfaction? (Well, Hm Hm

Also I must write one more it seems.

As usual I'm puzzled about many things. It would be a relief to talk to anyone sympathetic.

So if anywhere around do come & see me.

But bafflingly enough when the collection did appear in book form in 1976, 'Sleep It Off Lady' was printed in its 'weak' version. It's still my opinion that the story should end slightly before it does, with and on the word "consciousness." However, I find it so poignant and intimate like all Jean's work that I'm moved even by what seems a very slight blemish. Maybe she changed her mind after all, though I don't think so. (She also confirmed in conversation what she'd written in her letter.) I guess it's more likely she simply forgot, or grew too tired to check proofs: several years had elapsed, and she was eighty six and nearing her end. This was the last of her books published in Jean's lifetime, and certain of the stories in it rank with the best she ever wrote and the best anybody wrote. Who'd quibble with such a legacy?

Monsters and mistakes

> Let us remember that the word *monster* does not mean something
> horrible. Lope de Vega was called a 'Monster of Nature' by Cervantes.
>   – Jorge Luis Borges

The dead should be allowed to rest. Yet without absolute proof of complete
extinction, they do continue to exist – most certainly and obviously in the
memories of the living. If during their lives they achieved some fame, that
inevitable distortion of their continuance, towards legend and disputed
immortality, can sometimes sadden those who once knew them. Soon even the
famous may be misremembered and in the course of time they surely will be.
Their works, bones, ashes, words will all be picked clean, sifted and scattered.
For the moment, they avoid oblivion, but at a posthumous price. We lend them
our attention and they live again a while: all too often in this way they come
to haunt us.

Get that detail right. Be correct, insists one particular writer's ghost. *I never did
or said those things, I wasn't like that.... That wasn't exactly me, wasn't what I meant,*
the apparition goes on. *I'm being misread. They misread me, misread me...* I know
as she did that that last verb spells out past and present alike. So how should
I show my continuing respect? How to placate that friendly shade?

•

Let's start with what the publishers Longman describe as "the first extended
study of her work". This was a book by Louis James, appropriately enough in
their series of 'Critical Studies of Caribbean Writers', appearing in 1978, just
before Jean's death. The critic, who really could and should have checked, gives
her stage name as 'Jean Rhys' and has her marrying in 1919 "the Dutch poet
and translator Max Hamer"! Unfortunately this is by no means all he gets
wrong. Among other things, the stunning but very bleak conclusion to *Good
Morning Midnight* is interpreted as "a profound statement about the nature of
compassion", while James maintains that our author has brought her heroine
"miraculously, to a moment of love and meaning". I think his thinking wishful,

as seems also his next remark, that this most desolate of literary epiphanies "is the culmination of the search which has been passed through the four novels". James follows his curiously strained assertion with another odd and somewhat patronising comment: "It might be thought that it left its author with nothing further to say, for she published nothing more for some twenty years."

It might be thought that *festina lente* could have made a good motto for Louis James, but another scholar, Thomas Staley, was soon to rush in. The year of her death, this American academic published *Jean Rhys, A Critical Study* (Macmillan, 1979). Erroneously if gallantly, he makes Jean four years younger than she was on winning "the Smith Literary Award" [sic] and he also gives her "beautiful green eyes". In general Staley's writing is worthily stodgy and lets down its subject, apart from the fact that it's far too determinedly upbeat. Once again there are perpetrated (let's trust not perpetuated) some extraordinary misinterpretations. On learning, for instance: "At the end of *Voyage* Anna lies in bed thinking about starting over again", the mind reels at the bathos, the banality of such a summary. Understatement, misstatement, error – take your pick.

There existed however, then and still, an extensive Rhys collection at Staley's own workplace, the University of Tulsa, as the dull professor duly acknowledged. Yet it was rather more than 24 hours from Tulsa – not until 1985 in fact – before another American, Nancy Hemond Brown in the *London Magazine,* corrected such a fatuously optimistic reading as Staley's. She demonstrated in her long article, via sagacious and painstaking comparison with a Rhys typescript at Tulsa, that Jean's original ending (Part IV of *Voyage In The Dark*) had been much cut. But while Jean herself might have intended something even darker – Anna's actual death – the final section as published is hardly less harsh. Although Constable the publishers persuaded Jean to alter the novel (as Brown says), "in favour of an ending less bleak and pessimistic", it's scarcely an easy option that Jean provides. Anna's continuation in a hollow, loveless condition envisaged as hell on earth is far from the cynical resilience of a Dorothy Parker's "you might as well live" and closer to the relentless angst of existentialism, a style of thought it long predates. But as for endings and beginnings, a final note on Staley, upon whom irony or despair seem lost. Here's how he sees fit to start a paragraph to sum up *Good Morning Midnight*: "Although so profoundly different in ways too numerous and obvious to mention, *Good Morning Midnight* concludes on a note similar to Joyce's *Ulysses*." Comparisons may be odious, flattering or instructive (again, take your pick), but it's stale stuff indeed when academics aren't actually accurate, either.

If these were a pair of admittedly early books on Rhys, they did manage to make a few interesting points here and there. In the 1980s further books about Jean appeared on either side of the Atlantic. They fell into predictable styles. There were seriously worthy, stodgy Americademic tomes such as Arnold E. Davidson's *Jean Rhys* (Literature and Life Series, Ungar, 1985), compiled with some enthusiasm but a different sprinkling of errors. (For instance, Max Hamer, Jean's third husband, was sentenced to three years' prison, not six months, and died in 1966, not 1964...) The other mode of Rhys treatise tended to be teeth-gritting or unintentionally comic. An egregious example is *The Ladies And The Mammies: Jane Austen & Jean Rhys* (Falling Wall Press, 1983). According to its perpetratrix, a Selma James, Ford Madox Ford was "an American novelist living in Europe", and Jean "has pushed her way into English fiction and demanded her right not only to be heard as a woman but as a Third World Woman – even in the great halls, even on the battlements". Even in Devon, a woman less pushy than Jean would be hard to find, and she wouldn't have fallen for any pseudo-feminist rant without a pinch of salt – or, for that matter, a dash of tequila...

While Jean is much read, she's as widely misread, misrepresented. For instance, her little-known ghost story 'A Spiritualist' most definitely deserves reprint, but does it merit burial in an opportunist omnibus whose most macabre aspect is its clutch of strangely unworthy bedfellows? Within this feminist-angled anthology *Mistresses Of The Dark,* the hard gleam of Jean's 3-page gem is far from obscured amid the surrounding dross. But an unholy trinity of American editors it's kindest not to name commits in the space of a single paragraph a whole series of dismal errors concerning Jean and her work. Jean would have been amazed by such interest, if not amused by such absurdity. It's hard to be both assiduous and asinine, yet the transatlantic trio pulls off this difficult feat. The editors call Jean "a woman of Creole descent who moved from the Dominican Republic to England and eventually The Continent". Oh, and she "held a variety of clerical and modeling positions in her early years". We're told Jean wrote "*The Wide Sargasso Sea*, a prequel to Charlotte Brontë's *Jane Eyre*" and "she was awarded the prestigious Commander of the British Empire for her contributions to literature." (Sic, sic, sic!) We're then unhelpfully informed that "Her collected works include *Complete Novels* (1985) and *Complete Short Stories* (1987)" and – by a final inspired flight – her autobiography becomes *Smith Please…*

Adrift somewhere between the Scylla of hysterical fancy and the Charybdis of lumpen criticism, Jean Rhys's craft eluded them all. Not until Carole Angier's gigantic, finely researched and genuinely perceptive biography of her in 1990 did Jean receive just and extended appreciation. Yet I feel it's ironic if not unnecessary that many reviewers of this superb work chose to underline or deliberate upon Jean's character defects – evidence to be used, à la Plante, to display her 'difficult-ness' as a woman. And more than most it was the British literary women, supposedly her sisterly admirers (biographers like Claire Tomalin and Hilary Spurling) who pitched in with the punches as well as the praise. Under the headline ANGEL WORDS FROM A MONSTER'S MOUTH, the former began a lengthy Sunday broadsheet article: "When you feel you've had about all you can stand of Jean Rhys's behaviour – a feeling that comes over you pretty regularly…" Tomalin bustled and busked along towards a last paragraph labelling Jean "as much monster as she was victim". The first sentence of Spurling's weekend piece read "This is a horror story to chill the blood and turn the heart to stone." Jean was, be warned finally, "ruthless" and had "limitless and overwhelming needs".

Indeed the safely moralistic, tut-tutting approach to Jean's life-style, as distinct from her literary style, had itself become almost a cliché of criticism. Angier avoided that pitfall brilliantly, of course, realising that the life fed and led to the work, and that in Jean's case the two could not be separated. Far too many critics need to feel superior and so adopt some sort of rule with which to rap the artist's knuckles: it's even easier when awkward creative types are dead and can't answer back. Another woman academic writer, Lorna Sage, had earlier let fly at Jean: "she does sound ruthless – self-centred enough to make use of whatever class of 'attention' she could get." But then academics also are wholly pure and unselfish, earning enough to feel secure in judgement; creative writers may be less clever and worse off, but they can usually afford more generosity towards one another. To be fair to Sage, her opinion (from a 1983 *Times Literary Supplement*), assumes a coldly simplistic not a warmly sympathetic Jean, and even that assumption comes via various removes. The worthy young don was viewing an elderly woman in decline – reviewing the sad caricature of Jean in *Difficult Women*.

In the context of that peculiarly misogynistic work, Jean herself might well have declared with desperate, autocratic anger that writers were forced to be "monstrously selfish". So they are, in some ways. They need to survive as independently as possible, in order to get the writing done; yet the odds are stacked against, and often their struggle seems almost an impossibility. Desperation, quite as much as cheerfulness, keeps breaking in. We should anyhow remind ourselves of that significant and characteristic exchange in *Good Morning Midnight*, the discussion between the Rhys protagonist Sasha and the gigolo, where they reach a definition of 'a *cérébrale*'. According to the gigolo, the term denotes "a woman who doesn't like men or need them." Sasha retorts: "Oh, is that it? I've often wondered. Well, there are quite a lot of those, and the ranks are daily increasing." The gigolo's response is quite specific: "Ah, but a cérébrale doesn't like women either. Oh, no. The true cérébrale is a woman who likes nothing and nobody except herself and her own damned brain or what she thinks is her brain."

Jean believed that while you don't actually hate people, you must be wary of trusting them... For both as woman and writer you are safe only when alone. Then you can observe, being left free to think; you become inviolate and independent. But in other words too, you're only allowed freedom within your mind, inside your own head. You mustn't let any gleam of intelligence show or you will be suspect, if not yourself hated. To keep intact your secret self – the imagination, that inner beauty – you must keep up appearances, paint your pretty face, smile and behave as others expect of you... Gifted with beauty and brains, Jean knew she would have to pay. Hence the ageing and very vulnerable Sasha, adrift in Thirties Paris, can no longer take for granted either looks or money. She knows also that there is always a price to be paid and continues to analyse herself unsparingly. The scene ends wryly, with her own last words on what she perceives herself to be. She pronounces on that cérébrale the gigolo has depicted:

"In fact, a monster."

"Yes, a monster."

"Well, after all that it's very comforting to know that you think I'm stupid... Let's ask for the bill, shall we? Let's go."

The Thirties themselves are long gone, so are the Seventies, and Jean too. Before much longer the memories will blur, but if her words remain, stay clear and are read, then perhaps that's all she would have asked for. Did she really deserve, let alone ask for, those demeaning epithets? I recall a headline in yet another Sunday broadsheet article – THE OLD PUNK UPSTAIRS. Its author, that jovially vulgarian vocalist George Melly, dubbed her 'Johnny Rotten', and concentrated on the sloppier, slapstick elements of Jean's disintegration. He seems to have treated Jean – a Jean by then on her last legs, yet not going gentle into anybody's goodnight – with an uneasy *mélange* of kindly patience, frantic hospitality and sporadic insensitivity. But maybe I also misread him...

•

Let's now loop back into the labyrinth of words, via another departed mythmaker very much worth the reader's while. I quoted earlier that bookish storyteller, the blind seer Borges. So it's fitting to end here by again quoting him quoting one of his own favourite writers: "Enchantment, as Stevenson said, is one of the special qualities a writer must have. Without enchantment, the rest is useless." What Jean that wonderfully rare old woman possessed, and what possessed her, was a mysterious and captivating quality which somehow survives her. It's a strange fate being a spellbinder: others may well hate you for it. You may be rewarded with love, but for that you will always have paid. Jean sang for her supper; she paid with her books. Whatever else she did or did not do in life, the lovely lonely monster should be forgiven, since she surely won't be forgotten.

Dark visions of childhood

Who can judge what is phenomenal? Who decides what is a natural or 'unnatural' event? When nobody, adults included, can explain the general fear, nor refrains from showing their own – where is comfort found and what does one believe?

Our view of the world is irrevocably coloured by our earliest memories of childhood, and as we age these memories return, thronging around us like ghosts. Jean returned to her birthplace, the Roseau of her childhood, with a disquieting three-page reminiscence from her last collection *Sleep It Off Lady* (1976). Read carefully, 'Heat', a very concise, wistful yet doomladen piece of personal history, reveals a great deal about Jean. It shows how her West Indian background in one sense proved, imaginatively at least, inescapable, and how too in another, important dual aspects of her own character naturally cohere.

Her detached clear-eyed vision, simultaneously knowing and innocent, always seemed to retain something of the child's amoral objectivity of regard. A sublimely unconcerned concern, if it can be so described. Jean's focussed gaze remains unperturbed even when facing some or other extreme upheaval, and yet its very attentiveness belies that first impression of impassivity. Everything is being noticed, nothing escapes that stare. What is noted is not forgotten and in due course will disturb, given time... Ford Madox Ford had earlier praised the primary, 'writerly' side of Jean, the aspect to him most evident in her 1927 literary début, *The Left Bank.* He prefaces the collection by remarking on Jean's "singular instinct for form". The instinct, the shaping spirit, was never to change throughout Jean's long life. It's quite explicit in 'Heat' too, where this octogenarian describes her 12 year old self. She constantly stares at the twisted candlesticks her father has salvaged from the Martinique eruption. They hang on the dining-room wall and Jean's mealtimes are spent "trying to make sense of the shapes".

The other attribute of Jean, part and parcel of her oft-remarked 'helplessness', could exasperate those not prepared to understand or make allowances for it. This side of her temperament might sometimes be construed as a survival tactic, a ploy of complaisant femininity – the 'little woman' pose conveniently adopted for manipulating the more ingenuous type of male. It was a kind of *laissez-faire* attitude of passivity, a shrugged acceptance albeit sceptical, of whatever might happen. Again, this has also been read as emotional inertia, a quiescence somehow exotically tropical and part of her heritage – avoidance of the fierce sun as one moves slowly, as one must, in the heat. Hers was a curiously languid, blighted temperament, canny and quiet yet quick to blaze... (Ford it was again, ever perceptive, who identified that weird, becalmed aspect of hers. While Ford by 1931 was otherwise partial, if keen to settle literary accounts, it's recognizably Jean portrayed as 'Lola Porter' in his somewhat tepid novel *When The Wicked Man.*) Indolent colonial and tireless neutral observer, Celt and Creole, privileged underdog: Jean was all these things, a curious mass of contradictions, and always the outsider bemused by her fate yet aware of her own chronic inability to alter it... For Jean, The Book (apart from any merely temporal beauty) would be her only timeless weapon; that way she could slowly but surely express a distinctive, rueful *esprit de l'escalier.*

Interestingly, as far back as that first Ford-blest book, *The Left Bank,* there is one story narrated by a young woman named Roseau. In Roseau, we find a complex Rhysian mixture of impassive perception and even passivity, alongside a more active awareness within a character receptively openminded. Roseau means in French 'reed'. Jean's women narrators and protagonists are, through this ironic echo of Pascal's famous phrase for Man, always *thinking* reeds – with all the heightened consciousness implied. They are acutely and painfully aware, their philosophy that of the survival of the weakest. As women, they also need to bend before the wind, and thus survive, inevitably shaken but never quite broken.

As for Jean's younger self, in the supposed safety of her home, Roseau, she tells of "a huge black cloud over Martinique". What Jean recalls is the disaster that befell Dominica's sister island. St. Pierre, the capital of the nearby French colony, Martinique, had just been wiped out by volcanic eruption, with the loss of about 40,000 lives. This sort of cataclysmic destruction was by no means without precedent in the Caribbean at the turn of the century. No one in Roseau for instance could feel sanguine about such a catastrophe: the inhabitants must have experienced sheer dread and a sense of panic. "I know now they were all frightened", writes Jean. "They thought our volcano was going up."

Only a decade before Jean was born – and she must have heard plenty about it from her relatives on Dominica and from other islanders – her home town had been hit by a similarly awe-inspiring celestial onslaught. Here's how that provocative chronicler of the phenomenal, Charles Fort, described it in one of his poetic assemblages of inexplicable facts, *Lo!*:

> I take data of another occurrence, from the *Dominican*, and *The People*, published at Roseau, Dominica, BWI. About 11 o'clock, morning of January 4th [1880], the town of Roseau was bumped by midnight. People in the streets were attacked by darkness. People in houses heard the smash of their window panes. Night fell so heavily that it broke roofs. It was a daytime night of falling mud. With the mud came a deluge.
>
> The River Roseau rose, and there was a conflict. The river, armed with the detachables of an island, held up shields of mules, and pierced the savage darkness with spears of goats. Long lines of these things it flung through the black streets of Roseau.
>
> In the Boiling Lakes District of Dominica, there had been an eruption of mud, at the time of the deluge, which was like the fall of water upon St. Kitts, eight days later. There had, in recorded time, never been an eruption here before.

Jean writes of the grave of a heroic young Englishman who had lost his life in 'their' volcano, "called the boiling lake... a sheet of water that always boiled..." "I thought of it as a mysterious place that few people had ever seen", she continues, and when two little friends call by at Jean's house, she is surprised to see they are carrying carefully labelled bottles. One boy offers her a jar, but its label reads: "Ash collected from the streets of Roseau on May 8th, 1902" and she refuses in horror. "I didn't want to touch the ash". Later that night, her mother wakes her, to show her the "huge black cloud over Martinique" and tells the young girl "You will never see anything like this in your life again". Jean avers that she "couldn't ever describe that cloud... but I have never forgotten it." Then comes a kinder cut, a very personal black-out, perhaps just a simple lapse of memory: "That was all. I must have gone to sleep at the window or been carried to bed." In Victorian novels, any such 'fade' (often the immediate female reaction to shock or trauma), would have been described literally in terms of a faint. Jean, very contemporary and so cinematic in her pictorial and dramatic presentation, seems to have edited out any specific reference to her feelings here.

The rest of the piece, a page and a half or so, underlines what even a hasty reader can appreciate: Jean's usual understatement and her unerring selection of detail carry us through to a masterly last sentence built mainly on monosyllables, whose 'rightness' and skilful simplicity take the breath away. 'Heat' in its three pages sums up Jean's uniquely suggestive reticence. She revisits a crucial scene of her childhood, reinhabits it, and gives us a series of clues to her lifelong feeling of 'difference', her isolation and how indeed she sees the world. A young girl then as now must distinguish and deal with the doubtful gift: life cannot neatly be contained or explained, preserved or presented as ashes. Ashes are the innumerable signatures left by death, vestiges of fear and mortality, all borne inside a clear cold urn whose glassy prison in itself retains a spuriously attractive aura of regret for what is lost...

Moving out and away from that sinister microcosm, the fearful limited gift she was shown so long ago and recoiled from, Jean Rhys touches on the themes of morality and hypocrisy that always fascinated her. There's a telling, witty paragraph about the gossip surrounding the destruction of the "very wicked city" of St. Pierre (a home for theatre, opera, free love!), as though a form of heavenly vengeance had fallen upon this Caribbean Gomorrah. Life and death, she is saying, cannot of course be so glibly accounted for. There must however exist escape routes, imaginative journeys, intuitions if not explanations.

Then we read: "As I grew older I heard of a book by a man called Lafcadio Hearn, who had written about St. Pierre as it used to be... but I never found the book and stopped looking for it." The book in question, which she surely would have enjoyed, by the Greek-Irish-American wanderer Hearn (1850-1904) – a strange, displaced poetic spirit like herself – is *Two Years In The French West Indies*, first published the year Jean was born. It is still rather difficult to find. But more importantly, Jean didn't actually need it, as she herself must have realised. There never *is* enough time, though books do have an uncanny way of appearing out of the blue when the intending reader least expects them: that is invariably the right moment for them to be read.

Now, however, that Jean is long gone – and soon after her death Roseau too was razed by a hurricane – she has been given a new status and proudly adopted within a West Indian context, as a Caribbean writer. Like Hearn eventually was by the Japanese, or Lowry by the Canadians, the cherished prose stylists are welcomed home in the end. Besides, they have meanwhile created and discovered their own spiritual destinations. When Jean, at the story's conclusion, finds "a pile of old newspapers and magazines", these ephemera tell her (and us) little or nothing. What they present is "the English version of the eruption". Moralising, injustice, politics, narrowness. The lack of true vision: getting it *wrong* therefore... All the things Jean hated. No wonder she didn't feel English. She wasn't. She was stateless, like all artists. And thus resides, most memorably visible in her work. For she was lent this language, as gifted writers are, only in order to celebrate it. She learned to illuminate the darkness through it, and it made her aware of both brightest sun and blackest cloud: how to bring books back from shadow and give shape to life and letters.

Mr Mackenzie, Miss Martin and their shadows

My bitter enemy next door is now telling everybody very loud and clear that I'm an imposter "impersonating a dead writer called Jean Rhys"... It's a weird feeling being told you are impersonating yourself. Rather nightmarish. You think: perhaps I am!
    – Jean Rhys, letter to Peggy Kirkaldy, 1949

Of all Jean's books *After Leaving Mr Mackenzie* (1930) tends to be most misunderstood, or at any rate the least read and in consequence undervalued. The novel is a haunted and haunting work, subtler and rather more complex than it first appears. Its protagonist Julia Martin when first encountered seems to be another very precisely-placed projection of Jean Rhys. Julia is thirty six; her affair with Mr Mackenzie has ended the previous autumn. Jean was thirty six in the autumn of 1926, when her two-year affair with Ford Madox Ford ended.

But what is ever finished, and exactly who, at the beginning of the book, has finished with whom? The title is ambiguous, and as always with this author, especially important. This isn't an energetic, Henry Green-styled titular present participle, for *After Leaving Mr Mackenzie* suggests also that past parting... What happens next? asks the reader, wondering what can or will occur after intimacy has been superseded by formality, farewell and departure. For Julia/Jean, replaced, displaced, past and present have merged: while she may live still in the past and be reminded of it, yet she must inhabit the present and look forward to some kind of future; her life must go on, but what *kind* of life? Then the author of this ruthlessly intimate novel is bold enough to step out of herself and offer objectivity to the reader, opting for third-person narration.

Julia's detachment, and her awareness of it, seems to have been the story of her life. Her book, like her life, opens in the loveless limbo of a cheap Parisian hotel room. Reality is cruel, cruel as age and her own fading looks. She feels as Jean surely did when writing her story that – at least by Biblical average – over half her lifespan has vanished. Time is passing and has already passed her by. She is an outcast without identity (no longer defined, be it noted, by her relationship to or with a man), a creature unreal to herself. Left drained of feeling, Julia can barely exist, except as a pale shadow – a remittance-woman living, literally, off the past. And then the regular cheques stop, as they do, as Ford's did... Affection, kindness, pity dry up just as the wherewithal does, and so the soul dies too, before the body. The prisoner is condemned to life, becoming a ghost even before the possibility of death. Nothing seems real any longer: everything is reduced to empty gestures, to going through the motions of emotion. Jean is said to have slapped Ford's face in the restaurant; Julia is written here slapping Mackenzie's face in Chapter 2. With her glove, and numbed by an odd, perfunctory form of despair, "she hit his cheek with it, but so lightly that he did not even blink". There is no relief, no release, nor any sort of resolution in the act. It's as if she scarcely exists, either for him or for herself.

"Poor devil" (she makes Mackenzie think at the end of that chapter): "She's got damn all." Lover was probably the least of it: Jean herself had lost a respected mentor, father-figure, patron, tutor, editor and generous friend. Ford knew everyone who mattered in 1920s Paris: once again, security had slipped away from Jean. She had forfeited her status both as married woman and as mistress, and no longer had a function or place. She was cut adrift, outside the 'respectable' society she'd anyhow never aspired to, but Jean was now even worse off. She was deprived of further easy access to those charmed artistic circles, among which she must have hoped to become accepted. She would clearly have known she couldn't afford to antagonize someone so talented, influential and notably kind.

Envisaging herself as Julia, and setting down her alter ego's emptiness with such sharp honesty in so fine a novel was a remarkable achievement, and one of which Ford himself might well have been proud. For he surely cared for literature even more than he had cared for Jean... On this evidence, he of all people would have recognized, however uncomfortably, that the promise of his protegée's early work had been fulfilled. If at times Julia seems insubstantial or unreal to herself, she comes to life and lives fully in these pages: Jean here does justice to the ghost of her youth and her dead love.

•

The artist Paul Nash and his wife met Jean when she was with Ford in Paris, in December 1924. Apparently Nash referred to her as 'The Ghost'. It struck Nash that although Jean's had been "a very pathetic and eventful history" (as that other somewhat underrated artist Stella Bowen would also corroborate in her own memoir *Drawn From Life*), she'd seemed, even then, to have scarcely "any real existence". Mrs Nash too considered Jean "ghost-like".

Certainly Jean in later years never had a sense of belonging anywhere: she lived permanently rootless, exiled, a stranger in a strange land, prey to coldness of every kind. "I belong to a past age really or a future one", she wrote to her friend Peggy Kirkaldy in a 1950 letter: "Not now." There was no 'home' to go back to: Dominica was a lost paradise. As for family and relatives, she closely resembled Julia Martin returning from Paris to London – to see dying mother, resentful sister, censoriously mean uncle – and finding she inhabits almost a different planet. Julia visits in desperation the comfortably off 'Uncle Griffiths': "But Julia sat outside the sacred circle of warmth. She was cold..." Julia will never be welcome round anybody's hearth: she makes others uncomfortable and she knows it.

She gets nowhere with smug types and hypocrites, and invariably has to flee, poor ghost that she senses herself to be, haunted as she is (as Jean must have been) by her dead infant. She tells the more sympathetic 'Mr Horsfield' "about my baby who died and was buried in Hamburg", and of her feeling of unreality about her past life: "But it had all gone, as if it had never been. And I was there, like a ghost." Her anguish, fears and self-mocking honesty simultaneously disconcert and attract men. Decent or exploitative alike, the latter seem to feed off her far more, or anyhow more subtly, than she ever does off them: "Mr Horsfield was filled with a glow of warm humanity. He thought: 'Hang it all, one can't leave this unfortunate creature alone to go and drink herself dotty.'" He cannot, of course, "talk sense" to her, as he declares, for she is too close to the edge, inhabiting regions he may never even suspect, let alone know.

Jean though, as always, has let the careful reader know. On the first two pages of her novel there is a scrupulous and skilful description of Julia's mean hotel room. "Its gloom was touched with a fantasy accentuated by the pattern of the wallpaper." Thereon is a macabre confrontation between "a large bird" and "a strange, wingless creature". Julia finds in this frozen grotesquerie some sort of predatory parable, the (in)human condition symbolized. "The effect... was, oddly enough not sinister but cheerful and rather stimulating. Besides, Julia was tired of striped papers. She had discovered that they made her head ache worse when she awoke after she had been drinking." We are warned that this is an unbalanced spirit, but also that Julia herself is aware that her mental equilibrium is precarious. As for the unpleasant creatures in eternal contention, "The branch on which they were perched sprouted fungus and queerly shaped leaves and fruit". This calls to mind another pattern, not Jamesian, not in the carpet, but all around, on earlier confining walls: "a florid arabesque reminding one of a fungus. If you can imagine a toadstool in joints, an interminable string of toadstools, budding and sprouting in endless convolutions, – why, that is something like it."

Why yes indeed, something like that pattern memorably set on paper by the proto-feminist writer Charlotte Perkins Gilman in the decade of Jean's birth. Jean I'm convinced knew the American author's famously gruesome, much-anthologized 'one-off' short story 'The Yellow Wall-Paper', from which that last quotation is drawn. Gilman's concise description of a woman's descent into madness – as the result of and as a refuge from – male domination, is not strictly speaking a ghost story, but the singular panic and frisson of terror it evokes are quite in the 'supernatural' literary tradition. Jean was a shrewd judge of an uncanny story, and this opening can be read both as *hommage* and as indication that the author intends to tell a macabre story of a lost soul trying somehow to rescue or restore itself.

The novel is filled with ghostly images, with numerous references to death: death is discussed, various deaths are remembered, death itself brushes by or is even more closely encountered. Julia comes back in time to see her mother die and finds a dreadful void:

> Julia thought that her mother's sunken face, bound with white linen,
> looked frightening – horribly frightening, like a mask. Always masks
> had frightened and fascinated her.
> She forced herself to stoop and kiss the dead woman.

Even death seems without real significance, a mask to disguise a meaningless abyss. Prior to this nadir of desolation, Julia herself has wandered London like a ghost, haunted by her failures – the excruciating losses of lovers and babies, along with the disappearance of any joy or purpose in life. At one stage her hold on life is so shaky that she even meets, fatefully, her *doppelgänger*. (There is additional irony here, in that Ford's best biographer Max Saunders has recently written illuminatingly about this nervewracked 'doubling' process within Ford's own books.) Julia, who has written to her old lover dolefully referring to herself as "an importunate ghost" is appalled to see "the ghost of herself coming out of the fog to meet her.

The ghost was thin and eager. It wore a long, very tight check skirt, a short dark-blue coat, and a bunch of violets bought from the old man in Woburn Square. It drifted up to her and passed her in the fog. And she had the feeling that, like the old man, it looked at her coldly, without recognizing her."

For Julia there seems no escape from the prison of self, of her shadowy fugitive existence. She has only to enter the palatial Oxford Street Lyons, as if hoping to shelter in these totally mundane, brightly lit and banal surroundings, before some or other form of weirdness singles her out. A stranger at her table suddenly rushes off, forgetting his hat, and returns to regale her with a "most extraordinary thing! I've just seen a man I thought was dead. Well, that's an extraordinary thing. A thing like that doesn't happen every day to anybody, does it? A man I thought was killed in the Japanese earthquake." One must assume that nothing is ever ordinary: perhaps everything is equally meaningless or meaningful. This excited "little man" may well be a kind of disinterested harbinger, bringing Julia a hint of unexpected survival against the odds, relaying a hopeful message in code. What *is* the significant pattern to life, if any?

The numbed Julia continues seeking refuge in banality. She hastens from the harsh light of the restaurant and ducks into the neutral or possibly friendlier dark of a cinema showing *Hot Stuff From Paris*. Julia may be just over from Paris herself, but in colder London dwells no easy escapist consolation: "it was strange how many of the older women looked drab and hopeless, with timid, hunted expressions. They looked ashamed of themselves, as if they were begging the world in general not to notice that they were women or to hold it against them." Directly after this further piece of dislocation, this temporary plunge into an unreal darkness, Julia Martin will meet her sister. Then, obliged also to confront members of her family, Julia must face up to her mother's death and be cut still further adrift before she can have a chance to discover who she really is...

At the Crematorium, Julia "is obsessed with the feeling that she was so close to seeing the thing that was behind all this talking and posturing, and that the talking and posturing were there to prevent her from seeing it." When Julia abandons herself to true grief – while honest enough to know it isn't simply her mother's passing she mourns – she seems to have a moment's mystical illumination. "Then the flame sank down again, useless, having reached nothing." I find these two pages horribly anticipatory and thus especially poignant. They make me think of Jean's own blazing honesty and struggle towards truth, and of how she must have regarded Max's voyage beyond Exeter Crematorium. She followed him there finally in 1979. I'm glad no earth, no force of gravity can weigh her light bones down, for I can't imagine her composed in decomposition nor ever resting in peace.

•

Fire purifies and frees. Ancestral houses, family homes may burn down – in reality, on Dominica, or in literature, as in *Wide Sargasso Sea* – but thereby too the body lets go finally of the spirit dwelling within. There's no further rottenness and corruption, no Shakespearean "cold obstruction" either. The poor flesh is purged and released, escaping the curse of life; the dead at last are freed and need no longer walk. After the fire there can be no sad or frightful involuntary return: no more vampires and zombis. Such things matter and exist for Julia, who cannot joke about ghosts any more than she can laugh over reality. The chilling Chapter 13, entitled The Staircase, charts the protagonist at her lowest ebb, closer in touch with death than life. She splits from Horsfield, who has no idea of her precarious physical and mental condition, and returns to Paris, resisting suicidal impulses and struggling once again thereafter to survive…

Jean, according to Rebecca West, was "enamoured of gloom". Bravely and unwaveringly realistic might be nearer the mark, although as her long life continued her steadfast vision darkened. Later books grew more sombre still. While she knew that one had to live on, in some kind of hope, she also recognized that the coldest evil destroyed hope itself. Rochester, towards the end of *Wide Sargasso Sea* threatens Antoinette: "My hate is colder, stronger, and you'll have no hate to warm yourself. You will have nothing." He breaks her, he thinks, by depriving her even of hate (and with it, of any purpose); following that, her beauty and reason seem to capitulate. "She was only a ghost. A ghost in the grey daylight. Nothing left but hopelessness." His flat, cruelly staccato triumph is, as the reader learns in the end, an illusion. The dangerous light of truth remains with the weak and wretched of the earth; the real victory may always be Pyrrhic, but here it belongs to Antoinette as she comes into her own.

Such terrible clarity of vision is in a sense superhuman, supernatural: to reach that stage – the fearless purification, even through extinction, of the individual self – may in fact be the meaning not only of Antoinette's own life, but of life in general. This can only seem hard to the point of impossibility, earning one's death with a vengeance! You shall, she appears to suggest, hope for nothing, not even justice. Accounts are never settled in the way you might wish; business is always unfinished. As for love, the fire of passion only refines it: give up desire or give yourself up to it; either way the element follows you around and will find you and turn the page to ash.

•

So what can happen in the end, after leaving Mr Mackenzie? When Julia meets him again, back in Paris, they seem temporarily to repeat their roles. He remains ineffectually goodnatured and totally misunderstanding, and she accepts from him once again (but for the last time) alcohol and money. The acceptance, however, is a token one, a form of ritual, and a way of writing a fitting end to a chapter of Julia's life here concluded. Thus they are enabled to make their final farewells, and do.

What will become of Julia afterwards? Is she condemned to continue, existing rather than living, haunting the *quartier* as before, a poor thin ghost? The ending Jean suggests, for Julia and perhaps herself also, is like none of her other conclusions. There is a simple-seeming, strangely pure, 'all passion spent' last paragraph, rendered in a prose just short of poetic. Three magically economical sentences do the trick, bequeathing if not – God forbid! – a glib happy ending to *ses années folles*, at least a way forward out of the dark wood:

The street was cool and full of grey shadows. Lights were beginning to come out in the cafés. It was the hour between dog and wolf, as they say.

A wonderful end, to be read as positive, since full of potential – neither light nor dark, like the Gallic 'crepuscule' invoked. This dusky twilight (*entre chien et loup*, the French phrase places it), is not only 'the blind man's holiday' defined by Brewer's Dictionary, but an enchanted time when anything can happen. A time of miracles and meetings, where private and public meet.

Compare the *al fresco* conclusion of an earlier yet also unusually mystical and death-obsessed story. John Buchan's *Space* (first published in 1911) has his narrator-protagonists – more conventional male outdoor types, the pair of them – finally emerge from "a glen all swimming with dim purple shadows". Then at last is revealed their shared tale's weird *dénouement*. But Buchan's own observation, seemingly, precedes and paves the way for an ending which manages to be both canny and uncanny: "The world was not quite the same as an hour ago. It was the hour, as the French say, 'between dog and wolf', when the mind is disposed to marvels."

For the female of the species too, for Jean as for Julia – city-dwellers through circumstance at least, if no less threatened by mortality – this hour represents a real yet spectral time. A special conjunction, a brief spell of promise and possibility. A re-entry into the world of the living, where words take on life and Julia-Jean or any of us may rejoin the human race. There may be danger in those Rhysian "grey shadows" and the cool will inevitably turn to cold, but there's excitement and transformation too. Triumph and disaster alike are lurking. As for 'wolves', it is implied that Julia can cope – maybe the better for her past experiences; dogs, generally in the majority, can more easily be lived with. Nordic mythology tells how with the twilight of the gods (the end of the world) the monster-wolf breaks out of his prison to devour the sun. In alchemy, a dog devoured by a wolf represents the purification of gold by means of antimony. The greedy battles for the soul go on, while the soul aware or not, goes devoutly on its own quest...

Do I read too much in this? Can you ever read too much? (She might have been amused at that thought.) Jean Rhys was a fabulous artist, a weaver of dreams, and an ever-rewarding writer to reread. Reading her again, one learns to appreciate her more clearly, catching sight of subtle, unexpected truths and transmutations here and there. When brightness has all but fallen from the air and artificial lights start to appear, people often feel uneasy, sensing the approach of night. It's a transitional time I like to associate with Paris and Julia

Martin. Perhaps too, as Jean's artfully-drawn character intimates, that's the best time possible to re-encounter and come to terms with the ghosts inhabiting one's past.

Jane Eyre/Jean Rhys

Presentiments are strange things! and so are sympathies; and so are signs; and the three combined make one mystery to which humanity has not yet found the key.
  – Charlotte Brontë: *Jane Eyre*, 1847

The paired names, both invented. Women of letters. The letters simple yet very complex constituents linking these imagined and dead women, lettered individuals whose marks are left on their vanished worlds. These signs once almost united them; between them there was a coded, immediate balance. The letters signified something unknown and unrecognized: here disembodied intelligences were given form and enabled to meet in democratic space, outside dictatorial time. They found themselves being redirected and composed, written together, black on white. This way the dead walked with the living, the unreal became again real. It may be seen and heard how the names themselves (twinned echoes, haunting monosyllabic sounds redoubled) seem closely balanced now, forming a just, euphonious quartet. Two characters – one imaginary or created, one imaginative or self-creating – only connect on paper across two centuries. They are joined in a subtle relationship, entering into a mysterious symbiosis.

Yet it wasn't the respectable Jane Jean liked. It was the Other, that crazy creature – the plot-twist polite readers shouldn't mention or name, the hidden captive. That lunatic, the shunned disenfranchised wretch, the dangerous anarchic spirit which could never be totally suppressed. When revealed, she is duly identified as unrespectable – and therefore socially outcast, beyond the pale, incapable. Thus the hapless, sexually theatening Bertha (i.e. birther) has had to be locked away. Barred from any possibility of new life, denied all hope of creation... However, this blighted and benighted alien, this dark Gothic exile keeps her vestigial flicker of hope, retaining the terrible power of retribution through destruction. No wonder Jane pales beside her! ("Ghosts are usually pale, Jane", Rochester smugly informs his governess and carer-to-be, and on the whole they deserve each other, attaining the moralistic, unrealistic and thus only half-happy end.)

The issue of control is here at stake, of course, although never quite confronted. Nor can its corollary, male hypocrisy, yet be fully addressed. Relationships must function without love or challenge, safe households where one's place is known and assumed. But how shall wrongs be righted, righteous anger be repressed? Injustice can't be contained indefinitely nor ignored. Nor banished to the back of one's mind. Nor allowed only antics in an attic. Hence what is to become of the penned, cooped-up caricature, the *dea ex machina* her own creator couldn't make really convincing? The outrageous ghost of the past. The disturbing spirit. The fearful, vengeful *folle du logis*...

She it is who disposes of Thornfield Hall in the end, damaging credibility with her demise. The novel collapses around her in the blazing rubble: not so much a dying fall, as anticlimax thereafter, while loveknots and loose ends are piously tied. The madwoman in taking revenge becomes spectacular. She attains apotheosis – she who was set aside, never even acknowledged, let alone allowed *respect*. Victorian values are taken for granted: those persons granted respect rarely do change... Charlotte Brontë knew well enough who they were, but she herself finally had to draw back from the edge. The result was a flawed novel, if not great, often inspiring. As for the ones granted respect, novels never changed them, anyhow. They persist, the safely entrenched, power-crazed, uncreative types – versions of *homo Victorianus,* authoritarian, affluent yet grasping. They persist with their allies, alongside all those who would govern or teach while exacting obedience and respect that is neither fitting nor properly earned.

In vexed areas where her predecessor had not been bold enough to venture, Jean didn't fear to tread. She struggled for years towards her own inspired vision. It was just this Other, *her* Antoinette Jean loved:

She seemed such a poor ghost, I thought I'd like to write her a life.

•

'Bonds', 'vassalage', 'slavery' and many similar or related words recur in *Jane Eyre.* Women readers are therefore still bound to relate to the book and to react to its main elements of anguished satire and angered passion. Women writers too. Especially the more intelligent, such as Elizabeth Bowen, enquiring in 1942: "Might this be called the first feminist novel?" "Jane wants much more than love", wrote Bowen, "she wants human fullness of life – the book voiced, for the first time, woman's demand for this". Not anyway to be a drudge, a breeding-machine, a ghost, a creature living out its death-in-life, a prisoner without the 'reality' of gender, identity, or rights.

Jane Eyre seems to me most a novel of protest, a brave and bracing cry against passivity. But like nearly all the fiction of its time it was prolix and needed pruning. Jean's original achievement in *Wide Sargasso Sea* was to extend, explore and modernize, while also rendering timeless, that cry, that yearning, and all those other vital elements she rediscovered in Brontë's novel. Jean set into more concentrated, conciser form the poetry and pity of the sex war, precisely that which was left out of Brontë's (four or five times?) longer book. For Jean Rhys had the will and ability to move readers in fewer, more direct words. This is the poetic gift she possessed and by which she was possessed. It led other 'poetic' (read: 'boldly economical') women writers like Elizabeth Smart to praise *Wide Sargasso Sea*. Alan Ross, publisher of some of Jean's best stories, and a poet himself, saw in *Wide Sargasso Sea* "a haunting beauty, that has, in its genre, few equals".

What, though, *is* that genre? Perhaps we shouldn't even try to categorize any single genre, since the novel itself crosses into and cuts across so many... Like every ageless work it links up with, and is fertilized by and feeds off, the past: a great variety of traditions and sources, mainstream or alternative; mythical, mystical, historical or realistic; social-racial, etc. In truly contemporary style (avoiding the term Modernist and all its predictable prefixes and meaningless 'posts') Rhys collages, borrows, adapts, subverts, reconstructs, invents and finally unifies the most unlikely material within her unique creative sensibility.

The author will live with it, do her time on it, find due release only when agreeing to let it go: delivery and deliverance. A decade or more has been required fully to dream it and draft it and set it down. Her last husband's death, her own heart problems, prophetic intimations: variously distressing events seem to coincide with the birthpangs of the book. But this literary offspring will bring the seventy-six year old Jean honour and respect, although her own lonely journey is by no means done.

She'd never become respectable. Too much rage and sadness in the world, in her own world. She had wanted to be happy. Years of solitary work were required to dream it, draft it, set it down. Then Jean must have realised that at last her ghost was gone; given a new life, she could no longer haunt Jean. After the relief and the release, depression set in. Such respect, honours, money! It was *immaterial*. Too late anyhow, what with her real life all behind her, unravelled, fading into the past.

Those of Jean's friends and readers who survive to look back at her last years (the next thirteen) must wonder how she kept going. It was remarkable she did, and that she struggled on, writing, revising, publishing. Unlike her health, her standards did not decline. But retirement, comfort and silence weren't her style. It had taken so long to learn how to write: that knowledge could never be abandoned; deliberately abandoning it would have meant death unearned.

Anyone else, after writing a *Wide Sargasso Sea* (and who else could have?) might have rested on her laurels. Born to bear such a mature work, wearing beauty's terrible mask that might suit equally some youthful liberated spirit of the Sixties or an ancient classical Sibyl, she makes us a present of her gift and sends her wonderfully enigmatic missive to the future.

•

Who blames me? Many no doubt; and I shall be called discontented. I could not help it; the restlessness was in my nature; it agitated me to pain sometimes.
     – Charlotte Brontë: *Jane Eyre*

Those words Charlotte Brontë ascribed to Jane could have described Jean. "She does not attempt to solve the problems of human life; she is even unaware that such problems exist; all her force, and it is the more tremendous for being constricted, goes into the assertion, 'I love', 'I hate', 'I suffer'". Apart from the rather sweeping assertion in the second section of that sentence, the comments passed uncannily fitted Jean Rhys. In fact they stem from that very uncommon reader Virginia Woolf, referring to Charlotte Brontë. Woolf (herself a far superior critic than creator) continued accurately to characterize the kind of writer that both Brontë and Rhys were: "For the self-centred and self-limited writers have a power denied the more catholic and broad-minded. Their impressions are close-packed and strongly stamped between their narrow walls. Nothing issues from their minds which has not been marked with their own impress." Most strikingly, Woolf summarizes their shared hatred of injustice: "There is in them some untamed ferocity perpetually at war with the accepted order of things".

The intensity of such vision, fuelled by compassionate grief and rage at female helplessness, is distant and distinct from self-pity, far more active than passive. At least there is equality in words; one may be revenged in and by imagination, ordering events in a form of words that finally satisfies the soul and lets it rest in peace, delivered of its wrath. Here the weaker sex shall shed its burden and grow stronger: within books wrongs can be righted. Lives may be reinvented, just as lines are rearranged, lies revealed: to tell the truth means to tell your story as well as possible.

Brontë takes revenge on behalf of women ('the fair sex' as Victorian males liked to call it) for all the cruel unfairness and hypocrisy that a patriarchal status quo had inflicted upon them. A dangerous undercurrent of violent sexuality runs through the novel, reducing and damaging the spirit: men and women alike are crippled and contaminated by it. There is horror and disgust in Jane's description to Rochester of the creature simultaneously presumed unnatural and supernatural – the foreign body that's in fact human, all too human, his own lunatic wife. "Fearful... ghastly... discoloured... blackened... purple... the lips were swelled and dark; the brow furrowed: the black eyebrows widely raised over the bloodshot eyes," etc. That it is alien, darkly "savage", somehow subhuman (i.e. racially, sexually threatening, its bloodlines tainted) is underlined. So much so that when Jane eventually remarks that it reminded her "of the foul German spectre – the vampire", it seems an unconvincing afterthought, subverting with cliché the emotionally loaded description earlier provided. By the end of the book, savagery has got the better of Rochester too. Jane hears how "he grew savage – quite savage on his disappointment: he never was a mild man, but he got dangerous... shut himself up like a hermit... walked just like a ghost about the grounds and in the orchard, as if he had lost his senses", and so on.

But revenge and revelation are still to come. Rochester, who has not seen fit to explain to Jane "the mystery of that awful visitant", will himself be visited by far worse than mere "mental terrors". By virtue of a further irony the fair sex will revenge itself on the unfair one: for his sexual exploits and exploitation, his lying and philandering, Rochester must be punished. Crazed, crippled, blinded, one hand amputated – the final terrible vengeance falls just short of castration. The real spectre at the Victorian sexual feast was syphilis. Here, more likely, might have been the imagined fire that all but consumes him – via the rough justice of unmentionable metaphor, meted out to him by a triumphant female trinity of victim, narrator, creator.

So, reader: she married him. Do you easily accept that this damned and damaged man was rescued by the love of a good woman? That temperaments poles apart were joined together in connubial bliss? A first-born child gets a cursory mention in the closing paragraphs: male, resembles his father, and healthy – touch wood, thank God, etc. All in all, Jane protests too much: the mutual happiness seems most briskly insisted upon. The ironic measure of just how much Jane cares for him is that now she actually must. Edward acquiescently and necessarily ends up in Jane's power, although not *really* blind, not *really* emasculated, not *really* a wheelchair case: it's one of the more cheerfully gruesome endings in English literature.

A still more comfortable extension of – or variation on – this snug-and-smug, unconvincing uxorial scene was relatively soon supplied, and by a male writer. Indeed, Walter De La Mare ingenuously imagines his eponymous hero *Henry Brocken* (1904) as house-guest of 'Jane Rochester' and her "moody and taciturn" husband. If Jean ever read *Henry Brocken*, she must have thought its third chapter a piece of wilful whimsy, an encounter oddly gentle and genteel, altogether too fantastical.

By contrast, Jean was later to insist upon the blazing right of an oppressed individual to her own voice and say; *Wide Sargasso Sea* would let the dispossessed have the last word. Through restoration and exploration of such rights the novelist's method finds form and meaning. In the process are created fictive lives becoming distinct and finally separate from their creator's own.

But in Brontë's book, everybody must learn the lesson (marry or burn?) from governess Jane and henceforth behave well and politely. Men may stay put if immobilised; they are only to be trusted if women keep more than one eye on them. Genteel piety prevails; pity is suspended along with disbelief, while rage is well and truly banished. The fearful, fleshly side of relationships – the awesomely carnal element in fact, in all its savagery – will return, taking on conciser forms.

It's only further into the twentieth century, however, that we see this delirium hit the dysfunctional homestead: a doomed syphilitic domesticity focusses Bataille's *Histoire De L'Oeil* (1928). Then, quite as concentrated and as angrily bold, there follows the reviving and recuperation of Brontë – via her possession of *Jane Eyre*'s own avenging angel – by Jean Rhys.

Dark pictures moving in the mind

"Do you think that too," she said, "that I have slept too long in the moonlight?"

       – *Wide Sargasso Sea*

In *Wide Sargasso Sea*, Rochester and Antoinette contract a loveless arranged marriage that is by implication contaminated from the start. Such arrangements are bound to involve dishonesty, exploitation, struggles for power. How can self-respect, equality, let alone love, survive? The bait of money attracts to itself attendant evils of greed, snobbery, hypocrisy. "I have sold my soul or you have sold it", Rochester dreams of writing to his father... Trapped by (yet separately trying to resist) mammon, the illfated pair resort to various kinds of irrationalism and both have recourse to differently attractive 'magics'. They misread and misinterpret whatever truth might reside in the relationship and with their quite dissimilar egoisms, prejudices and superstitions not only blight love's possibility but turn it into loathing.

The hotblooded Antoinette dreads the prospect of being owned, used, and finally deserted by the chilly, mercenary stranger she has agreed reluctantly to marry. She who is destined to be made and held captive shows her fear of being made over into some safer, obscurely subservient, Anglo-Saxonised 'Bertha'. Such seems to be Edward Rochester's eventual, sardonic version of her. But she temporarily pretends to adopt, if not become, this alien-named persona ('"As you wish" she said.'), meanwhile hoping her drastic spiritual gamble will succeed. Through the power of her sex and the use of obeah, she may be able to re-enchant or even enslave the lover she needs and cannot bear to lose.

Rochester, having received information about her "bad blood", self-pityingly regards himself as a dupe of circumstances, rather than one acting from the first in dubious faith. He duly turns into the archetypal suspicious husband, cross-questioning 'Bertha' (since 'Antoinette' to him now signifies matrilineal madness) about "the white powder strewn on the floor". She answers that it's "to keep the cockroaches away" – ironic reference to her early reactions to being called "white cockroach" by the blacks. However, through desperately embracing the concept of 'blackness' and 'black magic' (read: instinctual, freely-indulged sensuality), Antoinette will initially succeed in her design...

Meanwhile there's an enthrallingly tricky piece of description, from Rochester's viewpoint, just before he succumbs to this newborn succubus. It's a neat twist on the Byronic "Love watching Madness with unalterable mien", for here the man implies that he still cares for her, regardless of potions and duplicity. His surrender is a knowing one, so this coldly calculating anti-hero claims, although its consequences may well be deadly: "The light changed her. I had never seen her look so gay or so beautiful. She poured wine into two glasses and handed me one but I swear it was before I drank that I longed to bury my face in her hair as I used to do. I said, 'We are letting ghosts trouble us.'"

A night of abandon, poisoned also thereafter by disgust: only the ghosts of love remain. The wrongs done to one another and to love itself are different in scale and intention, but in their mutual betrayal man and woman are unworthy equals. "You are trying to make me into someone else, calling me by another name," Antoinette reproaches him, just before the ashes of her passion turn to hatred and madness: "I know, that's obeah too." Rochester is later clearly informed about Antoinette (by Christophine, her nurse and accomplice, the savante of these 'black' arts): "It's she won't be satisfy. She is Creole girl and have the sun in her." And so the child of the tropics is summed up – the doomed Antoinette becoming an exotic object, a reduced lost creature who will only find herself in her final revenge. At least she is allowed apotheosis of a sort, that "poor ghost", the revenant whose life Rhys reclaimed.

She regains dignity and her terrible beauty at the end. The woman Rochester wishes to hide away and write off as "only a ghost, a ghost in the grey daylight. Nothing left but hopelessness", is granted a value and a vision greater than her fragile self. Madness it seems, so unacceptably destructive in purely social terms, may prove of prime importance to an individual's deeper creative development. Such a theme runs through literature and life, from Lear to Laing, as a 'poetic' or mystical *sine qua non*. The blazing illumination (here both symbolic and literal) is ultimately dearly won, its awesome lucidity painful in itself.

The experience of madness is no escape from the pain of life, merely a mental equivalent or metaphor for it. Mental anguish generally cuts deeper than physical hurt. For some tortured souls, it's a dreadful concomitant of their life's long journey; the craziness of existence is viewed as part of a meaningless pilgrimage towards an inevitable blank page and a release from suffering. Others regard madness differently: "Madness is nearly always a supernatural punishment. A *hungan* [priest] even told me", wrote Alfred Métraux in his classic work on *Voodoo* (1959), "that 'only those who resisted the will of the mysteries' go mad."

•

> ... there is diablerie in the business after all, then!
> — *Jane Eyre*

Antoinette is punished for that most female form of *hubris*, a desire for and belief in love. Yet her own past, and also how she is perceived, seems to conspire against her, rendering her ever more powerless. She seeks to redress the balance in her favour, but the means she chooses compound her folly and accelerate her tragedy. "Voodoo is a practical and utilitarian religion", Métraux points out, "which cares more for earthly than heavenly goings-on". Thus to consult Christophine appears to Antoinette a last resort as viable and logical as it is desperate... After all, "believers are in effect excellent Catholics, extremely pious", who generally (e.g. ninety per cent of Haitians, according to Métraux) "perceive no contradiction, no opposition, between the official religion of the country and the particular faith that they have inherited from their ancestors". Antoinette (like Jean herself) has been schooled among nuns. She remembers a convent as "my refuge, a place of sunshine and of death", and remains both devout and superstitious enough. But to use those darker forces which are not her ancestral rights (or rites) proves a forlorn and awful idiocy.

For she doesn't belong, and never has done, upon that island. There is no place for her there: 'white niggers' and 'cockroaches' are despised by the blacks whose aid she would enlist; to white society, she and her family are tainted, discredited; for her husband she has been property and is now liability... "Creole of pure English descent she may be, but they are not English or European either", her husband reflects. *They*. Who, though? Who *is* she? She has no true place, so how can she ever discover what or where that place might be? In lonely despair this outcast of love, betrayed and rejected by 'her' island, the familiar natural world, turns instead for solace and solution to the supernatural.

The terrible result is that she loses – not gains – control of life and love. Illusion and delusion meet. She is taken away, sent away, put away... Phrases whose various meanings Jean herself experienced only too well. To end placeless, displaced, isolated, marooned in England, out of time, having outlived hers. Here too I could feel for my old friend and still do, when rereading *Wide Sargasso Sea* – trying to appreciate how wisely and wonderfully she transferred that personal pain to Antoinette and gave it universal weight. And what pain Antoinette too in creation brought her! The lucid confrontation with a darker self, the rage and violence suppressed, the madness threatening always at the back of one's mind...

Finally I suspect she came to regard herself as a living ghost, just as Antoinette (*"that girl who lives in her own darkness"*) does in the novel. "Sometimes I looked to the right or to the left but I never looked behind me for I did not want to see that ghost of a woman whom they say haunts this place." But the younger, dead self, the double, is always there. Meet that spectre full-face without a mirror and you shall be twinned – being both mad and sane; seen to be dead... The two girls Antoinette thinks she has seen may be fantasies or reflections, real or fiction. What is truly perceived and remembered or merely imagined. Herself and/or another. Jean is properly ambiguous there: "She met another girl and the second girl said, 'Have you seen a ghost?' – 'I didn't see anything but I thought I felt something.' – 'That is the ghost,' the second one said and they went down the stairs together."

Jean envisioned herself as a revenant elsewhere, most directly in the late story I've mentioned, but also in earlier novels. One recalls for instance, 'Julia Martin' writing to a former lover in that rather rueful yet realistic way of hers: "I hope you won't think of me as an importunate ghost". It's almost as if, in order to preserve herself and her singular talent, Jean fell into the habit of playing down her true worth, being self-effacing and passive. Sometimes this façade of reticent compliance parodied itself, spelled out as a generalised form of helplessness; sometimes alcohol might fiercely erase it, drink enabling her freely to spill forth demons of anguish and anger alike.

By the time of her triumph with *Wide Sargasso Sea*, Jean must have felt she'd used up her life, had in fact died years before. But though friends and contemporaries, lovers and husbands were gone, along with her youth and looks, mind and talent remained intact. I wonder anyhow whether she herself believed what Antoinette tells Rochester: "There are always two deaths, the real one and the one people know about." He, for all his own version of a Faustian pact, is neither fool nor simplistic villain; Christophine has said as much to Antoinette: "The man not a bad man, even if he love money, but he hear so many stories he don't know what to believe." Rochester's own revelatory response to Antoinette is: "'Two at least', I said, 'for the fortunate.'"

Rochester nonetheless, manipulative gold-worshipper that he is, is also turned into a ghost before his time. He is drained, null and void, like everyone who denies love: "I was exhausted. All the mad conflicting emotions had gone and left me wearied and empty. Sane." By a bold reversal, we are led to question the whole concept of 'equality', of madness and sanity, and to understand that his cold, hate-filled reasoning – the wholly hypocritical mask of social acceptance and adjustment – is the real root of cruelty and injustice. Antoinette, that instinctual being and sensitive unworldly beauty, *did* deserve a place, as he is fully (emptily) aware: "Above all I hated her. For she belonged to the magic and the loveliness. She had left me thirsty and all my life would be thirst and longing for what I had lost before I found it." He realises they have left behind forever "the hidden place". It is one of the most poignant variations on the Edenic myth in twentieth century literature.

·

> Men all are shades, O Women...
> Apart from your kindness, life's at best but a snare.
> – Walter De La Mare: *The Revenant*

Loss and exile. Lack of love. Ghosts of unhappy loves. No escape. Except into further thirsts, other losses, more intense unreality. Voyages in the dark, towards the end of night. Towards the end of the last novel. Drawn like a moth to light, to find light in the final words – "the dark passage". Trying to forget the hidden place of the heart. Through temporary oblivion. Oblivious to all. Forgotten by the world, life passing by. But memory miraculous, not blotted out, never addled by alcohol. Preserved rather, to live to write another day.

Another, and another... "'I am not a forgetting person', said Antoinette." But somehow by good work one does forgive. And hopes to find forgiveness, in remembering what one can, in writing what one knows.

The oracular old crone has her own obeah. She tells Jane Eyre she is "very near happiness; yes, within reach of it. The materials are all prepared; there only wants a movement to combine them. Chance laid them somewhat apart; let them be once approached and bliss results." Here her message might have been spoken specifically for Jean, urging that journey via *Jane Eyre* towards *Wide Sargasso Sea*. It's just a matter of the right book read at the right time by the right reader... A life may be rewritten. Your life may change if you make your inspired guess at its meaning. Everything fits into place: one year, ten years, as long as it takes, the time will be there for you. You'll make it, you'll make the book, it'll be the making of you...

Not for nothing the crone asks Jane: "Then you have some secret hope to buoy you up and please you with whispers of the future?" Fictional Jane however is a conventional soul compared to the real-life Jean I knew. Jane requires only what the fortune-teller reprovingly labels "A mean nutriment for the spirit to exist on..."

So we should warm in any case to this wise old sibyl, this fireside sage. "[T]he glare, however, as she sat, only threw her face into deeper shadow: mine, it illumined", reflects Jane.

The mysterious chiaroscuro of good and evil, the fascinating paradoxes of light and darkness, glancingly hinted at in this short scene, continue to inspire. They will be depicted a century later in a new art-form altogether. Meanwhile, here's the crone again, after having briefly 'examined' Jane: "I wonder what thoughts are busy in your heart during all the hours you sit in yonder room with the fine people flitting before you like shapes in a magic-lantern: just as little sympathetic communion passing between you and them as if they were really mere shadows of human forms, and not the actual substance."

It put me in mind of the cinema, and *I* wonder whether *Jean* had seen any of the film adaptations of *Jane Eyre*. They're so flatly literal and inexpressive, shadowplay of the worst variety. By far the best is the one once least-regarded – but of course most poetic. It's a monochrome 1943 B-picture which in only 68 minutes still works its magic, and is now recognized as a minor classic in its own right: *I Walked With A Zombie*. This unique film (quite one of the most extraordinary to emerge from wartime Hollywood) was the brainchild of an emigré Russian writer-producer called Val Lewton (1907-1951). Together with the French director Jacques Tourneur and SF writer Curt Siodmak, working on the lowest of budgets, and using as basis both Brontë's book and Inez Wallace's recent newspaper articles on Haitian zombies, Lewton produced a masterpiece.

Its disparate elements are beautifully organized, stylishly fused, and so a dark, hypnotic, tragic vision prevails. No compromise necessary: only the title (foisted on Lewton) somewhat misleads. But, most surprisingly, there's no accommodating a commercial system, no sell-out. Methods painstaking, a scrupulously pure attention to detail. Each set-up superbly intricate, camera-movement fluid, editing swift, subtle, sure. Music, sparsest of dialogue, entranced performances – all cohere. Here it is, in a new variation, that hauntingly Protean, relentless tale. Related once again with weird conviction. This time totally un-Englished, filtered through many sensibilities, to be confined only to a West Indian island. Those perplexing relationships unfolded in a stifling atmosphere of alcoholism, mania and dark ritual. Shadows play out their doomed half-lives. Amid a complex web of faith and madness with, believe it or not, sanity and superstition hanging yoked together. Judgement can neither be reached nor be final, since different forms of madness rule both night and day. As for life and death (along with their transitional state, the enslaved purgatory of the zombie), these are inexplicable questions, presented as mysteries and accepted as such. Beauty and terror seem perfectly balanced and (certainly according to the eighteenth century's artistic formula for the Sublime) thereby sublimity is attained.

This concise and poetic work would have amazed Jean. Would have? Perhaps it did. *Jane Eyre* has been a source of inspiration to countless readers, countless artists. And in *Wide Sargasso Sea* a black girl tells the child Antoinette "you crazy like your mother", elaborating that "She have eyes like zombie and you have eyes like zombie too". Jean's own eyes were most unusual, as has often been remarked – slant and strange, hugely memorable: she was aware of that, and here and there wrote in her descriptive hints. (She was or had been a believer. She was superstitious too. I don't know if she specifically wished to be cremated, but she was.) It's curious and poignant also that she should have been variously persecuted for her differences and 'eccentricities', and that, despite final fame and fortune, she endured being maligned as the witch of Cheriton Fitz.

Which leads me back to the question of originality. Did Jean, herself such an original, ever see the Lewton film or remember it? All artistic 'originality' is a matter of making patterns, finding connections, spotting the secret links that unite humanity. If we recognize these, they can console or inspire us. Nothing else changes, nothing is new. There are shapes, shadows, figures in the carpet, pictures on the wall or in the fire, quilts of overlapping ancestral voices, prophesying or remembering, influences both verbal and visual, simultaneously music and mosaic. As for what or who came first, that's like the quizzing authors always get: *Q: Is the character based on X or Y or You, yourself? A: Je est un autre. His (or her) life is elsewhere. Q: But is it someone you know? A: Yes. Always. Never.*

So writers must repeat themselves, reminding themselves and readers too that all there is is freedom – finding one's own way onto the page. The perfect, pure democracy of the page where nothing is taken for granted and rarely at face value. The page, where it happens, where it matters, which it's all about. And what if someone were to ask: Yes, but how did Jean Rhys get there, how does one ever reach that *Wide Sargasso Sea?* There's no answer. I can't ask her now, and couldn't ask her then.

I can only conjecture, revisiting her here and trying to catch an echo. What might that wise old creature have told any new writer?

Go back to the beginning (perhaps), to that once upon a time... Then start again, cut and rewrite. Go back. Over and over again. A timeless book takes all the time you care to give it, all the time you have, all the time there is. Meanwhile you'll need to go back, back to talk to Lewton or converse with Brontë, go wherever necessary... To ancestors and friends, the living and the dead, back towards more distant mysteries and myths never written down. Originality – for you or anyone else – comes of having the courage to write them up, to seize the time whenever that time is right.

Beware, though. For you it may never be right; for her it proved so.

Different women

But in your bitter world, she said,
Face-joy's a costly mask to wear.
> – Elizabeth Barrett Browning: *The Mask*, 1850

While Jean was still alive, numerous critics were pointing out her resemblances to Colette. In 1970 one young magazine interviewer told her he thought of her as "an English Colette though with a different attitude, which shows most in your men" and inferred that she was "very irritated by the way men behave, perhaps irritated by men". Jean replied: "Yes, I do in my books but I feel far more irritated with women". The American professor responsible for the first full-length study of Jean, later in that same decade, also finds parallels with the French writer – "the knowing awareness of women and their motivations. the compression, the subtlety". Jean Rhys's women are, according to him (and at least in their pre-war incarnations) "devoid of Colette's sensuality... far less spirited, more resigned".

Jean herself pointed out the obvious differences: "I do admire Colette, her wonderful descriptions of flowers, trees and animals, animals especially. But she uses different subjects. Colette was a practical, a natural writer; she was brought up in the country whereas my life has been mostly lived in towns." Jean always maintained, both in conversation and in letters (such as this one from 1949): "I never wanted to write. I wished to be happy and peaceful and obscure. I was *dragged* into writing by a series of coincidences." Writing may after all have been what she found she was born to do; Jean in realising this became certainly an obsessive and a perfectionist. She knew also she was not, nor ever would be, the career professional Colette turned herself into.

Some similarities between these two remarkable women will inevitably continue to be remarked on nonetheless. When young, both for a time were 'kept' by men, older, influential mentors variously pushing and driving them to write almost despite themselves. Both of them were unusually attractive, both were actresses for a time, and both lived lengthy and promiscuous lives, disreputable before being honoured. But Cocteau memorably called Colette "a sort of little fox in a cyclist's outfit, a fox terrier in skirts": it seems clear that

Jean in her younger days was nothing like so energetic, doggedly resilient nor in any sense foxy. (Though that quiet, feline quality of 'sheathed claws', a watchful attraction she possessed even in old age was, to me as a fellow catlover at least, very evident.) Jean could learn and did from the stylish older writer's example, but compared to Colette, Jean's literary independence, that unique voice of hers, was haphazard and less organized, if in the end quite as stubbornly achieved.

Reviewing *Sleep It Off Lady*, Jill Neville observed that "Colette who also studies Bohemia makes her impoverished females fight back and often win. Jean Rhys women have only their ability to perceive, note, mark and inwardly digest. A dangerous and unpopular habit." Jean's studies of women are distinctively personal although these characters' helpless passivity may indeed seem irritating at first. But with their full (or empty) circumstances clear, with makeup removed, the individual souls caught inside these specific situations and persons are minutely explored and revealed to be profoundly human. We are all of us, the author is saying, full of imperfections. This is anyhow neither shallow 'feminine' nor aggressive femin*ist* writing, but something more deeply female, which manages to go even further finally, towards a finely balanced genderless art. Such economy of means deployed, without flirtatious frills or flourishes, results in no easy messages or conclusions; the Jean Rhys style is attentive, attractive, yet lethal. She never seeks to ingratiate and she doesn't miss a detail. Yet it is Jean's very scrupulous precision that has sometimes led critics of her work to linger overmuch on its descriptive, even painterly surface. Here the purely perceptive may be mistaken for the sleekly, materially passive.

Diana Trilling in her 1978 lecture 'The Liberated Heroine' made no such mistake. Everyone has a personal favourite Rhys book: Trilling thought best *After Leaving Mr Mackenzie*. But, she warned, "Today the woman's movement begins to focus on Miss Rhys as a diagnostician of female masochism", and while "her lady [Rhys's Julia Martin] is indeed a masochist", such an emphasis was misplaced. It was on a par with "labelling someone a proletarian novelist because there is a working-class character in her books". The critic felt that "Jean Rhys's dazed heroine was conceived only to serve her author's own frightening vision of emotional isolateness". That is in my view a perfectly just and viable conclusion.

Another admirer, novelist and short-story writer William Trevor, also seemed to be hearing "the bothersome voice of Jean Rhys" clearly in 1984. His article on Jean's *Letters 1931-1966* opened: "Jean Rhys, who never put a foot wrong in her writing, rarely put one right in her life. She was probably not more disaster-prone than most people, but she did not dissemble and although she hated ridicule and spitefulness she exposed herself to both: she lived as she wrote; honestly."

As regards the differences and difficulties of women, and Jean in particular, Trevor focussed tellingly upon a late but serious disaster in Jean's literary life, the Vaz Dias affair. This saga which I recall Jean still complaining about twenty years after the event illustrated how friendship can turn to enmity, how financial greed knows no bounds and, too, what problems alcohol may cause...

Selma Vaz Dias was a smalltime actress who as early as 1949 had wanted to adapt *Good Morning Midnight* for BBC radio. At that period, Jean's pre-war books were out of print and she was thought to be dead. Thanks, however, to that initial *New Statesman* advert inserted by a then obscure but enthusiastic actress in search of a good leading role for herself, Jean too was ultimately located, resurrected and reprinted. It wasn't until 1957 though, after the dramatisation was eventually broadcast and Francis Wyndham (then a reader for Deutsch) approached Jean, that her rediscovery gathered any momentum or any 'comeback' could be staged... Some time later, visited by Selma bearing whisky, Jean was persuaded by her to sign a none too clear, closely written piece of rough paper. Jean sobered up to discover that this was after all no joke. The half-cut Rhys had rashly signed an agreement whereby Vaz Dias herself would get a 50% cut of all proceeds from *any* dramatic adaptation in *any* medium of *any* of Jean's works *anywhere* in the world; Vaz Dias gained in addition sole artistic control over the said adaptations!

As can be imagined, after Jean's writing duly became applauded, translated and ever more lucrative, the problem of extricating the ingenuous and fecklessly generous author from the financial grip of her former friend became pressing indeed. To sort out a deal in the end (and perhaps rather fittingly) the services of another dramatic dragon lady were required. The fixer was the formidable Peggy Ramsay, *doyenne* of theatrical agents.

Ramsay, like Jean, was an immigrant from sunnier climes who'd 'put it about a bit' in her youth. She was twenty years or so Jean's junior and esteemed her work. Thanks to the agent's efforts, a settlement was reached, Jean was extricated in due course, and the publication of *Wide Sargasso Sea* could go ahead... It's sad to learn from the recent biography of Ramsay by Colin Chambers (Hern Books, 1997) that she was "not taken with the passive side of Rhys, the romantic victim". Ramsay, says her biographer, was repelled by Jean's "decayed femininity". This is perhaps in itself overly dramatic, but he also depicts a Ramsay who, on meeting Jean, is "shocked by what she saw... a painted doll, dressed in brocade, primped up against cushions and still trying to lure men". Ramsay the redoubtable, who ended up a millionairess, was apparently scared of ageing and loathed losing her own looks. We are told that this powerful woman, faced with the likes of Jean and seeing her now as a senile relic and an embarassment, was prompted to behave in most unsisterly fashion. Thus, "in her fright, she became utterly contemptuous of Rhys, the writer whom she so much admired, as if disgust might ward off the terrible fate that Rhys' frail figure presaged".

Sights not pretty, thoughts near ugly. What bitter scenes, women being meaner to one another than men are. Yet I doubt that Colette and Jean, had they ever met, would have behaved pettily towards each other. Above and beyond their own sex or sex appeal, they had in common rarer powers, an art to shore against their ruins. Uncommon and enviable consolation of a more lasting kind... But who among the promoters and go-betweens, the exploiters, expounders, big wheels and wheeler-dealers, will be remembered longest or best, and in what form?

Money and the chorus line

Gold is the idol they worship.
– *Wide Sargasso Sea*

...others thought she was a Dominicaine, which has been synonymous
in creole from earliest colonial days with 'fancy prostitute'.
– William Seabrook: *The Magic Island*, 1928

The 1968 Penguin edition, much reprinted thereafter, of *Wide Sargasso Sea,*
gets Jean's age wrong. It would not have worried her at the time. Knocking a
few years off that very long life, which itself had knocked her about, can't have
seemed important. I doubt however if Jean appreciated the second sentence:
"After her father died, she drifted into a series of hopeless jobs – chorus girl,
mannequin, artist's model..." With its flat, simplistic summary rather
inaccurately telescoping cause and effect, such a start to her CV might even
have rankled.

Besides, few artists like to recapitulate or be reminded of privations
undergone in their earlier days. Apart from those particular technical-creative
problems experienced in conjunction with their chosen life-style – and such
problems can prove both obsessive and curiously pleasurable – there is the
mundane matter of the daily struggle, getting (earning?) a living, actually
managing to survive. This struggle with its necessary sacrifices all too often
seems to invite dissatisfaction and disaster, not least where the financial or
sexual spheres are concerned.

A Salvador Dali may have dwindled into 'Avida Dollars' (Breton's cruelly apt
anagram for him), but even he wrote of earlier, straitened days, of being
disowned by one's family and haunted by "that exhausting phantom, the
constant worry about money". For an intelligent and artistic female like Jean,
cut adrift from the tropical childhood world she knew, and alone in "this cold
dark country, England" (*Smile Please*), life was inevitably difficult. It was, too,
Edwardian England, before the cataclysm of world war changed that smug,
comfortable, colonialist society for ever. In the male-dominated ethos of the
time, Jean's youth and looks were her only assets, and the theatre must have

seemed initially her best option for survival. "I had a complete conviction", she writes many years afterwards about her younger self, "that I was a useless person and that I could never get a job".

In every respect inexperienced and lacking in self-esteem, Jean joined the chorus of a touring musical show. She has concisely, poignantly and self-mockingly as always, described those travelling days of invariable hardship and varying humiliation. Perhaps this escape into theatre, towards a hoped-for independence, is one other reason why Jean has since been called "an English Colette". Apart from the general excellence of both women's writing, and their personal feline grace and beauty, both had to make strenuous efforts to free themselves from older, more worldly men – mentors who kept, controlled and exploited them in a variety of ways. (At least via a threefold or interrelated domination: mental, physical, fiscal.) Both women were, in the phrase of that distant time, free with their favours, though neither of course could truly be bought. But they themselves paid a harsh price for their apprenticeships. Gaining, using and indeed transforming their material the hard way (there's anyhow no easy way), both women effected the magical exchange, both underwent that sea-change into literature. Enriched, we as readers can only be grateful for what these great writers left us. And just what, for example, was left *After Leaving Mr McKenzie*, Jean herself – 'ex', exile and ex-showgirl, shows us...

●

"People talk about chorus girls as if they were all exactly alike, all immoral, all silly, all on the make", wrote Jean. She of course finds considerable differences in character and status between the "speciality dancer" – at odds with the other girls, themselves a very varied and surprising group – and the inevitable "company tart". As for the latter, Jean notes how they say merely that this woman "has a lot of friends". How strangely genteel theatrical life was then, on the surface at least, and how accepted this pretence of keeping up appearances! Yet everybody involved was clearly aware of that continuous sexual commerce which remained envied but unmentionable. It was after all the hierarchical heyday of stage-door johnnies clustering like flies on easy meat.

But the stereotypes don't change: this particular microcosm on display, this carnal carnival and market still obtains, persisting in ever more various and explicit forms. The chorus girl, observed Viennese psychoanalyst, Viktor Frankl, is not only "thoroughly depersonalized", but "a symbol of girls 'wholesale'". As just one component of a dance troupe or chorus, and thus merely a part of a collective group, she must in every sense keep in line: "in life as well she must keep in step". She cannot therefore burden the average male, whose erotic and aesthetic ideal she is, with any responsibility. She exists of course, to serve the greater cause of 'entertainment': take that (and her) how you will...

Frankl's *The Doctor And The Soul* (1945) may date from well before the breakthrough phase of international feminism, but nothing has significantly altered. "Just as one chorus girl in the revue can be replaced by any other, so in life this type of woman is easily replaceable. The chorus-girl type is impersonal woman with whom a man need have no personal relationship, no obligations; a woman he can 'have' and therefore need not love. She is property, without personal traits, without personal value. Only the human person can be loved; the impersonality of the chorus-girl type cannot be loved. With her, no question of faithfulness is involved; infidelity follows from impersonality. Not only is infidelity in such erotic relationships feasible; it is necessary. For where the quality of happiness in love is lacking, the lack must be compensated by quantity of sexual pleasure".

That, I thought, spelt out various aspects of Jean's unhappy lot prior to World War One. A woman on her own, needing money...What for? Why, to exist or subsist as a sort of sub-species whose members are nonetheless viewed as attractive acquisitions yet need to enhance their own prospects by being bought. Meanwhile she tries to keep body and soul together, to keep up appearances, to keep on living. And so she finds herself kept. A kept woman, who needn't be kept long... And what lies ahead for her later? Two out of three husbands imprisoned for financial peculation! Ironic catastrophes these must have seemed to Jean, looking back. For here were failed gestures towards security: if marriage means one is more 'respectably' bought, so entering bourgeois domesticity, Jean perhaps hoped thereby to forget or ignore the inescapably loathsome cash-and-sex nexus.

Frankl notes too that "it is amazing how frequently women resist the temptation to prostitution in spite of economic necessity". Often though, how often, there may be no hope and no other course but that desolate *Voyage In The Dark*. It is scarcely surprising if (as she mentioned) this harrowingly bleak book was her personal favourite. Jean in old age could still write with startling honesty: "It seems to me now that the whole business of money and sex is mixed up with something very primitive and deep. When you take money directly from someone you love it becomes not money but a symbol. The bond is now there. The bond has been established. I am sure the woman's deep-down feeling is 'I belong to this man, I want to belong to him completely'. It is at once humiliating and exciting."

No wonder she told me she knew all about being a black sheep. The impossible, greatly resented, disreputable dream of writing what one wants – and somehow managing to live within, on, off one's work – *could* come true in the end. But what a long and difficult journey it would always prove. To live, and transfer that life or another to the page; to make the page live. What a hope, some hope! And yet, *dum spiro spero*: Jean was right. She is well-regarded, valued now because she told truth, uneasy truth. Everyone has stories to tell; rarely does anyone tell them so beautifully. Somewhere along the line, most artists sell out, body and soul. Male or female, they strut and prance and try to please; by drawing attention to themselves, they hope to be chosen, to be bought. But without the necessary strength and talent, they end up slaves.

Free yourself. No compromise. You never, never rest on your laurels, and you keep on keeping on. These were other unspoken lessons learned from Jean. She hardly ever offered direct advice, but one was welcome to share what she knew. As for farewells, spoken or written, such occasions were always lightened with expressions and wishes of good luck. It went without saying that the best of luck was already mine, since I'd begun to know Jean Rhys.

Names and music

As with most autobiographical writers – and particularly those so self-consciously so, like Jean – she would bring into play games and private jokes when deciding on the selection of names. Thus writers memorialize, teasing the reader by all too thinly disguising places and characters. Their various transparent devices of 'concealment' used may include similarities of sound-patterning, reversing a few letters of a name, and so on. This is rarely only a simple authorial tactic – a matter of avoiding acrimony or not prompting grief, anger or libel. More often it's a very personal code that hints at some hidden discourse on another more intimate level. It's a further invitation to that longed-for ideal reader, clues planted as a form of secret-sharing, almost flirtatiously playful in intent and practice.

One of Jean's best stories, 'Till September Petronella' appeared in the *London Magazine* in 1960 long before I met her. Looking back now at my younger self, twenty four or so, on first reading it – this septuagenarian's extraordinary revelation of her enchanting youthful persona (it's set in 1914) – I can better understand my, and its, fascination. What's instantly and enduringly recognizable is that teasing, tantalising sexual power beneath the tale's deceptive, calmly described surface; it all seems to have been lived through, fully experienced not simply imagined...

Indeed, years after Jean's death, when reading the exhaustive 762-page biography of her by Carole Angier (Deutsch, 1990), I found those talented, edgy young protagonists convincingly identified. The artist Adrian Allinson, for whom Jean once modelled, is here himself the model for 'Andy Marston', while composer Philip Heseltine, later best-known as 'Peter Warlock' (self-styled), appears as 'Julian Oakes'. The mutual attraction-repulsion between Heseltine and Jean is but one facet of a hard, glittering gem of a narrative: their world, the old world, Jean's own world, was going to change utterly and very soon, and this inexorable drift towards disaster is subtly, lethally conveyed.

Jean is seen with the usual unsparing detachment, as both victim and catalyst, the passive object of desire or loathing. Yet she is well aware of her own very real magnetism, her sex appeal and ability to manipulate others, along with her own inclination (parlous as much as powerless) to let herself be manipulated by them. Jean presents inescapably – within this haunted framework of brief retreats from London and of wouldbe rural idylls fated to turn into sour defeats – her impulsive younger self, whom she calls here 'Petronella Gray'. Ella of course was the first of her two Christian names, while 'Ella Gray' was just one of various stage-names she'd adopted. Jean's favourite Soho club of the time, The Crabtree, is turned into 'The Apple Tree', while the arboreal motif is suitably, musically echoed by the links she suggests between oak and hazel. (Heseltine himself is an enchanter, attractive, resilient yet relentless. And despite Jean's clear dislike of him, this enigmatic man was also, she suggests, a genuine talent if not a force of nature.) As always, hers is an honest and unsettling vision, not merely a re-vision of the facts, such as they were. Events are never revised in her own favour: she may make up her face, but as for making up stories, the teller of tales must play straight and stay true.

But the music of truth is always there to be heard and recaptured, in its infinite variations, and all (all!) that's required is to ring and run the changes, tell the story, solo in one's own original voice. Just like jazz. An improvisation, ideally, that seems easy and fluent and spontaneous. Where everything falls perfectly, rhythmically, movingly into place, and in the course of which even extremes (such as protest or satire) can become inspired, highly personal celebrations of individual lives. A form through which, however momentarily or illusorily, life's energy and rhythm may be felt to be contained, with common or uncommon experience shared. Jean had, as good writers should have, an ear for music. She who enjoyed listening could make her own words dance. And she caught, first person (let it not be forgotten), the fine defiant lilt of Selina – black West Indian immigrant to 1950s London – in 'Let Them Call It Jazz'.

The song inside Selina's head travels with her via Holloway Prison and loss and racial hatred. It sounds to her like a fragment of truth and hope, but she comes to learn that it can't be stolen from her: neither theft nor distortion can destroy it, nor can money in the end buy it. Certainties are elusive though and invariably hard-fought. Nothing is quite what it seems. Selina is the daughter of a white man and a "fair coloured woman", but in Notting Hill she is seen as irredeemably black. This unjust burden to be borne renders her additionally vulnerable: as a stranger to the city, a trusting woman, poor and alone, she is anyhow fair game for oppression. Motives, like racial origins, are mixed and complex. Beauty is a prized illusion, not even skin deep, nor in the beholder's eye – but as for the unalloyed and truly ugly darkness, it lies mostly in the hearts of whites. Pure whiteness which (because there's no such thing) the realistic Jean hated, was the self-righteous province of her arch-enemy in the world – that whited sepulchre, the hypocrite!

"I've been a black sheep for so long" Jean wrote to me in 1970, "that I'm used to it & don't care any more". And certainly she (and two husbands) had had unpleasant firsthand experiences of prison and being outside the law. She'd always, from her earliest days in Dominica, identified with the oppressed, the underdog and the black, and the rest of her long life in Europe never caused her to change her views on that score. I think I might have complained to her at that time about some minor hassle with an agent or publisher. Or maybe I'd mentioned my own feelings of alienation as a foreigner in England (or Devon), or my estrangement from most of the family, in particular my fascistic father. Perhaps I'd only been lamenting, as authors tend to do, a lack of either money or current inspiration; it's the unfortunate if usually fraught relationship between these concerns which causes so many crack-ups and creates so many outcasts. At any rate she lent a sympathetic ear, as always... "So just get on with it, get with it, no need to worry about those trumpets", I tell myself now, rereading 'Let Them Call It Jazz'. And I remember Jean and recall snatches of music we'd listen to on that 'jinxed' record-player of hers which she swore she could never get to work as it ought...

At the end of her story, Selina finds herself complaining: "Even if they played it on trumpets, even if they played it just right, like I wanted – no walls would fall so soon". That music I hear in my head – be it something like Selina's song, or Jean's – becomes my own. A song I may invent to keep spirits high and senses clear, to keep me buoyant, and at best, in love with life. For now let's call it jazz, let's call it art, let's simply call it the pulse of hope. Or call it if you wish an inspired surge of virtue, this special-delivery, precious discovery, long-gone-and-still-here virtuoso version by Sidney Bechet – powerfully poetic and sublime as any horn there ever was. Hear that soprano sax wail away for us all. Feel it vibrate in the memory, even while it hits those ecstatic top notes to spill out a torrential last chorus of bliss and sheer exaltation. Never mind birdsong, trumpets or the likes of Gabriel – here's the lyrical and generous Creole spirit that Jean loved. Yes indeed, Joshua *is* fighting the Battle of Jericho, and the walls *will* come tumbling down!

Bechet and Zelli:
the music behind names

Sidney Bechet, "the wizard of jazz", as his British biographer, trumpeter John Chilton has dubbed him, was born seven years after Jean, towards the end of the last decade of the nineteenth century. (And was as secretive as Jean about the real date.) Like her, he came to know and love France – which proved and provided a spiritual and geographical refuge, a home for both these wonderful artists over a number of crucial years. There too, also like Jean, Bechet experienced pain and disgrace, as well as pleasure and success. And it was in France where the belated but ever-increasing recognition of such exceptional talents eventually led to legendary status in their latter years, continuing now to their posthumous near-canonisation.

Bechet, it's clear, could be as temperamental and awkward to deal with as Jean at her worst ever was. Paranoid, truculent, superstitious, proud, and given to bouts of violent rage, he would demand and command centre stage and the best spotlight – yet he deserved no less. He was an instantly identifiable, fiercely emotional solo voice, one whose awesome technical skill fused raw passion and a subtle, sublime poetic gift. This unique stylist could invariably inspire other musicians, overwhelming them or lifting them all towards his own rare heights. As for audiences, young and old (but especially the young) treasured that Dionysiac drive and directness, the beautiful, blazing sincerity that could kindle the coldest heart.

In 1959, not long after the death of "le grand Sidney, notre cher ami", I attended a memorial concert for him in Paris. A stream of musicians of all nationalities and ages gradually filled the stage; some among them, like so many others in the audience, did not hide their tears. It was inevitably, unforgettably, an evening for the blues: that's what everyone felt and what they all played... On and on that keening, elegiac mood continued, the heat of solos and ensembles trying to exorcise the cold shock of loss. Finally it was too much to bear – too much emotion cut adrift, floating free yet in every sense lamentably uncontrolled. I remember wandering away before the end. I couldn't take any more. My head and heart were full. I was nineteen then. But

I think I understood that neither individual nor collective grief could begin to shape (let alone with any truly loving art), what anyhow was impossible, an appropriate gesture of farewell. Nobody wanted to stop playing the blues – really the blues at that, and in the Parisian night, but it was not enough and now never would be.

Bechet was gone, himself swept away. All his most individual, special onrush of energy, all the flowing creative grandeur stopped. What survived wasn't necessarily the flawed, fallible, lovable essence – humanity, but (as in Jean's own chill story of that title, describing her husband's death) "the sound of the river". Only that perpetual river-sound: now hardly audible, like one's own breath; now to be heard finally as an inescapable threat outside oneself, something which enlarges absence and underlines the greater silence, desolation without end...

Sidney like Jean was irreplaceable. Both were creoles. Jean used the term in the old sense, without connotation of colour, referring to herself in particular, who happened to be white – or in general to people born and bred in the West Indies. (*Personne de pure race née dans les colonies* as Larousse has it...) True creoles, by the American definition, were usually whites of French origin born in New Orleans or neighbouring Louisiana. Interracial relationships then produced the 'café au lait' mulatto – also rather confusingly called creole, and generally denoting lighter skin. Such creoles, like Jelly Roll Morton, Kid Ory or Bechet himself, were all proud of their ancestral French connections. Bechet and these fellow 'musicianers' (as *he* referred to them) used the term in the looser, traditional, jazz sense, having less to do with pigmentation than with denoting the origin of a specific musical style.

And what style and technique Sidney Bechet had! His star white pupil, Bob Wilber wrote something about the maestro which put me in mind of Jean: "He was very concerned about telling a story... In other words, the start, the theme, the development, the variations, and coming to a definite conclusion. The idea of the form was very important to him". "The singular instinct for form possessed by this young lady" was of course precisely what Ford Madox Ford praised in his Preface to Jean's first book of stories, *The Left Bank* (1927). Ford – so dedicated, as he confessed, to "the technical side" – went on to perceive of "an instinct for form being possessed by singularly few writers of English and by almost no English women writers". Whereas Jean's stories "begin exactly where they should and end exactly when their job is done". Despite hectic lives lived 'to the full' (a euphemism) and including travels, sex, booze, blues and disasters of every kind, both she and Bechet were always creatively consistent: neither seems ever to have produced work by any standards less than good.

Reading once again Bechet's splendid autobiography *Treat It Gentle*, I find on the final page: "I'm an old man now; I can't keep hanging on. I'm even wanting to go; I'm waiting, longing to hear my peace." There too I hear Jean's voice, but she lived to be almost ninety. Bechet, when that was written, was not even sixty. (Nor am I – not quite yet, I realise as I write this. In fact, at fifty-seven, I must make the most of whatever time remains, living from day to day if no longer from hand to mouth.) At least now I expect to manage to bid Jean goodbye in spirit – on the page. And give her a kind of last literary wave, if not that actual farewell we missed out on... As for Bechet himself, he died in the City of Light on what's thought to have been his sixty-second birthday. The story ends thus on a kind of beginning and, recalling those wonderful solos, seems to close on a climactic high note of supreme symmetry.

"Me, I want to explain myself so bad", his book concludes. "I want to have myself understood. And the music, it can do that. The music, it's my whole story".

•

It's very possible she heard him play, in Twenties Paris, since all these paths seem to intersect.

At any rate, there's a story or two more to be told here. What's in the name Zelli, for instance? This is the surname chosen for the mirror-image or projection of Jean, her 'heroine' Marya in the first Jean Rhys novel, *Quartet*, published in 1928. It's unusual enough for one to speculate a little about its provenance. Knowing our author and her sly sense of humour and care for detail, you can bet it's not simply a matter of 'doing a Simenon' and plucking names for one's characters out of the telephone directory... Just a random gesture towards the exotic, to difference and 'foreignness'? Maybe. A hint perhaps, since its initial letter comes alphabetically last, that the bearer of such a name will also be always last in line, fated to be some kind of loser? Zed with its hint of bed-heat, drowsiness, even of Caribbean torpor... Does Z have some ultimate, waspish suggestion of loucheness, of not-quite-straightness, of zigzagging indirection? Well, perhaps I'm spelling out too much, but some authors, the best and most literate ones, have ways of reminding readers that one reads not only from, but into, the page.

Jean describes how "From the balcony Marya could see one side of the Place Blanche" and a few sentences later she underlines her meaning: "The Place Blanche, Paris. Life itself. One realised all sorts of things. The value of an illusion, for instance, and that the shadow can be more important than the substance. All sorts of things". This is the Place Blanche indeed – the white place, the *page* itself – where she will find her true identity as woman and writer.

What, then, from her temporarily privileged viewpoint might Marya-Jean have seen? "The nightclubs", observes that acute chronicler of expatriate life in the Twenties, Malcolm Cowley, "clustered near the Place Blanche". "In those days" he goes on, "Zelli's was the most popular with Americans". Another historian of the literary Bohemia of the time describes Zelli's as "an American-style bar in Montmartre with a jazz band and large dance floor, frequented mostly by English and Americans". Artists and addicts and socialites all regularly wound up at Zelli's – the likes of Cocteau, Princess Murat, Nina Hamnett, Christopher Wood – and despite its evident attractions, musical or otherwise, it was generally considered "not the most salubrious of places". Every member of that 'quartet' of her title – Jean, her first husband Jean Lenglet, Ford, Stella Bowen – either individually or in one or another grouping, would have been familiar with it.

A place, in fact where almost anything might happen… One with a name that spelt notoriety… Martin Williams takes up the story in *Jazz Masters Of New Orleans*: "In Paris in 1928, Sidney Bechet was arrested, jailed for eleven months, and ultimately deported because of his involvement in a shooting scrape in Montmartre at a nightclub called Joe Zelli's Royal Box. In the fight, Bechet had been verbally goaded and was shot at before he defended himself". Bechet was to admit: "I'm not for covering up any part of what's true: I can be mean. It takes an awful lot; someone's got to do a lot to me. But when I do get mean, I can get powerful mean. That's the way I was right then on the street outside that cabaret".

Bechet did his time and in time made his name. He was to become an international name – and almost a household name in the country which had once expelled him. The French would name streets and squares after this all too sensitive artist, the outcast and black sheep who turned into their own folk-hero... Such public commemoration has not yet happened in Jean's case. England is not the place for wild enthusiasms, nor is the West Country, which drowses on in its damp time-warp. There's not the ghost of a blue plaque at Cheriton Fitzpaine, though even that chimera may possibly appear in time. For the moment, it pleases me to recall how Jean and I sat there together, one afternoon of rare sunshine, listening to a lilting creole tune. Her 'temperamental' player worked fine that day. So we heard, soaring above his band of devoted young French musicians, their "powerful mean" but beloved mentor. Bechet had never really left, he was back now with another of his unique compositions, and we were glad to hear him tell his pretty tale. Such a nice musical bouquet for the equally disreputable Ms. Zelli, that unforgettable *Petite Fleur*.

Translating

And yet however far it may be from Montmartre to the Latin Quarter, the same ghosts are there, everywhere, alive and smiling and quick to touch me with the heady bitterness that rises from the past. But for them, I should not have been tempted to write this book.
— Francis Carco: *The Last Bohemia*, 1927

Really it's an impossible quest, the search for some fixed yet always elusive truth... Doing your best to find the right meaning, as if there ever were one. The multiple choices involved, the involved choices multiplying, when words in order should be so simple, seeming so natural. Trying to establish a relationship that will appear inevitable. Tuning into a stranger's voice and turning out its approximation, while hearing at all times a very particular tone, an individual style that speaks to you clearly or obscurely but which must be heard. The voice demands immediate conveyance for its story – however plain or fancy, trite or true – through the movement of that other chosen language, learned as your own.

Adopting a sound and rhythmic pattern foreign to you, you move to enter that imaginary world. In this land of startled shadows and ill-defined unease, doubt reigns and only the shifting shapes of words surround and bemuse the traveller. Guided by that tantalising ghost of a text – some long dead creation now distant, unfamiliar, dancing ahead out of reach, or at any rate never clearly visible in its paper-thin shroud – you try to grasp its fantastic will-o' the-wisp dance. But who can seize hold of another's fantasy, another imagination albeit compatible, so as to possess that bygone makebelieve which must be made believable all over again?

Make it breathe, make it new, give it a current life, get real, find guidance from the dead. You are still at the mercy of the approximate, bound for inevitable betrayal by being doomed to compromise. This is in no way an exalted task, although occasionally choice and scope are extended: some privilege is granted you, and you find you're in touch with a kindred spirit.

More likely you're boiling the pot, keeping your hand in, just doing a job as best you can. Once in a while there's an enthusiastic discovery, illumination ensues, an adjustment is made that's an improvement. You may be able to seek advice, if you're lucky: more often, you're exiled to silence and cunning. Any honest effort at communication is condemned to failure: depressing enough admission... And there arrives a necessary time or deadline when it is let go and lets you go at last. The effort of sharing another language and an unimaginable mind is done. What you have achieved is not yours in any case, but you may meanwhile have learned something.

•

Jean told me she learned something particularly valuable from Ford. It was a tip she seems to have passed on to writers generally, having found it useful herself. (Alan Judd, for instance, mentions it in his very readable 1990 Ford biography.) Jean said it was simply a question of first translating into French any sentence she had doubts about. This practice helped her 'decide' whether or not the sentence worked: if it went into French, it would also work in English. I don't know how rigorously she kept to this rule, but if a precise, objective prose like hers was the result, the procedure might seem worthwhile.

Ford himself had swung her the commission to translate *Perversity* by Francis Carco, and Jean's version of this novel of Parisian vice and its victims was originally published by Covici in the USA in 1928. There followed (hardly surprisingly) an unholy row between the ex-lovers, when Ford's name appeared on the translation, not Jean's. The quarrel has been well documented. It now seems the publisher alone was most probably at fault. Ford, whose generosity was legendary, could hardly have been petty enough to cheat his former protegée out of the credit for work he himself had put her way. (And to be fair, he only reinvented her as 'Lola Porter' some years after she had pilloried him as 'Heidler'.) At any rate, this claustrophobic Carco novel of pimps, prostitutes, petty crooks and escalating violence is scarcely one that the highminded Ford would himself have hastened to embrace.

Jean was quite diffident when I asked her about the book. She maintained she'd done the translation relatively rapidly and needed the money. She wasn't especially eager to see it reissued. (In 1987, eight years after her death, it was paperbacked by an American firm.) But *Perversity* still 'reads well' as a portrait of that Parisian underworld Carco knew intimately, while the descriptions of the bars and brothels of that era ring true enough. It's a limited slice of lowlife, a narrow enough segment of a small, amoral world, but the murderous climax is pathetically convincing. Francis Carco (1888-1958) was by no means a bad writer and certainly an intelligent one, yet by contrast with Jean's own work, his novel – if on the surface more explicit than hers – has dated. Somewhat lacking in pace and tension, it ultimately fails to lodge in the memory.

I am curious to see what Jean made of her first husband's book *Sous Les Verrous* (*Barred*, tr. Rhys, London, 1932). This even rarer fiction is a *roman à clef* by Lenglet writing as 'Edouard de Nève', and Jean is reckoned to have altered it considerably in the translation. As it dealt with much the same time-span and events covered by her own *Quartet*, it might be well worth reissue, proving of more general interest these days than hitherto assumed.

Jean loved the French language anyhow, and was sympathetic about my own efforts at translation from it. She fully appreciated the personal and technical problems such work entailed, and that the varieties of translations were clearly differentiated. They could be categorised as labours of love or money, but the former usually precluded the latter.

Since the mid-1960's I've published in both categories, translating occasionally on spec but mostly on commission, and it's been an invaluable help to my own work. One of my earliest versions of a French classic proved in many ways the most ambitious and hardest of tasks: translating Lautréamont (1846-1870). What with extensive reading and research, it took several years, and the *Complete Works* initially required two separate annotated volumes. Since Jean first read my version, it's been several times corrected, revised, reprinted and lately reissued as a single weighty tome. The better the book, the harder to translate... This rule obtains, no matter whether the style is dense or transparent, whether sentences are obliquely tortuous or tautly direct. Translators can scarcely ever consider their work finished, anyhow, nor feel it is that ideally accurate rendering originally hoped for.

It'd be folly to be fully satisfied with a translation: the process is as maddeningly slow as creating any good new work. A myriad meanings dance across that unfamiliar music. Enough to drive you mad, though you assume you're partly mad to be attempting the impossible in the first place. No problem here about being perpetually dissatisfied! You can't help but attain a somewhat anguished level of creative dissatisfaction. Creative dissatisfaction:

part and parcel of the whole struggle to make words mean what you want them to... Creative dissatisfaction is something else I learned from Jean – as expressed most obviously through her own methods, tireless, obsessive rewrites, longhand without short-cuts. Keeping on, keeping on-track, seeing it through...

•

"I don't know Lautréamont's work", she wrote in summer 1969. "But I'll be much interested to read your translation when it comes out next year. I'll watch out for it." Jean did, but later told me, typically, of abortive attempts in London bookshops to locate a copy. After sending her one, I received, as so often, some encouraging and helpful comments. They were especially welcome because, having worked my way through hundreds of hallucinated pages of sonorous, scandalous poetic prose, I could scarcely retain balance, let alone ask its longdead author for guidance or blessing. Jean though, always a level-headed and committed reader, seemed to take Lautréamont's resolutely un-English creations – all those youthful incandescent blasphemies and surreal nightmares – in her stride.

The important thing was that the book lived; it didn't need to be loved. It had set out to alienate the unwary and to subvert and shock its time, yet it should survive for the present. Of course it wasn't 'readable', in the sense that her own books so deceptively were. But Jean realised that the French style quite as much as the content was extraordinary. Most gratifying where I was concerned: she thought I'd managed to preserve the necessary foreignness of this Gallic vision of the Gothic while finding for it an equivalent English-language style.

Jean's comments went deeper in their quiet way than the fulsome and extensive reviews. So many years later, I can understand what I was looking for at the time. It wasn't praise or even reassurance. I had enough confidence and self-belief, but I felt then (far more than now) a profound, desperate loneliness. Writing was what I loved most, my life's main aim, yet life itself seemed pointless. I could make no sense of it, finding far more meaning in words than events. I seemed to myself, if not to others, less anti-social than dissociated, detached. Where or what was my real life, did it exist only on paper? The demands of this inescapable solitude appeared to poison relationships: my inner isolation was read as aloofness or vanity, and such misinterpretations I was never even aware of. I felt naturally gregarious yet unnaturally reticent. How should such a one begin to communicate? Endlessly, I'd be driven back towards the page, to try to translate the loneliness there.

Asceticism or excess: again, it's a matter of style. The highs and lows of drink and drugs had marked my twenties – during the Sixties, that is. Luckily for me I'd survived and lived to write another day. Now I can better comprehend the reasons for what Marguerite Duras described (in *La Vie Matérielle*, 1987): "I drank all the time and I was never drunk. I was withdrawn from the world – inaccessible but not intoxicated." Delaying tactics, rather than considered strategy. If taken for strategy, an addiction of any kind is just a slower, easier form of suicide ('What's *your* poison?'). Something to blot out the most uneasy questions about yourself, while creating the illusion that you are still in control. That you can cope – simultaneously feeling perhaps even good, or at least less bad. An easy anaesthesia, then, being numbed from further potential pain.

Always for a writer the best habit, the best high, is using words. You may make a nonsense of relationships, but there's always the pure literary fix, meaning and peace on the whiteness of the page. Jean knew it, so did Marguerite Duras. "Alcoholism is scandalous in a woman, and a female alcoholic is rare, a serious matter" said Duras. "It's a slur on the divine in our nature. I realised the scandal I was causing around me". Duras, a self-aware, serious writer, managed to regulate life and work, intake and inspiration. Keep drinking as you would keep dreaming. Destroy yourself if you must, but you must still create. As to the reasons for doing either, women at least have some strong certainty in creation. Who can question a basic physiological role and fate as a creator? To translate this presumed creativity, the essence of being, into achievement (a child, an artwork) seems at once natural, admirable, difficult.

In order to make sense of that purpose or any great gift, a certain way of looking at life (be it French or English: a *regard*) is called for. It's an endurance test for an ungodly age: a highly sceptical love gazing on emptiness yet given the form of respectful objectivity. A strange beleaguered version of optimism, a desperately literal looking forward, like trying to read ahead to the end of one's own unwritten but predestined book. Everyone is the happier for a personal vision, but few seek to articulate it: is that desire merely a wilful intuition, a disreputable kind of ersatz mysticism available to the likes of authors and atheists, to wellmeaning materialists and the mad? How is the capacity for inspiration – creative sympathies and intentions – best directed? How do you even *translate* (in that word's wonderfully rapturous sense) such thoughts?

If Jean's own expressive poetic vision, via her Celtic ancestry, sometimes seemed innate, she was generally reserved on the subject, wary of assuming any inherited creative spark. Gifts might someday be called in as debts: there were no short-cuts, no glib affiliations. Thus she never easily reclaimed for herself a Welsh identity as, for instance, 'Margiad Evans' – the Uxbridge-born Peggy Eileen Whistler (1909-1958) – most emphatically did. But Jean might well have endorsed that creative rapture approached in the conclusion of Evans's *Autobiography*, published during the darker days of World War Two: "I am not lonely. I should only be lonely if I happened alone, if I existed alone, if I had to make myself breathe. If I had created myself and must decide for myself when to die, *then* I should be lonely... on earth I find myself in everything, because in view of death we are all the same age."

Translating a different form or a difficult life to the page means temporary liberation from and for oneself. You learn by a closer reading than ever, through another's language. An extra dimension entered, experience gained. And if genuine greatness is rare, its magic remains unmistakeable: when met with, it must be respected. More often, a translator encounters the predictable or dull and has to resist any urge towards embellishment. 'If in doubt, cut it out' is a sensible maxim, but you cannot make good what may simply be bad. Even a vexed text shouldn't betray anger or confusion, though; rendered with skill it will still read well.

The best work is always a different matter, presenting more creatively valuable difficulties. It enlivens, enlightens those ideal readers it deserves, each set of words gradually giving up its ghostly secrets. Within such books our lives are discerned, their difficulties shared and explored: beliefs, dreams and the lack of them; the lonely problems of love. Creators and characters alike suffer there, becoming inseparably linked – difficult women (and men) trying to explore and inhabit their impossible solitudes, making clear to themselves and others that what should be easiest to understand is also hardest to express.

Hunger and some thirst

Hamsun, as I have often said, is one of the authors who vitally affected me *as writer*.

  – Henry Miller: *The Books In My Life*, 1952

The first published book by Jean Rhys appeared when she was in her thirties, her collection entitled *The Left Bank* (1927). It contains a grim little sketch, stark self-portrait rather than short story, called 'Hunger'.

In 1890, the year of Jean's birth, an unknown Norwegian writer had published *his* first book. Knut Hamsun was then in his thirties too and his extraordinary novel was called *Hunger*.

The earlier book describes the sufferings and stubborn endurance of a starving young would-be writer as he wanders around the bleak townscape of Kristiania (Oslo). This unnamed but blazingly honest narrator encounters mental and physical coldness everywhere. In search naturally of himself – via any friendly face or halfway responsive editor – yet increasingly desperate to earn a literary or actual crust, he meets with ridicule, distrust, contempt or incomprehension. The result is an anguished if aggressive tragicomedy, a lonely plea for survival in a cold zone of the spirit. Here the getting of a living, one's daily bread, and the meaning of a life are all called into question, with an individual's persistence and self-belief coming under attack from the inhumane and mostly beastly bourgeoisie.

But the bitter wit precludes self-pity. The protagonist's tone of pained intimacy sounds a new note. It's a voice of unusual candour which ensures that we trust the teller through the tale. In this original, very personal voice, surviving time and translators alike, Hamsun manages a miraculous transformation, whereby extreme or depressing experiences become something of a joyous assertion against the worst odds. Down but not out, bloodied by the bloody awfulness of life, but unbowed, individual authors find themselves hungering always for the spirit that gives life, the word that goes beyond flesh and sustains both life and letters...

It's a pioneering and properly inspiriting book still. Over the years, that resilient hungry narrator singlemindedly, singlehandedly fighting off urban angst and avarice, wholly in search of existential meaning or a more meaningful existence, has had a multiplicity of influences: similarities and parallels may be traced from Hamsun through to Joyce, Céline, Miller and many of the heroes and villains of Modernism.

Hunger has certain qualities, however, which particularly remind me of Jean's Paris-based works. There's the blend of stark realism and imaginative fancy (or fanciful imagination), and within the narrative the artful contrast and interplay of these polarities. The framework, since the 'plot' as such is minimal, is both lucidly detached yet very taut; it seems so freewheeling, so loose, yet it's highly controlled. The tone of voice is intimately personal, but remains understated, while not actually giving the impression of reticence in its selection of detail. And whether modulating from a whisper to a scream, that voice insinuates, takes you into its confidence and weaves its spell so that you listen, riveted. Included in the work – the same applies to Jean's books – are dreams, hallucinations, omens, fetishes of varying kinds, premonitions. These pointers towards the unconscious; literary-psychological signposts; fantasies, obsessions – whatever they are, are seamlessly, unerringly deployed. And yet the mysterious buttonholing process of the narration has been glassily objective all the way, as the reader comes to realise in the end.

Jean in a 1934 letter to an American friend, the novelist Evelyn Scott, discusses various related problems: drink, the difficulties of paying the rent and, of course, writing. "Last week I spent most of my time in bed." She doesn't explain why – February cold, booze, poverty, depression, convenience or pleasure? – but continues: "Read 'Hunger' by Knut Hamsun that gave me a great kick. Translated 1899 and might have been written yesterday." Jean has read the first, and at that time the only available, English translation. (By 'George Egerton', pen name of early feminist author Mary Chavelita Dunne.) It goes to show that a great author remains great, or retains some of the greatness, even in a mangled and inaccurate translation.

This is also true alas, of the edition I knew, the 1967 version of *Hunger* (the next into English) by the American poet Robert Bly. Nonetheless, as a young man early on in his writing life, I found the book unputdownable: a courageous, concise, emotional experience, inspiring and inspired. There was a sardonic immediacy, a timeless quality about it, and that strange, distanced sense of intimacy I was to discover in Jean's own books. The leap of seventy years in time had resulted in a new book, even more moving and modern. Now, thirty years further on – Jean long dead, and myself no longer a young man reading a young man's book – I've acquired the third English version of this masterpiece, and by it again am amused and moved.

Sverre Lyngstad's new translation (Canongate, 1996), most appropriately Scandinavian, catches the tense-changes, the pace and the staccato rhythms his precursors missed. There's no bogus romanticism here: it's true as ever, and as affecting. I wish Jean could have read this more accurate and hard-edged vision of all artistic apprenticeships. I wish I could have talked about it with her: I should have guessed she loved the book as I did. At any rate, this latest and best of versions of the unsinkable 'hunger artist' made me return to Jean's own 'Hunger'.

"It doesn't matter. I am not hungry either: that's a good thing as there is not the slightest prospect of my having anything to eat…" "Starvation – or rather semi-starvation – coffee in the morning, bread at midday, is exactly like everything else. It has its compensations, but they do not come at once… To begin with it is a frankly awful business." "No money: nothing to eat… *Nothing!…* But that's farcical. There must be something one can do. Full of practical common sense you rush about; you search for the elusive 'something'. At night you have long dreams about food." "On the second day you have a bad headache. You feel pugnacious. You argue all day with an invisible and sceptical listener."

Arguments, hallucinations, excuses, detachment, weakness, anger, sarcasm, desperation. How she resembles Hamsun here, foodless for five days, and how touching her humour at her own expense:

> Lying in bed, my arm over my eyes, I despise, utterly, my futile struggles of the last two years. What on earth have I been making such a fuss about? What does it matter, anyway? Women are always ridiculous when they struggle.
> It is like being suspended over a precipice. You cling for dear life with people walking on your fingers. Women do not only walk: they stamp.
> Primitive beings, most women.

She writes too, of "nerves strung tight. Like violin strings. Anything: lovely words, or the sound of a concertina from the street: even a badly played piano can make one cry. Not with hunger or sadness. No! But with the extraordinary beauty of life." Jean, like the mystics, like Hamsun in his greatest book, knew what was truly valuable, what was not delusion. These writings are not about starvation so much as salvation. How does one fulfil oneself or fully express what one believes? How except through art, the great consoler, can one make sense of life or share insights into its meaning?

"Ah, but has he starved?" Gissing used to ask, whenever any writer's name would be mentioned. Gissing himself quite literally had, of course, and he knew how to cut through romantic affectation: there were no short cuts, ever, nor 'overnight successes' and other such unlikely stories. There is naturally a sort of morality of apprenticeship involved here. (Jazz musicians will ask "Has he paid his dues?" which boils down to the same.) Gissing perceived all this too, in *New Grub Street,* a novel Jean and I once agreed should be required reading for every tyro writer. In 1893 Gissing wrote to his brother: "The struggle of life gets harder as one goes on, instead of being lightened. It would be a strange sensation to look forward with easy confidence for a year or two." Gissing in his short life more or less burnt himself out – overworked, underpaid. But in his lifetime he was valued by his peers, as Jean was, and he too will surely continue to gain not mere readers but devotees.

As for 'easy confidence', I doubt whether genuine writers experience much of that. But they may well *read*, and be read so, as though that's a magical quality they always did possess. At any rate, the unsettling creative hunger (being thirsty for experience, greedy for knowledge...) never leaves an artist. Jean, however old and tired she became, never lost it. Everyone knows that drinking too much inevitably involves eating too little. Under the circumstances, and until the very end, it was Jean's stamina rather than her gait that staggered. I never saw her too much the worse for wear. Anyhow, whenever visiting, I'd generally make sure of bringing along something for us to eat on that occasion. Sometimes we'd eat there with her, or we'd take her out to lunch or tea, or the affable Mr Greenslade would drive her to a prearranged pub or hotel at a halfway point between Axminster and Cheriton. But in truth, the food was of little importance: somehow or other, we were surviving; the company was what mattered.

As for the famished Jean familiar to Stella Bowen and Ford Madox Ford, hungry for literary success and a meaningful life in the Paris of the 1920s, here's how she closed those early pages of her own 'Hunger': "I have never gone without food for longer than five days, so I cannot amuse you any longer". That's telling 'em! And telling it like it is, too… I want to cheer her – raise a glass to her brave ghost.

When the wicked man (or woman)

Literature is a place for generosity and affection and hunger for equals
– not a prizefight ring. We are increased, confirmed in our medium,
roused to do our best, by every good writer, every fine achievement.
  – Tillie Olsen: *Silences*, 1980

The publication of Jean's first and very accomplished novel *Quartet* (originally,
Postures,1928), with its lethal, unflattering portrait of her ex-lover and mentor,
Ford Madox Ford, was surely bound to incite some form of literary reprisal,
some novelistic tit-for-tat. Indeed, Ford wasted no time time before beginning
his own riposte.

Although *When The Wicked Man* wasn't finally published until 1931, Ford's
vengeful *roman à clef* still holds considerable fascination for anyone interested
in either of these brilliant writers. Ford must have been stung and hurt by the
irony of the situation: pupil rounding on master, youth attacking age, beginner
beginning by using *him*. (The fact that it was Ford who had unceremoniously
ditched Jean was in his view probably beside the point. She had now delivered
the first and worst blow.) Most hurtfully too, Jean – in a sense his 'creation' –
had appropriated him, pinning him onto the page, within a deadly permanence
Ford cannot at all have appreciated. He who so prided himself on his ability to
make art, had himself been made over and remade: he'd become a 'character'.
Witchlike, she'd stolen something of his soul, used it for material and made it
hers! Most writers – especially when sensitive, struggling, or in sundry ways
insecure – can become somewhat paranoid, and Ford and Jean themselves were
no exceptions.

Perhaps Ford was put on his mettle, seeing it also as a matter of honour, a kind
of literary duel and exorcism. In his terms, he it was who had been goaded,
maligned and challenged. Their affair might be dead and buried, but there
remained no point in digging up the past as *she* had done: so the maestro would
invent, make it new, tell a new tale or two involving Jean. After all, Ford was
the one with a firm, established reputation as mythmaker and fabulist. How
else then – and how fittingly – could he demonstrate his lofty superiority over
ingratitude but by a new piece of work? One is tempted, wellnigh invited, to

read Ford's book as an Olympian form of condescension – teacher looking down on fractious pupil who demands not to be overlooked.

The venomous residue of any relationship, he must have imagined, may be distilled and put to significant use. It's perfectly possible to settle scores in fiction, rebuking somebody by a very public slap in the face – like that notorious, literal one Jean is supposed to have handed Ford. So in Ford's book, he's destined at the very least to be ungallant. Given Jean's and Ford's previous linked histories, *When The Wicked Man* must inevitably prove a name-calling work.

Hence Ella Lenglet whom Ford had published and prefaced and promoted – re-naming her Jean Rhys – will appear here in Ford's novel as 'Lola Porter'. Encoded here in her new Christian name is echolalia worth exploring, some suggestive resonance. Behold her, Lo! says Ford – 'introducing' her ironically from his lofty authorial-Biblical-patriarchal height. *There* she is (là) – the woman bearing the name *he's* given her. There in *his* book, 'la porter' (we'll reach the surname shortly): Ella-Lola, languid yet violent, the slow Creole, the dangerously alluring tropical plant, the role-playing creature both unholy and lowly… Ford's femme fatale has a hint too (Ooh, la la) of Belle Epoque spice; Jean's showgirl past is turned against her and into an obscure theatrical taint. For Ford (b.1873) in his heavy Victorian role, such an alien and exotic name implied all the seductive villainy and glamorous corruption of the most dramatic of courtesans, Lola Montez herself. (I'm also irresistibly reminded of the famous *Hello Lola*. And must add, after *hearing* Mr *Red* McKenzie & co. on that 1929 recording, a curious audiovisual image, via hindsight: the professorial old buffer-Hueffer obsessed by showgirl Marlene-Jean in *The Blue Angel*, 1930.) So here's how Jean is seen, as a hard-drinking, Jazz Age floozy. The superior FMF reads Rhys as a slippery player of low tricks.

He writes her surname *Porter*. Hence by association – bearer, coolie, colonial. Somebody lacking all constraint and decency, yet obsequious and lowly, hired to do an English gentleman's bidding. Someone mercenary, passive, idle. Someone like Jean, in fact, from the Caribbean… Ford early on remarks of Jean's first husband (also a writer, and portrayed here as such, and as a suicide): "Perhaps both he and his thin, blackamoor wife were both starving". The contemptuous racial references are continued through the novel: there's even mention of "a darky porter in the building on the hill" to compound the jest.

A further coded 'identifying quip' against Jean (Ford's 'black amour', in the sense too of a deceiving and adulterous love) is later offered as if for her personal benefit. The Ford figure, a 'fat fool' of a publisher, as she calls him, reflects on her drunken, abusive language: "conversation commonly indulged in by loose women – or possibly by loose English schoolgirls. He had heard her say that her father – the descendant of the gipsy horse-whisperer – had sent her to England to a finishing school. Finishing!" Jean's father, a doctor on Dominica, had of course sent his daughter to England to the Perse School for girls, Cambridge. In Ford's novel, Lola Porter's name, via her previous husband, is Homerton. Homerton is a village on the outskirts of Cambridge.

It must be said for Ford, however, that the jokes are very often on or against him. He was too serious an artist not to see relationships from other angles than his own, as if from 'outside' himself. *When The Wicked Man* does not in any case focus only upon drink, sexuality, writing, business ethics, or America, but includes what may be rationally inexplicable – elements of disturbance that verge upon the supernatural. It's a strangely tormented and hallucinated book also. 'Nightmare' and 'farce' are words used in the first paragraph, while in the opening sentence its protagonist is "experiencing physical and mental sensations that were unfamiliar to him". So who is this Fordian alter ego the author calls 'Notterdam'?

Ford informs us he's descended from Nostradamus, and is "haunted", "after moments of extreme depression, fatigue or alcoholic indulgence", by "a sort of devil, called up involuntarily by him[self]". At the same time, Ford is suggesting, he purports to give *not a damn*... It's as if Ford himself wants to exist invulnerable within his own book, no longer open to be haunted by Jean, never again affected by her any more. He has only himself to fear, that side of him manifested as shadowy *doppelgänger* or baser self (the ghost of his guilt?). Meanwhile his 'enlightened' ancestry – parallelling Ford's own artistic forebears – will protect him from any malevolent spells which Lola-Jean with her voodoo world might work. In his writing Ford intends to take both refuge and revenge. Notterdam-Ford is presented as a publisher-mage, what's more, one who has power over a writer, as he himself wielded power over the Porters (Lenglets). He is a main cause of Porter's suicide in this very curious novel; in actuality, Ford might well have found himself wishing Jean Lenglet dead. (The tangled relationships, atmosphere of violence and threats, circumstances of Lenglet's imprisonment, etc, are fully and magisterially dealt with in the mammoth biographies of Ford and Jean Rhys by Max Saunders and Carole Angier respectively.) Here, in literary terms, Ford simply kills him off as 'Edward Porter', and concentrates on getting even with Jean.

Notterdam-Ford in the meantime shall be protected and saved from Jean-Lola by this, his confession. Notre Dame – and Ford wants noted the additional talismanic resonance of his names – rescues all good Catholics and good soldiers from their wickedness and guilt. Anyhow, in his own eyes Ford means well: Jean's jealousy and anger at her abandonment by him are turned into Lola's far less convincing vindictive rage – here motivated, Ford would have readers believe, by frustrated desire! It's a ludicrously diluted, rather unconvincing misrepresentation of the fraught drama these people originally lived through. Throughout the novel, secret references (scarcely in-jokes) to Jean abound, as if Ford is anxiously, additionally, casting runes, or laying a trail of arcane literary charms whose presence is to ward off her future wrath. For instance, out of the blue on page 23, we find that one of publisher Notterdam's "pet books [which] had not yet made up their advances" is called *Triple Sec*. This was of course a story of Jean's, which Ford himself had retitled, and which he as editor of *transatlantic review* first published. He seems here to be reminding his protegée of the inestimable triple assistance (literary, financial, amatory) which he has generously afforded her; at the same time, he snidely implies that her own work is and will continue to be uncommercial. Simultaneously, in this context of a book in which nothing is quite what it seems, the very ambiguous "pet" and "advances" might suggest (and might then have been suggesting) that he still retained a certain affection for her.

At times is heard an intimate, confidential whisper, at times hysteria and wild outbursts. That's like Ford's book itself and also, one infers, a fairly truthful portrait of how Jean behaved in those distant days. Ford shows us the extremes of Jean's nature: "Her voice was extraordinarily soft and stealthy"; "...she had clung to him. She begged and begged in her soft stealthy voice... She caught one of his hands and leaning on his breast kissed it continuously as if she had been a slave imploring a boon of a sultan." She "had told some really dreadful sob stories as to the privations she and Porter had gone through... The idea that this beautiful, flashing, lithe creature was actually starving remained almost his strongest and most shuddering impression of that night. He had actually promised to take her home and have his wife look after her." Which is what 'really' happened, as Stella Bowen in her memoir corroborates, at the start of the one and a half year affair between Ford and Jean.

Yet Ford depicts the alien, violent side of Jean too. "From one of the West Indian islands", she has "A taste only for toughs and low life". He cunningly gives his most wounding lines to 'Henrietta Felise' (Ford's new love-interest at that time) who says of Lola-Jean: "She is quite a star journalist, but she can't hold down jobs because of drink. I don't mean that she is sodden but when she does drink she is terrible... Abandoned, you know. And with such... oh, toughs. You see, her first husband died in jail. And his associates... Well, she rather keeps in with them. And poor Mr Porter..." Under the circumstances – Lenglet jailed and Ford faithless – that word 'Abandoned' is piercing ambiguity indeed.

With hurtful condescension, this other 'other woman' character continues: "When she isn't – oh, under the weather – she is quite a nice person. But these Creoles... I don't mean of coloured origin...The real Creoles of French descent... From Martinique and such places. They say she has even gipsy blood." The blithely prejudicial references are carried onward by Ford at his most authorially omniscient: "Creoles are as noted for their indolence as for their passion. On that basis, she became entirely comprehensible." Poor Jean, without moral fibre or backbone, "as limp as if her limbs were of India-rubber", is depicted as the woman who came to dinner, staying on eternally like a tropical vampire-doll to sponge off Ford and Elspeth-Stella! And Lola-Jean does indeed want to drain them dry: "Once Mrs Porter stopped him in the hall after dinner and asked listlessly if he would not advance her some more money."

Ford more than hints, via Notterdam, that he has fallen under her sexual spell, and ultimately "he found Lola Porter too disturbing to himself, so that he wanted her gone. Exactly what she did to him he did not know except that she made him tongue-tied, like a schoolboy". He admits and tries to explain his enchantment by frequent references to exoticism and magic. At one point Notterdam's children take "a great fancy to Mrs Porter who told them fantastic and horrible details of obi and the voodoo practices of the coloured people of her childhood's home". Later, Notterdam labels her "that devil", her eyes are "baleful", and there's an extraordinary passage about her riding ability (subtle skills of horse-whispering inherited from her West Indian past), in which the equine equation (woman-as-mare, animality/sexuality) is strikingly spelt out. When the reader reaches: "She was snorting like a wild mare herself, her breath pouring in and out of her large nostrils: her breasts heaved...", even the famous Fordian ellipsis can neither contain nor suggest what might follow. The text duly breaks, and there's a cut to next morning and the pair off riding together!

The scene that follows between Notterdam and Lola can't merely be read, in psychological terms, as some form of displacement activity. Ford cannot have missed nor meant us to miss the sexual significance of his use of equestrian metaphor: "The riding soothed her, whereas the longing for it, the evening before, had rather ominously let the tiger peep out from beneath her Creole nonchalance". (And *Tigers Are Better Looking*, Jean entitled her story collection, many years later. Some have long memories, some do not...) "But she was one with her horse" Ford goes on. "She had, she said, passed by far the major part of her girlhood in the islands of the Caribbean Sea on horseback. Even she would sit in the saddle all day in the dark stables during hot weather. She would be waiting for the evening breeze." Highly-sexed, inviting and, whether or not such needs needed spelling out, finding release and relief only in orgasm. Too hot, in other words, for Notterdam if not Ford to handle...

This bewitching woman herself spelt danger to Ford and Stella's relationship because of her intelligence and talent. Neither of these factors would have been as obvious initially as her extreme helplessness and beauty. When finally ejected and rejected by the couple, Jean was forced to find herself as a writer, and this she did, working out her anguish and her anger via her first novel. Ford, on the other hand, had to come to terms with the failure and folly of an older man's involvement with a young siren. Then, worse still, he had also to answer if not outdo her, in literary terms. How was he to justify himself or his actions, when what he wanted was both revenge and the last word? He needed to appear convincing, showing himself objective not objectionable, artistically honest into the bargain.

It's a tall order, and hardly surprising that Ford can't bring it off. There's an element of 'blame it on the booze' (this was, after all, the 1920s), and the novel is awash with alcohol and hangovers. But that's not enough, of course, and Ford knows it. So he shows us the paradoxical Jean who fascinates still. Sometimes she seems passive, unappealingly weak: "She was in one of her halting, india-rubber Creole moods. As if her hips were limp. There were dark rims under her eyes". On another occasion, he admits: "An extraordinary woman. You never knew what she really felt. It was eternal histrionics! You would say she was a simple, primitive being. Not she. She had the appetites of a Caribbean savage. But when she suffered from one appetite she superimposed over it the pretense of another. Even with liquor taken. For he did not believe – he was beginning not to believe – that by nature she was as obscene as she pretended to be when she was drunk. At ordinary times she was rather delicate, and languidly fastidious about her body... But there was no knowing."

In a revealing tableau towards the end of the book, Lola flings herself at Notterdam and somewhat masochistically proclaims her frustrated love for him. She taunts him with talk of another lover lined up, though: "He's a proper lover... He'll no doubt treat me badly... All men treat girls badly... I wouldn't marry another man for all the tears of Christ himself entreating me." She changes tack to plead: "Don't I deserve a twelve-months' happiness and perhaps a kid as well as any other woman?... I've suffered enough..." Then, with a sort of desperate ecstasy of passion the scene is brought to a close: "She fell on her knees before him and caught his hand. 'Say that you're going to do it...' she said. 'For God's sake say that you are going to do it...' She kissed his hand again and again, whispering the most fantastic offers of herself." But she can't cajole or indeed ho(a)rse-whisper Ford – formerly Hueffer, pronounced 'Hoofer' – who confesses "she made him feel so fatuous" before dismissing her. He won't dance to her tune any longer, as scared of her as he's scared of her passion.

The mention of the child is interesting because many years later Jean was still furious at the imputation that she had had a child by Ford. Ford's 1972 biographer, the American academic Arthur Mizener, for instance, was just one who incurred her wrath on this score. I remember her several times in the 1970s holding forth angrily about it. The subject evidently rankled, but the truth may have been that Jean adored Ford and did want a child by him, or had thought of it as a way of keeping his love.

Ford himself seems to have feared commitment (or any further commitment) just as much as Notterdam is shown to fear "Lola Porter's voodoo practices". Hence Ford's self-punishing character and alter ego in the novel is portrayed as hallucinating under stress – one who involuntarily summons a sort of *doppelgänger*-cum-demon. (Representing jealousy or guilt, one wonders?) At any rate: "She had perhaps willed the apparition on him. Perhaps it was not his descent from Nostradamus that gave him the power, very much against his will, to call up this disagreeable devil." Then we learn that such an unwelcome "appearance was always somehow connected with Lola Porter", and that this familiar is manifestly part of a classic psychological pattern – the money-sex-power-potency nexus. The first glimpse of it, of this darker side to Ford's anti-hero, comes, as its creator fittingly recognizes "Just about that time she had been considering offering to go to bed with him if he paid over the money."

But it is Lola-Jean of course, who is needy, greedy and venial. Ford therefore determines to give her no more, neither money nor importance, giving not a damn.

"He had horribly deteriorated!" he tells us, resisting "the seductions of this blackamoor!" (The exclamation marks are Ford's, and indeed he insists too much throughout. The problem with the book is that this insistence could not, like their affair, be properly resolved or dissolved.) "Listen: I know things… Oh, from the tropics", half-wheedles, half-threatens Lola-Jean. The occult power of obsessive sex or the guilty clutch of voodoo? The violence of love scorned, perhaps? Anyhow, it gives Ford pause, cause for alarm. "She's quite a good writer really", he is bound to admit in placatory self-justification, having soon afterwards noted "The arrangement was perfectly rotten for Elspeth, having that devil in the house."

Is one saved or damned however, and can one have one's cake and eat it? Maybe the solution, in literary terms (Ford must have agonised over this) is to pretend that it didn't really happen, it was all fiction. Ford was good at fiction, masterly in making fictions, and he wrote fluently and much. Hence he would convert almost anything to literature, and could accommodate Jean within this fictive context as he had and had not done in life. And within this highly personal, artful fiction he could appear and not appear at will, as if by the magic of his own pen. Showing himself – if not in the best possible light – at least to be a generous, honest, decent, Godfearing fellow…

The rants and rages of Rhys are here in some blistering pages, rendered honestly and earnestly enough, one suspects, and pretty much verbatim. It's an odd curate's egg of a book though – amid Ford's oeuvre a shaky artefact: overdone yet understated, going too far yet not far enough. As if he couldn't contain himself or his annoyance. Regretful sniping to the bitter end. A very personal, name-calling book and a way of settling scores. Yet at the conclusion of this messy narrative he sees fit to date the process most precisely. The last page of the novel is laid to rest thus: "Paris, 17th December, 1928; New York, 15th May, 1929; R.M.S. *Mauretania*, off the Scillies, 1st December, 1930."

Why the dates and places? Is it obscure showing off, or a clear form of reassertion for Ford – that he was busy, a hardworking professional, and exact? A man of the world, moreover…The mature, roving cosmopolitan, dedicated to his Art. The old war-hero, proof against all further injury and not to be assailed by any feral fly-by-night, not by some frivolous young floozy. Dates: beginnings and endings. See how absolutely, unassailably the author remembers! You can trust him completely, therefore. (What you have read was not just a fable. It had life, it *was* life…) It's ironic that the novel is so dead, so hard to read now. A curio, dry as dust, preserved in a poisoned time-capsule…

The dates alone seem like a seal or charm, but one which cannot mysteriously confer finality or immortality. Contemporaries didn't need to know them, nor did readers of the future. Ford tells us anyway. He wasn't going to be George Moore, and not kiss and not tell. Ford did both, wanting to justify himself into the bargain. These writing-dates are the real epitaph on the Rhys affair as far as Ford's concerned. Pen picked up, pen set down. So much for the end and the epitaph.

For epigraph, the book's 'framed' beginning, we get given Ezekiel: "Again, when the wicked man turneth away from his wickedness that he hath committed, and doeth that which is lawful and right…" When all's said and done, this doesn't seem to have very much connection with the real plot, with whatever has happened, with what was really said and done. Ford didn't like (who would?) appearing in the role of cad or *wicked* uncle to les jeunes, or even as weak villain of the piece in Jean's re-vision of events. (Those *Postures* – by implication too Aretinian? – Jean later retitled *Quartet*.) The highly susceptible yet highminded Ford must also have felt guilt concerning his behaviour to Stella Bowen as well as toward Jean…

According to his own lights, ancient or otherwise, Ford was an old-style gentleman, one keen to do the right and honourable thing, a good ex-soldier and a good sort; he liked to nurture talent and help the young. As to younger women, adultery and promiscuity, well, the flesh was weak. Yet not *wicked*. The word might feature in his title and his novel, but didn't imply any inherently negative quality in his own soul. God was Good, Ford believed, and he himself struggled to be. Hence this moralist gives us the sententious Biblical stuff, huffing and puffing at the start of *When The Wicked Man*. Jean, he must have thought by the end, was exorcised.

But *When The Wicked Man* appears a muddled exercise rather than expiation or exorcism. By Ford's own highest standards, and for most general readers of today, it is his own book, more rueful than ruthless, whose unfocussed force fades by the year. In comparison with Jean's, Ford's novel fails and falls somewhere in a shadow-region, a purgatorial limbo. Caught halfway between explanation and exploration, between pride and abasement, it's work sadly flawed. Ford's book isn't currently in print, and only his admirers or Jean's may find and open it. When they do, *When The Wicked Man* will prove an unsatisfactory if spasmodically illuminating read.

Alcohol, always

There were a lot of gulls swooping about the other day. Near the
window. They looked very lovely but I think the little birds were afraid.
They all lied
> — Jean Rhys to author, 28 Jan 1970

> On golden seas of drink, so the Greek poet said,
> Rich and poor are alike.
> > — Louis MacNeice: *Alcohol*, 1942

At the start of 1970, Jean ends a letter: "There is no news except that I'm trying
hard to drink less whisky and not succeeding". The following month she's
complaining: "I haven't done much work alas. The cold makes me so useless.
Also I've been switched on to something else which I'm finding difficult." The
last sentence presumably refers to medication. I don't know, and never asked,
what she was being prescribed or whether continuing to drink while also on
prescription drugs was a good idea. On March 14 she writes: "I heard today that
I'm not to go to the hospital after all. Such a relief as I loathe & dread hospitals.
Pills & injections instead. I daresay I'll be quite all right soon".

By summer of the next year she was sounding much stronger, if not happier.
Diane and I were always amazed by her stamina and powers of recuperation. On
23 July 1971 Jean writes: "I'd ask you both to come over & see me. It would
be fine. But whatever changes I make, & I have made a few, Cheriton Fitz
remains a dull spot. Even drink can't enliven it much! The other day I started
planning a grand farewell party, then had to give up the idea. Too difficult.
However we must arrange something. [...] I've got a small fridge now, so
drinks are cool." The next month she declares: "It will be nice if you both can
come & see me. This is really one of the dullest places under heaven, but I've
improved it a bit & have some records I like, & whisky as a rule. No always."

Looking through my letters from Jean I find numerous references to drink
and various invitations from her, especially in Jean's latter days, to drinks and
parties during her visits to London. On occasions, Diane and I would try to
make sure she was eating properly, and that we could share a meal with her

somewhere locally, if not at Cheriton. On 28 June 1972 Jean writes: "Diane & yourself must come & have lunch with me one day & cheer me up! I'm getting to be quite an enthusiastic cook – find it really interesting. I can do better than the damned old Rougemont anyway. Besides people are always giving me exotic things like Malaysian curry which they say are quite delicious. <u>But for six people</u>. Also my usual assortment of drinks!"

So most of the time it was back to drink. Yet neither Diane nor I ever saw Jean out of control, maudlin or aggressive. Drink was just something Jean was used to, something she needed. I've known plenty of alcoholics before and since our friendship with Jean, but among them all she was the one who functioned best and continued working most coherently almost until the end. It's also exceptional that Jean should have lived so long under the circumstances, and this says much for her stamina and will. Physiologically too, women cannot usually drink as much as men without loss of health and sobriety: this is one area in which the sexes are not equal, wherein the male is at a dubious 'advantage'. But Jean had lived through the thirstiest eras of the century, including both World Wars; she'd lived too with men like Ford, who drank a great deal.

Jean found in alcohol both consolation and stimulus; it can after all numb or tranquillize, excite the mind and increase one's confidence. Alcohol – the process as much as the actual effects of drinking – provided Jean, as it did Lowry, among many others, with subject matter, with material that might be used. The notably inebriate poet Hart Crane perceived in 1921 "the Subconscious rioting out through gates that only alcohol has the power to open". This contrasts with the non-drinker's view: "Alcohol confuses everything, gives free rein to the most pitiful subjectivism and sentimentalism. And afterwards one remembers nothing – and if one does, it is worse! Everything that one thinks while in a state of intoxication appears to one to have the touch of genius: and afterwards one is ashamed of it." But Salvador Dali, writing thus twenty years after Crane, could not himself be described as the most soberly balanced of artists: having evidently so many phobias, Dali's abstention from alcohol was more likely prompted by fear of it.

The fear of lost control, or of inability to work, doesn't seem to have entered into Jean's own drinking. She appears to have indulged in binges from time to time, but hard drinking over many years must have given her a strong head.

Such drinkers need simply and steadily to top up their habit, in order to stay in popular yet appropriate terms, pickled. It's perfectly feasible for them to function well on most levels, remaining compos mentis, without their being 'drunk' in the sense of incapacitated. True, there were sporadic attempts at detox, but Jean didn't want to give up drink and why should she have? Some self-destructive souls use alcohol as a slow but sure form of suicide, a gradual and licensed poisoning. Lowry was one such; Crane and Berryman finally couldn't wait: they took flying leaps at death. Jean unlike them had progressed beyond the suicidal impulse; that dangerously attractive extreme was a part of her youth. And yet, till the end, she could write so movingly of desperation, loneliness, and the inevitability of what awaits us all!

Jean felt as she expressed it at the poignant close of her autobiographical *Smile Please*, that you had to earn death. Perhaps this rigorous and very moral view served her as a kind of religious imperative. As an atheist (believing, with MacNeice, that "The beautiful ideologies have burst"), I hope so: it may have saved her in the end, for the end.

Before concluding here, let's bear in mind someone else who existed once and whose shade requires a libation. She is or was someone Jean could well have met and in 1920s Paris might certainly have known by sight. I mean the manic, extraordinary Baroness Elsa von Freytag Loringhoven (1874-1927). The Baroness, outrageous avant-gardist in everything, may now be described as a proto-punk poet, a one-woman Happening. She also pursued poets – most infamously and haplessly, William Carlos Williams – and starved in Paris too, ending in despair as a suicide. This footnote to literary history, this ill-starred Baroness and friend of Djuna Barnes, made a statement that deserves to be remembered. "True death is wealth tremendous, but it must be earned with life; that is why I still live". Her words urge us to praise human endurance, as a kind of heroism, a persistent struggle to make sense of what after all may be meaningless. What price success or failure? I recall writer-friends dead and gone. Especially Jean, to whom as ever I raise my glass.

Being personal

The writer does not apologise for the fact that this book takes the form of REMINISCENCES rather than that of HISTORY. To arrogate to oneself the title of Historian is to lay claim to Impartiality – and this is a book of Propaganda.

    – Ford Madox Ford: *Thus To Revisit*, 1921

As I am writing this book in the form of 'Souvenirs', I must cheerfully accept the rules of memoir writing and dredge up a few facts.

    – Jean Genet: *Prisoner Of Love*, 1986

How does one writer write about another? And not just 'another', in the sense of 'any other writer', but of a special writer, such a one as Jean? You are young, and wish neither to flatter nor intrude. You feel you need to wait therefore, to learn and write more of other matters... Also you have your own work, other priorities. Time is on your side, if not hers, yet it slips by almost without your noticing, swifter than a lost opportunity. Soon enough death demands admittance, surprising everybody as it always does.

You'd intended to write *to* Jean, not *about* her. But circumstances changed: you found you had to sell your Devon cottage; you paid off your debts, packed away boxes of books, put things in store, and put your life on hold. Then you left England, travelling through Europe until you discovered a place to stay awhile.

Yours was a search for breathing space. With each day there a poem. The living not easy but simple. In that beach shack at the edge of a small fishing village on southern Samos. It was 1979 and you were thirtynine. No longer a young writer, as Jean was no longer an old writer. Card or letter, posted or postponed, could never reach her again.

In the spring of that same year, unknown to you, Jean died in Devon. You on your Greek island couldn't then have predicted that you'd ever return to live in an English city, let alone the very place where she had died. In Exeter today it still seems odd and sad to think of the lonely old woman marooned at Landboat Bungalows, awash with booze and the blues, stranded there a few miles away at cheerless Cheriton. Fits of *le cafard* plaguing her last days along with mortal fear of that final and only escape.

At least the trouble she'd seen and all her angry, painful solitude had drifted towards a conclusion; she had made an end.

•

As for myself beginning to write anything about Jean, many years were to pass before I could even start. But in one of the earliest letters I wrote her, dating from 1969, there are the following two paragraphs:

> A writer friend to whom I'd talked enthusiastically about your books, a year or so ago, happened to mention the fact at a party recently to Michael George of Deutsch. (I expect you know him? I don't.) George, it seems, wondered if I'd be interested in writing something about you. Well I would, of course. When I have my translation sorted out and delivered, by the start of December if not before, I'd like to try writing an article on your work.
>
> Would you like me to do this? And if I did, could I ask you any relevant technical/biographical questions? (I don't want to divert you from your own work-in-progress, naturally.) Anyway, I certainly won't contact Michael George or consider such a project until I hear from you.

Deutsch of course were Jean's publishers. I can't remember who was the writer friend mentioned. At any rate, Jean replied later that month:

> I've not been very well & while I was in bed all my letters got jumbled up – answered & unanswered. (I haven't got a desk – no room.) So I've had to apologize all round – giving various excuses (but this is the real one).
>
> So far as I can remember you suggested writing an article about my work. Of course I'd be very pleased.
>
> But if you mean an article about my_life – well it's exactly what I'm trying to do myself in an autobiography. I'm not quite well yet but hope to go on with it fairly soon.

A month later she reiterated: "If you do write anything about my work I'll be delighted of course & very interested. I wish it all the luck possible."

As things turned out we were both sidetracked, and the subject was never discussed again. Maybe the idea remained in the back of her mind or mine. Yet when I came to know Jean better, it never even occurred to me that this was what I might eventually do. I couldn't see Jean as 'material' in any way: I thought of her as indomitable and indestructible, so that writing about her would have seemed like some kind of premature obituary.

Like Jean and like most other writers, I'm aware of my own set of superstitions. To write too specifically about living friends often courts disaster, for you tend to end up losing them, one way or another. Nor, writing of the living, can you utter unpalatable truths: it's easier to give offence than offer objectivity. Jean already had my respect; perhaps she also deserved my tact. If as she'd said she was writing her autobiography, it was therefore pointless and presumptuous for me to write anything personal about her. Nor could I see much point in simply adding to the already accumulating stack of dry review articles and Eng. Lit. essays on her work. I'd spent three years of a full degree course criticising the world's classics, this during the heyday of the Cambridge English school in the 1950s and 1960s. I felt accordingly that I was done too with academic analysis of texts: I'd put in the time, got the First, been there, done that... So, after going down from University in 1962, it took years of what I called 'the unlearning process' and others call 'real life', before I could become a writer myself. None of the books I'd published by 1969 when I met Jean had pleased me, but I certainly didn't want to displease her. The wide gulf of fifty years between us awed me at first, and I knew myself a mere apprentice.

To be writing anything about Jean, I'd need more skill than I'd then acquired. That much I must have guessed, and so the article or magazine feature or whatever it was I'd been thinking of was shelved. After all, I wasn't don, publisher or PR-man to be expounding, selling or promoting Jean. It wasn't for me to become anything other than a potential friend. At that time I was happy enough to establish contact with virtually any writer: we were all of us absorbed in a difficult, if not impossible pursuit, whose prolonged isolation could often prove almost unbearable. Under the circumstances, those working with words generally have enough in common to give fellow-writers more than just the time of day. At best, envy and sycophancy and log-rolling don't enter into it. As far as I was concerned, Jean was the best around; her work was alive and would live, and that was why I'd wanted to meet her in the first place.

I had no other expectations: she'd fulfilled them all, on the page, and continued to do so. Hence I couldn't be disappointed in her, and I never was. "It is often asserted that writers should only be known through their books, and that when met in the flesh they prove a disappointment; but I found that few commonplaces could be less true". Such was Simone de Beauvoir's view in her autobiography *The Prime Of Life* (1962), and this shrewd but herself rather unlikeable woman then goes on: "I was never once disappointed by my first encounter with any author whose works I admired, whatever might come of our meeting later. They all had an idiosyncratic manner, a keen eye for the world about them, a marked warmth – or bitchiness – of character, and a tone and manner which slashed right through the usual conventions and platitudes. Their charm might after a while wear thin or become mechanical, but it was always *there*, and imposed itself upon me from the start."

Speaking personally, for me Jean's charm like her talent, never failed. I was lucky I suppose not to have been shown the 'bad' side of her. Others were not so lucky. But then, I ask myself, what did those others want from Jean, and how did they meet her demands? Too many people in any case find it easier or preferable to remember the bad. Beauty of words however, the distinctive style which makes up a writer's literary personality, is all that matters. What anyhow will be read and remembered when the years have tested the work?

Conventional morality, common mortality: only the last ever applies. As for conventional, linear or 'straight' biography and its insoluble problems, another genuine original – Jean Genet, with some justice observed: "They remain dead, the people I try to resuscitate by straining to hear what they say. But the illusion is not pointless, or not quite, even if the reader knows all this better than I do. One thing a book tries to do is show, beneath the disguise of words and causes and clothes and even grief, the skeleton and skeleton dust to come. The author too, like those he speaks of, is dead."

Dreaming of other lives

Finally, it may be observed that the atmosphere into which genius leads us, and indeed all art, is the atmosphere of the world of dreams.
     – Havelock Ellis: *The World Of Dreams*, 1911

March 1966 was a desperate month for Jean. She did not regard *Wide Sargasso Sea*, on which she had worked for so many years, as yet quite ready for the publishers. Her husband was dying, and she wrote in a letter "I feel buried alive down here, everything moves with great slowness and I don't know what is happening." It was also "bitterly cold" in her "ramshackle cottage" and her situation must have seemed dreamlike and unreal. "I am shivering as I write" Jean told her daughter, who was coming over from Holland to see her. While Jean's delight and relief were evident she added, typically, "I can hardly believe it".

Less than a week later Max Hamer died. So the last few lines of Jean's *Selected Letters 1931-1966*, addressed to her publisher, Diana Athill of Deutsch, lament her husband's loss then conclude with that famous dream I quoted earlier. The omens were there for her to read: death and a recurrent dream of birth. Then numb relief, release, a letting go, and in every sense an acceptance. "So remote are we today from the world of our dreams," wrote Havelock Ellis, "that we very rarely draw from them the inspiration of our waking lives." But Jean was wise enough to heed the hint from a fate which gives with one hand what it takes away with the other.

For many reasons her life could never seem the same again: there would be more ends and beginnings and false starts, thirteen years of life still to run. Signs and portents – of sadness and satisfaction, loneliness and fame... Francis Wyndham has characterized the Anna Morgan of *Voyage In The Dark* as "a shivering dreaming creature" – a phrase acutely applicable also to her unconventional creator. "Little nervous subject!" Rochester calls Jane Eyre, when she tells him of her dream of being in the rain, "burdened with the charge of a little child: a very small creature, too young and feeble to walk, and which shivered in my cold arms, and wailed piteously in my ear." Meanwhile the man she loves is moving inexorably out of her reach, further and further away... Jane tells Rochester of her other dream, prophesying Thornfield Hall "a dreary ruin, the retreat of bats and owls", and of losing "the scared infant in my lap" as "I lost my balance, fell, and woke." There is too, an earlier "baby-phantom" to trouble Jane Eyre – "this strange recurrence of one image" – and further meaningful dreams and nightmares lie ahead.

In *Wide Sargasso Sea* Jean has Antoinette seek meanings and answers from Rochester: "Is it true... that England is like a dream? Because one of my friends who married an Englishman wrote and told me so. She said this place London is like a cold dark dream sometimes. I want to wake up." Rochester (at this stage the narration is from his point of view) retorts in annoyance that it is precisely *her* island that seems to him "quite unreal and like a dream". They continue the argument, and it's clearly yet delicately implied that the relationship will be disastrous since their respective ways of seeing, and being in, the world, are opposed. Later, shifting back to Antoinette, the poor heiress is shown daydreaming about England. Prophetically she thinks of "that house where I will be cold and not belonging". She foresees the end of her life's dark voyage, the fate dreamed and written for her by two very different women. "In that bed I will dream the end of my dream", imagines Jean's later, braver and altogether more attractive creation. And yet there is no easy answer, as Jean knew. That distant dream will soon turn to nightmare, the final ordeal before Antoinette can be released.

In 1959, years before Bertha's rebirth as Antoinette, Jean wrote from Cornwall to Selma Vaz Dias: "I start with a dream in Mrs R. [i.e. *Wide Sargasso Sea*] but no ghosts – All the same my dream must stand for it is the only thing I'm sure of." There's a typical Rhysian postscript: "The newspapers make me shiver and life too."

There are different levels of writing as there are different levels of life. Some receive and respond to inspiration, some do not. We can only imagine how others live and try to understand them and do them justice. That cold yet compassionate eye, that warm but undeceived heart, that mind telling truthful dreams – the rarest writers alone have all of these.

Most of us must trust to luck and work, remembering that as Robert Lowell has observed, "Dreams lose their color faster than cut flowers..." As for trying to understand the illustrious dead, it is fittest to celebrate the work, not denigrate the life. Who is to say how we ourselves should have behaved, or how they did? What is it we presume we can reveal? Perhaps only what, after all, has already been revealed. Personal truth, painfully acquired over time... Finally, one must dream up the correct answer to that haunting question which in his inimitable poetic rhetoric Lowell asked:

> Should revelation be sealed like private letters,
> till all the beneficiaries are dead,
> and our proper names become improper Lives?

Jean Rhys prior to World War Two

Jean Rhys at Landboat Bungalows, 1970s,
where she lived from 1960 to her death in 1979

Jean Rhys at Landboat Bungalows, 1970s

Jean Rhys in Exeter, 1972

Jean Rhys, late 1960s

Jean Rhys at Landboat Bungalows, 1970s

Jean Rhys at Landboat Bungalows, 1970s

6 Landboat Bungalows, Cheriton Fitzpaine, 1998

Alexis Lykiard and Maryvonne Moerman at Apt, 1999

R.C. Dunning, late 1920s

An academic approach

He doesn't understand about books. Very few people do. They are
mysterious not mechanical. And always will be. I do think writers have
a tough time and nobody likes them either! Till they are dead. Then
they become quite respectable and useful.

    – Jean Rhys, letter to her daughter Maryvonne, 1958

There's a ponderously titled book that adopts the sneer-and-smear approach
where Jean is concerned. It's easy to be controversial by speaking only ill of the
dead, upping your sales by doing them down. Professor John Carey proves a dab
hand at this in his 1992 opus, *The Intellectuals And The Masses: Pride And
Prejudice Among The Literary Intelligentsia, 1880-1939*.

    Knowing Jean, I doubt that she ever consciously thought of herself as an
'intellectual' or member of any general or particular 'intelligentsia'. A misfit
she certainly may have been, but she was both unpretentious and straightforward,
resistant to labels of most kinds. They neither suited nor convinced her. What
she was was original: no mention of that. In any case, Jean Rhys rates only three
sentences in this lofty thesis of Carey's. These are quite inappropriate and
vindictive. Out of all of Angier's vast biography and Jean's long life and
considerable *oeuvre*, Oxford don Carey saw fit to pick a neat couple of
professorial plums. It seems he wanted to advance his own book's case – that
creative (as opposed to critical) types are not just difficult but utterly horrid,
their particular arrogance and excesses leading from ivory tower to gas
chamber! Something in fact, of a controversial if not hysterical revision of
literary history. But here's J.C's holy writ on Jean:

> The novelist Jean Rhys left her first child, a son, near an open window
> in midwinter, so that it [sic] caught pneumonia. It [sic, ditto] was sent
> to a hospice for the poor and died there aged three weeks while Rhys and
> her husband, the Dutch writer Jean Lenglet, were drinking champagne
> in their Paris flat. Rhys's second child, a daughter, spent much of her
> early life in institutions.

This is poor stuff, richly selective, a condescension indeed so distorted and 'economical with the truth' that one scarcely knows where to begin correcting the rarefied and airy Carey. Can it be convincingly credible for instance, even in academic circles, that "Literary intellectuals in the first half of the twentieth century", *pace* Carey, "tended to opt for childlessness or child neglect"?

Such callousness or calculation certainly wasn't true of Jean. She and Lenglet adored their child: the implication that they intended him any harm or were culpably involved in his death is rather a cheap shot. As is the reference to champagne, a far cheaper and less fashionable drink in 1920s Paris than anywhere now. Reckless and maybe deliberate irresponsibility, if not worse, is presumed.

Actually this beleaguered young family was living near the edge, in abject poverty. "Near an open window" is "near the door to the balcony" in Angier, who should be read for her meticulous research and realistic compassion regarding the tragic sequence of events. As for the true, wretched circumstances of Jean's own struggle to survive at all, these of course have been very concisely Careyfied. By which I mean compressed, wrenched and misrepresented – the reference to Maryvonne's "institutions" too... Carey funnels the lot into a fine trio of sentences, Olympian, judgemental and final.

Misinterpreted by Carey and denied any proper context Jean is naturally spared compassion or understanding. It is, though, Carey's own carelessly artful, chilly intellectualising – caring only to diminish Jean both as woman and writer – that should be questioned. The good Professor wants good copy? Questionable selection always does the trick: stick the boot into those you doubtless never knew! Who's left, anyhow, to raise a voice of protest? Who can argue with life's caddish hackademic point-scorers?

•

It would be hard to sound such a sour note as his, even if I tried. But then I like Jean am primarily a writer not a pedagogue... Oddly enough, our distinguished Merton Professor of English at Oxford University "came to my notice" (as those intellectuals enjoy saying in their learned epistolary exchanges) well before he'd sounded off at Jean in the book above.

In 1980 other intemperate comments by Carey filled a lengthy *Sunday Times* article. Now academics are always allowed generous space by the 'quality' press, and perhaps they should be so indulged, since they form after all the intelligentsia. At any rate I sent a short rejoinder in verse. Predictably the newspaper didn't print it. A retort in such form is itself considered bad form, too eccentric or flippant probably. Yet I was quite serious, no less flippant than the Professor at least: the latter appears during these later, millennial days as dismissive of people as he was once of animals.

As for Jean – friend and fellow human being who loved both words and cats – she was one who more naturally enjoyed verse than vilification. She died six years before the collection including this poem appeared. But I offer it now to general readers, readers in general, both hers and mine. (The piece won't appeal to academic tastes.) For another thing I learned via the theorizing Professor's Faberized volume: he delivered the 1989 T.S.Eliot Memorial Lectures.

Hence, pondering the posthumous fame of Old Possum, poet and cat-lover like Jean, I find an extra appropriate pretext (and context) for reprinting here a playful piece. It may serve to round off some sombre reflections on a lighter note:

Calling The Kitten Black

An Oxford academic called John Carey
deemed cats repulsive and insanitary.

The villains defecated, then saw fit to scratch
neatly at earth across his cabbage-patch!

Sagely to cultivate your garden is one thing,
but tell us Doctor, who invented trespassing?

Profess respect for property, while grabbing more;
pollute the whole world – left far poorer than before;

note the vile traces of that dirtier killer, Man,
acting more viciously in his short span
than any cat in an allotment can.

Prisons

...a terrifying insight and a terrific – an almost lurid! – passion for
stating the case of the underdog...
  – Ford Madox Ford: Preface, *The Left Bank* by Jean Rhys, 1927

She shows us different kinds of prisons, barriers, restriction and condemnation,
with the caged spirit everywhere struggling to be free. She knows the socially-
approved worlds we construct are largely composed of lives routine or
hypocritical, safe-and-sound. Such worlds can be comforting or complacent,
but are unreally incomplete without their baser limits. Those lower depths she
had horribly personal experience of. Yet she's also aware that co-existent with
this underworld is its uplifting counterpart, an elusive if not necessarily
illusive, area of vision.

Two of her three husbands, she herself and her daughter all underwent
extreme versions of deprivation, arrest and confinement. John (Johan) Lenglet
was incarcerated in La Santé and other prisons; during the Second World War
he survived a concentration camp. The teenaged Maryvonne, in the Dutch
resistance like her father, was interrogated by the SD (Sicherheitsdienst) and
briefly jailed. Max Hamer served his sentence in Maidstone. Jean fictionalised
her own experiences of British courts and of Holloway, doing her time the best
way she could, rendering her life and times as honestly as possible.

From her 1920s writings like 'The Sidi' and 'From A French Prison' (in *The
Left Bank*), on towards longer, fully realised stories like 'Let Them Call It Jazz',
written in old age, Jean's values did not waver. In the former pieces, she
describes the wretched fate of an Arab, very possibly wrongfully imprisoned;
next, a purblind old man leading, but in the end led by, a small boy, undergoes
the ritual humiliations of a jail visit. By 1962 Jean had honed her style without
altering her sympathies: there is neither condescension nor compromise about
the way she 'gets inside' a young black woman sent to Holloway. Jean, like the
West Indian immigrant Selina Davis, had wound up there for a brief spell, via
a similarly escalating set of minor charges and confrontations: neighbour feuds,
drunkenness, petty assault, unpaid fines. Her neighbour's dog, Jean claimed,
had killed Jean's cats: there'd been months of bad feeling, 'insulting behaviour'

(face-slapping, again!) on either side. One thing led to another, and through a sort of tragicomic inevitability Jean found herself remanded in Holloway for psychiatric and medical reports. Out of which, years afterwards, developed in time – it did not escape – one of her best stories...

Displacement, exile compounded by poverty and exacerbated by prejudice and sexism: faced with all this, who would not sometimes weaken, becoming almost paranoid or at least defensive? Jean needed to find ways of dealing with the most depressing or extreme experiences. They happened, so there was scarcely any need to invent them. What she had to do, both in order to cope and to fulfil herself, was seize hold of circumstances whether arbitrary, unjust or inexplicable. Events and feelings could be drained of venom, given new form, turned into 'fiction' which, while it might heal or solve nothing, could create meaning or pleasure out of pain. This sort of transmutation – raw, messy life into polished yet still lively literature – is unusually hard to achieve, requiring the evolution of a personal style. By discovering, developing, finally inhabiting such a style, the author exists and survives.

It's a kind of translation process, accurate as regards meaning yet composed of necessity into a new, imaginative musical pattern. Jean actually did translate her first husband's *Sous Les Verrous* (as *Barred,* by 'Edouard de Nève'), which dealt with Lenglet's prison experiences and the break-up of their marriage in 1927, the period also covered in her own first novel, *Quartet* . She also worked hard to make sure the book's London publication in 1932 was a success, as indeed it was, advancing Lenglet's literary and journalistic career immeasurably, and changing the course of his life. The fact that at that time he would agree neither to a divorce, nor to letting Jean have their daughter, seems to have made no difference to Jean's proffered help and loyalty. Jean (as Angier suggests) "often found it easier to give than to receive help". They had shared hard times, terrible times, and she must have realised that on this occasion she could significantly assist a friend in need.

•

Jean could indeed be selfless when it came to manifesting concern for those in trouble. In April 1970, just as I was moving from London to Devon, I heard from her as follows:

I meant to write before – but I'm still not very well & I had a rather worrying letter from a man in prison in Lyon, who says he is innocent but can't get a lawyer though he has money. Politics?

So I spent a lot of time writing around to anybody I thought would help for I felt very much at sea myself.

I have found out something about him that he is genuine & really in trouble. But now I can only wait for more news.

I was very touched by his writing to me – I wonder why he thought I could help though. I wish I could.

A week later, she wrote again: "Yes I hope that through Pierre Leyris I've got a lawyer for the man who wrote to me. I think of him & wish him so much luck". As far as I recall, the outcome was satisfactory. But I was even more impressed that a woman of almost eighty and in poor health could commit herself to the cause of a complete stranger.

I'd never been 'inside' then, not even as a visitor. Giving a reading in Lincoln jail in 1973 allowed me my first taste of what being deprived of liberty could mean. (It confirmed what I'd previously suspected, that as far as lives and letters go, I'd always feel closer to old lags than Old Radleians.) Since those early freelance days I've done several years of work based on Prison Writing Residencies. Inside one jail in particular, now retitled a 'holding centre', the naive and unfortunate – victims rather than villains – made up the norm. That rendered the job even less viable than writing itself can often seem. I had somehow to entertain or educate, to communicate and commiserate with, ever-increasing numbers of asylum seekers and suspected illegal immigrants. In their bizarre new British surroundings all of them, intellectuals or illiterates alike, were (literally) unsentenced. If pointlessness is part of the order of the day within these hope-starved places, how can words or writing ever help their inmates? How shall 'the wretched of the earth' find ways to resist or endure, let alone play or beat, the system?

The older I get the less I am sure. It's certain only that no magic formula exists for inner liberation. Jean knew judgements must never be glib, that somewhere a justice beyond words existed, unerringly in favour of the weak and dispossessed. All of us, inside and out, prisoners together for a time, get moved on. Ghosted in the small hours, appeals or cries unheard. Souls condemned to spend decades in anxious rehearsal, awaiting the unknowable moment of release. By all means search for meanings, though there may be no more than this to impart... So much she says and doesn't say, that now vanished "old Hollowayan" – as Jean Rhys once upon a time termed herself. Marooned at Cheriton, she would see out there the last and perhaps hardest part of her own long sentence.

On the brink of Bohemia

It was best to stay away from other writers and just do your work, or just not do your work.
     – Charles Bukowski: *Women*, 1978

Jean only twice prefaced any of her books with quotations. Epigraphs, it seemed, were as little to her liking as epitaphs. Endings so often proved fearfully misplaced or misjudged – no conclusive finish or clean break, whether in art or life. The book couldn't be closed, while one's own epitaph lay tantalisingly unreadable in the dark: a blank page out of reach, rather than a voyage toward any truly final release or full stop... As for beginnings, they themselves might only be forms of death too, abortions, empty tricks not empathetic magic, false starts, beckoning fair illusions, tokens of unrealised promise or dreams falling far short of fulfilment.

On reflection, Jean's pair of epigraphs are subtly, absolutely apposite. Both belong to their newfound contexts, serving simultaneously as helpful pointers to the reader, and as unique mnemonics or totemic charms for the writer. Both quotations derive from poets once deemed 'unsuccessful'. Both those poets managed to remain obscure and unknown during their lifetimes; both seemed unconcerned with poetic fashion and reputation. One has been redeemed and rediscovered posthumously, the other has not.

Emily Dickinson (1830-1886), in life completely unpublished, lives on, no longer a New England recluse but now recognized as the greatest of all women poets. Dickinson, who never titled her own poems, supplied Jean with the actual title for her novel *Good Morning Midnight* (1939). Jean also cites half the Dickinson poem – its memorable first two quatrains – rejecting the second part, one infers, as being open to a somewhat sentimental interpretation. At any rate, Jean feels she doesn't require the next eight lines and so like every good writer, selects for use just what she does need. Ironically, it was after this extraordinary novel, now increasingly regarded as her greatest, that Jean Rhys disappeared from view. Over two dark decades of near-oblivion and silence awaited her. In terms of career and reputation such a disappearance was akin to a death-wish; in publishers' eyes then and now such a prolonged lacuna must verge upon professional suicide.

But it was at the head of Jean's dramatic first novel (*Postures/Quartet*,1928) that the other verses were placed. Jean had been cut adrift by Ford Madox Ford and would later be literally 'written off' by Stella Bowen as "a doomed soul, violent and demoralised". The better-balanced, better-off artistic couple closed ranks against the interloper and tried rather ineffectually to send her packing. "We finally got her a job to 'ghost' a book for someone on the Riviera", wrote Bowen. Out of sight, out of mind... The tactic in the end didn't work (nor according to Bowen did Bohemian types, or waifs and strays): *Drawn From Life* is marred by the painter's own insecure censoriousness. Fourteen years after *Quartet*, a bitchery almost bourgeoise overwhelms Bowen as she recollects in hostility. Laissez-faire becomes letting fly, when she reflects on getting rid of Rhys-the-rival, "a woman who has become an incubus" [sic].

•

Lost loves and no love lost... When Jean recovered, she wrote her own hurt out of her system. It's no surprise that both 'Heidlers' are pinned down and pilloried in this very un-frivolous Twenties novel. Heidler is a neat conflation of Ford's original surname 'Hueffer', 'high' (and mighty?), and 'idler' – doubtless a name Stella called Jean: here the kettle answers the pot back! The truly *un*familiar name belongs to the author of the novel's poetic epigraph, R.C.Dunning. Was Jean being still more mischievous towards her former lover, by deliberately digging up or inventing a name slyly suggestive of Ford's twin Achilles' heels – Roman Catholicism and debts?

Yet there once *was* a poet called Ralph Cheever Dunning: Ford had published 'The Hermit' (the very poem Jean quotes) in *transatlantic review*, and Ezra Pound thought highly of him. But Dunning vanished into limbo: he's not now mentioned in any reference books, and even the meticulous Angier mistakes his Christian name. His was an ill-fated and ghostly existence, a kind of living death or half-life – itself oddly eremitical within that gregarious Parisian Bohemia.

I've found only one photograph of Dunning (in Sisley Huddleston's *Back To*

Montparnasse, 1931) and it's singular indeed. Against a sunny wall leans a tall, gaunt character in a threequarter-length coat with collar upturned, white shirt, dark tie, left hand clutching a trilby. The right is thrust into his pocket. His dark trousers are at half-mast. He has a small moustache and receding hair. He looks fixedly away from the camera. His eyes are half-shut, and he appears anxious, perhaps irritated by both occasion and pose. The gangling figure is weirdly staid and rigid but, owing to the angle at which he stands, his shadow against the wall is also visible. The impression this awkward posture gives – with the sombre silhouette beside him to which he seems only partially attached – is of stiff, studied nonchalance, an assumed hauteur. He stands on his dignity, having seen better days, yet remains unsettled and somewhat absurd. That strange frame behind his head, however, is a drainpipe plus *its* shadow: these parallel vertical bars evoke an odd, elongated creature skewered unwilling to the pavement. However, he won't be pinned down in his discomfort, he has more pressing matters to attend to, this peevish, formally-clad clerk interrupted in his far from naked lunch hour. This long forgotten poet...

Deceptive expatriate respectability, with something hauntingly askew. In the far right hand corner of the photograph (can such things be?) a segment of net curtain is being twitched aside. Or is it? Unseen observers, questions about to be asked, the shadowlines of paranoia... Here then is shown one with not enough will, not enough talent: a portrait of the artist as middleaged failure, and as addict. (A Burroughs would have surely sussed this invisible man at once.) Dunning's twin addictions were poetry and opium and the latter destroyed him. Did he, as some have said, starve himself to death, or 'simply' starve to death? (An academic question, perhaps.) At the opening of Jean's book, her inclusion of the excluded Dunning – exemplar of the hungry artist, determinedly masochistic maybe, but still uncompromising and honest – must have come across like a warning shot. Dunning, an underdog's deviant icon if ever there was, is enlisted to help Jean deliver a pointed yet poignant message to the 'Heidlers', her ideal readers for this very particular book.

As for undelivered messages, Hemingway himself was sent Dunningwards by Pound, on an errand to convey some raw opium in a cold-cream jar. Dunning, dubbed by Ford "the living Buddha of Montparnasse", subsisted mainly on milk and had uttered barely a score of sentences in as many years.

This Montparnassian bard would haunt the busiest cafés, always mutely impassive, but most of the time, death-obsessed and skeletal, he worked in his tiny lair that was "virtually a wooden box". Dunning, furious to be disturbed, flung the jar and several milk bottles at the Porlockian tough person, who beat a quick retreat… Hemingway belatedly fired back – from beyond the grave as it were – in that sourly unfair yet funny memoir, *A Moveable Feast* (1964): "For a poet he threw a very accurate milk bottle".

The great man's four pages on Dunning, who died in 1930, are sharply uncharitable and condescending, like so many of Hemingway's Parisian reminiscences. But in *Paris Was Our Mistress* (1947), author-publisher Samuel Putnam told a different tale of this "poet of the old school whose name is wholly forgotten now". He relates how, "in the last stages of tuberculosis and living in a room that resembled the traditional garret, Cheever was hungry most of the time and, some of us discovered, would actually go about picking up scraps out of the gutter. Pound and others helped him when they could do so without hurting his feelings; for he was extremely proud and reticent and endeavoured always to conceal his penury by putting on an air of cheerfulness or detachment. There was, simply, no means by which he could make a living." A few further sentences, before the chartered buses full of mourners drive to Dunning's interment at a cemetery just outside Paris. Putnam concludes: "Here was the starving artist legend of the old days taking on reality, and it was a reality we did not relish."

Friends and good Samaritans had not saved Dunning from the sad inevitability of his demise. A handful of poems, a couple of slim volumes, a modest poetry prize, the praise of his peers: none of these were enough. Starved of the wider success or inner fulfilment everyone craves, he first went underground, then literally went under. Jean's reference to him in her novel was a dreadful and prophetic reminder to Ford and Stella Bowen, those 'good Samaritans' who'd taken her in when she was starving, but who she felt ultimately used and exploited her for their own devious purposes. Jean was able neither to 'walk to the right' of them, nor 'hide' from them, nor 'greet them with the smile that villains wear': they were those very deceptive dogooders mentioned in Dunning's poem. Jean, who was always loath to lie or dissemble, had found herself in an emotional impasse – a situation in which everybody involved, out of self-preservation had to do just that. Masquerades, false pretences, postures.

Out of it, though – and this was consolingly true for any potential writer – could be made literature. Somehow or other one had to survive; one had a need and obligation to write such things down. She wanted to refute what might be said of her, even to pre-empt the strike, knowing none of that quartet had escaped unscathed nor ever should. Maybe, deep down, Jean agreed with Stella Bowen, believing that Bohemians come to bad ends; by not fulfilling themselves and their talent failed artists do not earn their deaths, any more than they can earn a living.

•

Yet who's to know what is deserved? Impossible to tell. And how or when should a halt be called? While it can't bypass or make sense of the desperate messiness of life, art should at least try to explore new forms and patterns, to summon up some (con)temporarily persuasive beauty. The artist must keep functioning despite lack of outlets, markets, appreciation. Poverty and hunger walk arm-in-arm by your side, stringing along, familiar fellow travellers to put up with or ignore. But if there's an inner need for the journey, there's also a will and a way. Jean travelled hopefully, and with extraordinary stamina, but all too many frustrated souls soon tire of a road seemingly interminable. Seeking changes of route they make false starts; they're seduced by short-cuts and diversions until, misdirected, they drift. Then their misery brings decision at last and they opt out.

To grant oneself premature oblivion may not mean one is remembered: that must remain a gamble; besides, it is relief – release from pain, which is sought. Other lives thus cut short, but touching upon Jean's own far longer voyage in the dark, belonged to Philip Heseltine (1894-1930) and William Buehler Seabrook (1886-1945). Neither was a complete failure like Dunning, nor exactly a household name like Hemingway, yet each achieved a fair amount in his respective field. Heseltine (whose *nom de guerre* became 'Peter Warlock') and W.B. Seabrook still have their admirers, and abide in the reference books. These were deeply moody men, whose wit and charm showed as the sociable reverse of a restless, dark inner violence: their schizoid natures never settled into 'normality' or playing safe, nor did their undoubted talents quite match their ambitions. Like Dunning, both were addicts, though most notoriously of alcohol, and in addition devotees of the occult: none of which can have helped them balance their lives or their art, and probably contributed to their downfall.

The enigmatic Heseltine, a larger-than-life character who appears as such in novels by Huxley and D.H.Lawrence, has his own place now as a minor but distinctive British composer. Jean (in one of her best 1960s stories, 'Till September Petronella', discussed elsewhere in this memoir) wrote about encountering Heseltine in the Twenties. The 'Julian Oakes' she describes is sardonic enough, but doesn't reveal the manic practical joker, a Rabelaisian roisterer who adopted with glee yet another pseudonym – Rab Noolas – and lived the Bohemian life with considerable relish. That dangerously excessive aspect of Heseltine has been chronicled by another louche minor talent of the time, one who also fell out with him – and who knew Jean from way back as "Ford's girl" – the artist Nina Hamnett. (Hamnett's second autobiographical volume *Is She A Lady?*, 1955, also discusses Seabrook, of whom more, shortly.)

One of Heseltine's boon male companions was the Australian author Jack Lindsay, and Lindsay's descriptions of the Warlockian diabolism, drinking and depressions that led up to his composer friend's suicide are sobering enough. There is a chastening account of the aelurophile musician putting out his cat and turning on the gas, thus avoiding for once and for all the Christmas festivities he abominated. "He united the highest ideals in art with a cynical view of human life and died despairing – apparently by his own hand", as the *Oxford Companion To Music* put it. Undisciplined or unexamined lives, the art never quite enough, nor quite good enough, to save them from the wrecks of their existences.

Nina Hamnett's own violent end – defenestration followed by impalement on railings beneath – merits a footnote from Jack Lindsay. Hamnett, formerly 'Queen of Bohemia', but by then a shabby and pathetic sight in Soho drinking clubs, was, Lindsay suggests, a haunted woman. Poor Hamnett apparently imagined herself victim to the unwelcome attentions of an old acquaintance – visited by none other than the long-deceased poseur and black magician Aleister Crowley…

Lindsay, a more down to earth male, was one of the rarer Bohemians who managed to survive, living productively, and for as long as Jean herself. William Seabrook, however, was another of the Roaring Twenties artistic expatriate bunch who did not. There was a high casualty rate of course, yet this American author deserves a few words here: not a bad writer, and certainly an unusual one. While he did not approach Jean's literary skill nor, as is clear, her longevity or physical and spiritual resilience, their lives, concerns and friendships meet at times and occasionally overlap.

Seabrook was an American minister's son and like Ford Madox Ford a Francophile who volunteered rather quixotically for service in World War One. Like Ford too he was later gassed – but at Verdun, for it was the French army Seabrook joined. As with Ford his gruesome experiences marked him for life and, after the war, alcohol proved also for Seabrook effective in keeping the worst of those memories at bay. This "amusing and most intelligent man" (as Hamnett thought him), took over Stella Bowen's Parisian studio when Bowen and Ford eventually moved on. But Seabrook was too restless to stay long in one place; a compulsive traveller, he published in 1929 his best-known book, a pioneering study of Haitian voodoo, *The Magic Island*.

By 1933, when Seabrook committed himself to a New York mental hospital in order to try to treat his alcoholism, he he'd published further accounts of his travels – in the Sahara, assorted jungles, Timbuctoo and Arabia. Seabrook was by then notorious, the author who "participated in voodoo rites in Haiti and ate human flesh in Africa". But he prefaces the controversial account of his own detoxification, *Asylum* (1935), thus: "I am an adventure writer of sorts, and I write this mainly as the story of a strange adventure in a strange place". In other words, here is the more secret narrative of a spiritual quest, the exploration of 'inner space' that every writer draws upon, observing oneself as objectively as possible. Until that point (and unlike Jean) Seabrook did not even try to transmute 'life' into 'art' – that is, a lived truth dramatised or converted into an autobiographical fiction. He had concentrated upon the exoticism of travel per se and the impact upon the traveller of unfamiliar or alien cultures. Nor is such direct autobiography as Seabrook wrote shaped for fictional purposes, but served up rather as in *Asylum*, provocative raw confession.

Seabrook therefore remains an obstinately minor writer, one who does not often move the reader or always hold your interest. He can come across as indulgent, formless, skippable: quite distinct in fact from Jean, the genuinely rigorous artist who'd nonetheless have been fascinated by his harrowing material. For instance, he writes of his carefully unnamed 'mental hospital', the eponymous asylum: "They don't like to take cases which they may not be able to cure, and contrary to some impressions, the whisky habit is harder to cure than the general run of ordinary derangements." But is one ever cured, and of what precisely? Midway through, Seabrook admits: "I still think whisky is a grand thing. I still believe that no man has ever become a victim of whisky – but only of some weakness within himself". Jean, who'd known such places and regimes, would have recognized and might even have applauded the wry honesty of that conclusion.

But Seabrook never really 'recovered' nor resolved to; neither did he possess the skill and style to deal satisfactorily with the rest of his life. There were three marriages, several more books (including the spasmodically readable *Witchcraft* of 1941, wherein he discusses his old crony Crowley with something close to affection if not admiration), more drink, and various sadomasochistic dabblings in the occult before he chose to write himself an end. Home on his farm near New York in 1945, W. B. Seabrook took an overdose.

His contemporary, the American critic Clifton Fadiman, put him into perspective as "a man who has spent his life doing the unconventional and writing about it... his disregard for convention, instead of interesting us by its amorality, too often amuses us by its absurdity." This may be unduly harsh, but it suggests also a curious loss of nerve or confidence on the part of Seabrook himself. The man seemed invariably to want to go too far, testing himself finally to destruction; the vicissitudes of his life, however often self-induced, took their toll of his art, whose expression was thereby flawed. Content and tone, substance and style, never quite cohere: the mismatch ultimately spells literary failure.

Jean Rhys did not skirt round or shirk this key problem. She managed to experience yet survive the Bohemian circles in which all these players moved. Her life was as variously hard as any and longer than most, but she still achieved fine work successfully rescued from the brink. Bohemia has its attractions; it frequently proves enticing to the creative traveller (no seacoast, but more than one abyss!), although within its dangerously intimate landscapes talent itself may be dissipated. The dilemmas involved there are as much practical as moral: poverty and popularity alike must be avoided if possible, since these entail further complex perils – destruction, distraction, indirection. But the Muse, "belle dame" to the poet, may remain "sans merci": the trio discussed above could not adequately summon nor romance her. Failing in courtship, knowing their gifts insufficient, they themselves saw fit to close the page.

Who knows where Jean's own Muse came from, or what androgynous form it took, that beckoning fair one which led to the very brink? But the timeless voice and inspiration proved true to the end. It was quite another poet, himself in his day scandalously aberrant, who now seems absurd and unreadable as he boasted: "We have drunken of things Lethean, and fed on the fullness of death".

Dedication

If you want to be a novelist you must first be a poet and it is impossible to be a poet and lack human sympathies or generosity of outlook.
— Ford Madox Ford: *The English Novel*, 1930

During 1972 I wrote my fifth novel *The Stump*. This book, so different from any of the other eight novels I've written to date, remains one which, despite its flaws, I still value. It's a highly personal story – if not absolutely autobiographical, although much of it is based on fact. And it was dedicated to Jean. The reasons for the dedication, like the theme of the book itself, were both complex and almost ingenuously simple.

The Stump also marks – as I now see, with hindsight – the beginning of the end of my 'successful' career as a novelist. By which I mean that it would no longer be possible for me to exist as before, living from book to book. Until then, and through most of the 1960s, I'd delivered a novel every couple of years or so. I'd managed to get by on all too modest hardback advances, supplemented with paperback sales and royalties from previously published titles. The novels thus far were well-reviewed and prompted some controversy: they had a wide readership, averaging six-figure sales. I was told I was commercial, since the lettering of my very un-English name now dwarfed each book's actual title. At this point I should have got the coded message, which clearly spelled danger ahead. I was on course to being promoted as Young Author Product. Sold by brand-name (Call me Yap, short for good doggy), I'd guarantee to offer a familiar formula, in their current favourite flavour and format, to consumers. And the latter would lap up whatever the paperback publishers in particular cared to push under their noses...

So what is a success? Was I one? Malcolm Lowry, a chronically accident-prone literary hero of mine, once opined that "success is a disaster" and, drunk or sober, his was astute advice. But if I really were successful – and this at least I failed to ask myself – why then should I be changing publishers every other book, while still struggling to make ends meet? It was all very well for fiction and literary editors to skip breezily from firm to firm, salaries and lunches expanding as they played their merry game of musico-fiscal chairs. That 1970s crop of ambitious opportunists and charming gamblers could afford to take such chances. As for the various agents dealing with the several publishers entrusted to promote my novelistic career, they all lived, I noticed, distinctly high off the hog. Who was supporting whom? I was young enough and naive enough to think novel-writing (like poetry) a vocation. Now I'm older, if not much the wiser, I suspect it's become more of an occupation, just a business after all. Serious authors should not be looking to the world of commercial publishing for honesty or truth, let alone a living. Alas, the literary (aka unformulaic or risk-taking) novel, along with the slim volume of verse, may dwindle further on their separate routes toward the new millennium, until consigned together to the specialised ethos of small presses and even smaller readerships.

Jean, though, was one of the last of the twentieth century's great names. She managed to combine subtlety and directness; the skill and quality of her writing concisely conveyed its author's refinement of feeling and thought. Thus her books are accessible without compromise, like all good storytelling, and linger in the mind. I'd known her three or four years when I started work on *The Stump*. She'd always been helpful and encouraging. By her survival alone she set me an example. I reckoned she had succeeded in that long, thankless, alchemical process of making art out of her own life. This, for a writer, was true success – was in fact the art of life itself.

My own life until then had been muddled and unsettled. So much so, that the four novels preceding *The Stump* all reflected one young man's desire to form meaningful attachments – indeed to find any alternative, or additional, purpose in continuing to exist. The protagonists and narrators, whether first- or third-person, were generally youthful, confused and bookish, as I was. They were also more often than not successful with women. Yet they could be callous as well as naive or sensitive, frequently finding chronic difficulties, innate or external, in sustaining relationships. Their experiences in fiction were on the whole both better and worse, and certainly more extreme, than my own in reality.

I think I was only too aware, as a Greek writing in English, that I myself did not 'belong' to any British literary tradition or group or class. Thus all these books happened to deal with outsiders, those variously at odds with their surroundings, misfits on the move, characters marginal to or marginalised by, society. As with most supposedly outspoken novels of the 1960s, considerable (and for some critics, undue) attention was paid to drugs and sex, topics I still find of interest. The books did tell their fragmented and rather downbeat tales with some fledgling energy, although my restless and sometimes reckless eclecticism meant that problems of form and content were not fully resolved. I seemed to possess the ability to shock or at least disturb people: this capacity first puzzled, next pleased, then finally bored me.

By the Seventies my novels had been banned for various reasons in half a dozen countries; praise and blame came in extreme if equal measure. In the UK then the books continued to reprint and sell well in paperback. Without my realising it, I must have been deemed a *success*, and envied accordingly. I myself remained blithely unaware of what this elusive word meant – or of the likeliest reactions towards and against it. Summertime it might seem, but the living wasn't easy: one needs to fund oneself as well as find oneself! While wishing to avoid typecasting, I knew I had to try to develop as a writer, to experiment and improve. I'd become more exacting, and quite rightly so, the fifth time around.

The trouble was that advances were small and novels (not only mine) had an obsessive way of turning into inexorable, accretive monsters whose substantial demands on time, health, wealth, energy could bring their creators more pain than pleasure. And I was always being told by agents that novels (not only mine) were becoming harder to place. And by publishers that novels (not only mine) were becoming harder to sell. However good the reviews, however many copies sold, the tyro author would bafflingly end up being paid proportionately less for each successive book. The strange tricks (or were they laws?) of the book trade at that time effectively prevented 'rising' or 'promising' writers ever feeling secure enough to become in any way 'established'. As for me, why should I complain: I was a success, wasn't I? What more did I want, then – readers might ask, now – an honest living?

Then and now, the response might be: a living of some kind, of any kind. "How is work going?" one agent enquired in a letter. "You ask how work is going", I answered: "to be quite candid, since March I have been working as warehouseman for a removals firm." (No complaint intended, though I think offence might have been taken, for this agent nurtured a strange view of how best to represent me; he was later to inform me that I was paranoid!) With the latest book, with *The Stump*, I'd promised myself I'd risk something different, indeed difficult. The hell with all commercial interests: the only interest that mattered was keeping mine and gaining the reader's.

My sole aim was to write a work for a singular, ideal reader – something shared for our own future pleasure, in order to ease and erase past pain. And that ideal reader appeared to be a woman, whoever, wherever she might be. I could hear her voice, a distant disembodied voice new to me, which sought now to be summoned. If I listened hard enough I might be prompted by this voice with its indistinct, unfamiliar tone growing clearer by the day. In those days I was still a young man at once too literary- and literal-minded, who was working on a veneer of cynicism. I certainly didn't recognize that what I was hearing might be the voice of the spirit. I'd done, and done with, my English degree, and knew that plenty of writers had referred to their angels, guides, muses and the like. I'd pondered these unverifiable materialisations or personifications, willed or wilful, and had found them wanting. Whatever such things were or weren't, they could more simply be seen, and so explained, as dubious props in those writers' own personal dramas. And they would be written off, finally, as manifestations of whimsicality, unnecessary self-indulgence, uncontrolled eccentricity. I myself of course was neither so fey nor so highfaluting.

If I'd stopped to think, analysed myself maybe, I'd have acknowledged that everything I – and Jean, and every other writer – wrote turned out to be generally or particularly autobiographical. I might have grown even more self-conscious than usual, and aborted the project in mind. Any additional angst about facing up to my anima I didn't need! But I didn't stop and got started instead. I began listening to the voice being lent me, until I could discern its owner. And "in a manner of speaking", "in a matter of time", she herself would begin to matter. She'd matter, be completely and wholly mine. Persona would invest person, become matter. And I'd find the right words: through them and in that manner she could turn corporeal and real at least to me. I was ready for her to show herself. I sensed her approach...

•

In my writing life (the life of the spirit, if you prefer), this inspiration (or visitation, as I prefer) offered something of great significance. Here appeared the first woman I'd wholeheartedly believed in. Here close to me was 'my' first feminine character, my first real woman revealing herself. It was the first time I'd assumed the first person female, taking on a woman's point of view, and trying to see the world through different eyes. The shock of this altered vision was as shattering to me as certain drugs, LSD for example, have proved to others.

The woman destined to haunt me – that wraith who would be both alter ego and familiar for as long as it took to be delivered of her – had, naturally, features of a powerful attraction. I'd seen her face just once before, a decade ago and under different circumstances. She and I, via a capital irony, had come face to face in the very public context of a central London bookshop.

We were shortly to share one private, telling insight. A tiny if sharp enough splinter of time was somehow displaced, if you like, and unexpectedly lodged within my psyche... I'd no choice but to wait in humility, to accept and note the moment that would soon arrive and be all there was between us. 'Our' anonymous encounter – of looks and gestures to which words were ill-suited – was not simply brief but most disturbingly elusive. It did happen however; a sort of confrontation occurred, beyond my control, which bestowed on me thereafter an inescapable consciousness of anguish.

I who had so long and so blithely assumed the right to observe, had not proved observant enough. As Author I was accustomed to being Observer; suddenly now I knew myself observed. And worse: at fault. Faced with her beauty, I'd been blind to her pain, seeing only what I wanted to see. I'd missed the obvious, and my careless, selfish, blinkered vision had disregarded or been unaware of it. Of what was missing and of what, wilfully, I'd missed... Whatever was next staring me in the face I felt scarcely able to deal with. For as I'd moved towards the till, to take my place at the front, I'd flinched involuntarily. My all too immediate reaction – rather than response – was duly, coolly noted. There was nowhere else to look, amid those rows of books, and the customers queueing behind me. I wanted to avert my gaze, but could not.

I'd first seen a slender, beautiful girl with brown shoulder-length hair. I guessed she was in her early twenties, as I was. She wore a bright short-sleeved summer dress, patterned in red and blue. She stood at the cash register, intent on what she was doing. She was busy and efficient, pleasant without being at all ingratiating to anyone. I felt, perhaps perversely, in the mood to draw her into conversation: that self-contained quality of hers, reserve rather than shyness, only enhanced the 'English rose' style of beauty which had initially caught my eye. Then, catching sight of what, incredibly, I'd originally failed to notice, I flinched.

There was no way to make amends or to pretend it had never happened. I was the one, as it appeared, who needed to be defensive, self-conscious and awkward. This grave beauty had evidently come to terms with irretrievable loss: what graceless, insensitive male could imagine the extent of such a fate? Her right arm ended at the elbow. Its stump appeared pinkish and raw, yet she was using it adroitly to operate the till. No disguise was required, no apology, and no explanation necessary. Why should she hide? If there's nothing and nowhere to hide, she seemed to be saying to herself, what's the good of hiding? She would show, not tell, and that was and would be the end of her story.

It became impossible finally not to look into her eyes. The look given me in return by her was impervious, impassively calm. I'd feared the anger of Medusa and found only the sadness of Eurydice. Yet something I thought I read in her face meant so much that I remembered it across the years.

Although I'd partially buried the memory, there seemed no escaping it. That enigma from the past existed like the undead, waiting to be recalled. So I summoned it at last: its image of nightmare and aura of grief could no longer trouble me. When I began the novel called *The Stump*, I hoped I might be enabled to bring some true and fitting end to 'our' journeys of flesh and spirit. Through the existence of a woman I should never meet again, my book would be brought to life, given its end as well as its beginning.

•

"Although the English girl who is its narrator is a long way removed from the Greek man who is its author," wrote one magazine critic, "there is an air of reality about *The Stump*". Indeed there was – and must be, if any fiction is to convince. For a start, whether adapting or focussing some of the ideas and images I have described above, a considerable amount of groundwork was necessary. On a mundane level, this involved much preliminary research into amputation and the so-called 'phantom limb phenomenon'. I accumulated a mass of medical detail, little of which I would in fact use.

There's also, as may be guessed, a more intuitive or imaginative form of groundwork. The last term is itself an apt word for preparation required before ideas can rise to their own personalised life. It reminds me of a conversation I had with Angela Carter. This novelist was a cat-lover like myself, and she recounted how, in order to essay something from a cat's point of view, she'd once spent a day crawling wordless and spectacleless around her darkened flat. Barefoot, her fingers tied together with string, she became absorbed in ferrying objects here and there, always and only between her teeth. All done, of course, in order to vary the angle of vision, to define and try to appreciate how one might see life from floor-level...

A similar kind of experience helped me to find my own way towards that other Angela, Angela Todd, narrator of my novel. She was also, in a sense, in her innocence, its heroine – a teenage angel and highflyer, soon brought down to earth, struggling to deal with that material world and forced to grow through and out of pain. To be surprised by pain rather than by joy, I could easily understand: it was a hard enough lesson and one never forgotten. On my first day at a British school, aged six and unable to speak much English, I severely fractured an arm. I was lucky, ultimately, to regain its use. Operations, orthopaedics, months in various hospitals. Half a century later, I see the past has flown, fragmented, and how precious a process is recovery, is life. Time that heals may be an illusion however, for so often it lies heavy and, to tell the truth, even with its passing some wounds appear never to heal. Yet writers have gone on hoping to identify and salvage certain particles of lost time, reassembling them in patterns that may or may not prove meaningful. The mosaic of memory is thus re-set, curiously preserved and protected by a structure of words as hard, as unyielding, as any plaster-cast...

We all have individual ways of surviving sudden change – unfamiliar, unforeseen or 'unfair' circumstances. Some go under, others go underground. The latter seek to resist their fate, whatever the odds against them: as misfits or outsiders they must resort to limited, variably effective forms of *ad hoc* response, trying to evolve a personal set of guerrilla tactics aimed at the tyranny of existence. Such is my avenging 'angelic' heroine – someone young, attractive and talented, who therefore in worldly terms seems to have everything. She then loses in quick and disastrous succession what life has given her: her innocence, her lover, her child and her hand. Her career 'prospects' as a promising athlete have meanwhile vanished. All she can see for herself ahead is pain; how others will now inevitably see her is further cause for pain. What do you do after losing everything except your sanity? Let go or fight? In the long run, we all lose the war of course, and death may even come to seem kind. But mostly everybody struggles on, endeavouring to find consolation if not meaning.

Angela is a fighter, she doesn't give up, and she gives as good or as bad as she gets. The world tests the beautiful and the brave: they are made to pay dearly along the way. Angela goes on; she reacts, resists, endures – and for her then I felt something close to love. An odd sensation to experience towards a simulacrum, a mere fiction! And yet anyone who has tried to 'create' a character will understand the feeling. Finally, almost as if I couldn't bear to let her go, I gave the book its purposely 'open' ending. For how could any life-line, imaginary or otherwise, too fittingly and neatly conclude? The transparent creatures of the spirit, once glimpsed and summoned, cannot stay trapped within any page; they seem to seek their own liberation, they must be allowed to fly free, however frail their wings. Authors aren't gods and were never omniscient; they're mere mortals, earthbound lovers who may briefly accommodate and release a fine-spun vision: such insights as they receive remain mysterious even to themselves, and are earned though not owned.

She haunted me for a few years afterwards, my angel and, insubstantial presence, phantasm that she was, was a strange comfort through some dark days. I no longer worried about her or my being misunderstood. I'd written her as best I could, the only way possible and open for me. No thought for career, marketplace and what was expected of me. Reading the completely divided reactions of some very far-flung and far off the mark critics, I was glad to have heeded this young woman's voice, so different from the one I and they had previously known. What to one English newspaper was *honest and moving*, was to its South African counterpart *a sick story*. Other UK papers and journals used phrases like *not enjoyable reading*, *painfully accurate*, *a chilling experience*, *a savage little tale*, and words like *ferocious* and *brutal*. Some 'quality' nationals and Sundays called me *a metallic young writer*, at the same time as they praised *an intelligent study of human responses to personal misfortune* and the book as *genuinely felt*. Most gratifying and down to earth perhaps was an Australian weekly's view of *The Stump* as *a very striking and hard-hitting comment on society's attitude to physically disabled people. It is a book which once you start you will want to read from cover to cover.*

Unfortunately, bearing in mind that last sentence, the sales were the worst I'd ever had. My latest publishers, the third I'd had in five novels, had just been taken over. Their new fiction editor's bright idea of salesmanship was to clap a tacky nude photo on both front *and* back covers, and to write an abbreviated blurb that nevertheless managed to divulge an important plot twist. I protested at all this, to no avail. No one listened: changes were not to be made. I realised to my dismay that I was property, to be marked and marketed with a label currently reading 'outspoken'...A similar sequence of events – including my reaction, and the publishers' non-reaction – would in due course unfold with regard to the paperback. It was ironically clear to me that I'd been saddled with a kind of macho writer's image, which I'd wanted to shed with *The Stump*. Writing this novel had given me an alternative option, a direction out and away from a stereotyped, assertive masculinity.

That Angela is an athlete, a tennis-player, was intended to be a ludic metaphor – ready, I suppose, to be misread. She's thus a good sport, a sporty type, rather than as men choose to see her: via the old, offensive slang of 'sporting girl'. She doesn't in the masculine sense play games; she's healthy, honest, up front, and fatally naive. She is naturally talented and attractively natural, and without too much reflection or self-questioning enjoys what she does: hence she's born – made – to pay the price for her gifts. I thought of her too as a female variant of Philoctetes, wielding racquet not bow. When weapon and hand alike are denied her, she is obliged to turn her wound to her advantage, for her own survival. Did I unbalance her with symbols – or 'emblems', as literary fashion currently prefers – and tilt the scales too heavily against her?

It's possible. Yet thirteen years on, in 1986, the publisher and translator Anthony Wood – founder of the fittingly named Angel Books – was absolutely on the ball when he called it "a 'poetic' novel in its total war approach" and "a theatre for psychic descent". Appropriately too, it was Wood who'd introduced me in our undergraduate days to the works of Lautréamont, which I was later to translate. And one quotation from Lautréamont's *Maldoror* – "I know my annihilation will be total" – is epigraph to *The Stump*. "I think the lopped hand is a very potent thing for its symbolism", Wood wrote to me: "Have you read

Götz Von Berlichingen? When Goethe did a revision of it... the changes revolved around the question of sensitivity; in the first version the iron hand was a complete and isolating bar, but somehow in the second version, some feeling got flowing again." I hadn't read the Goethe text, though there was a suggestion of Germanic doom – death's presence indeed hovering about this maiden and her surname 'Todd'. Angela had been for me a most personal poetic muse, akin to a Rilkean angel of inspiration. A dangerous if very *necessary* angel, recalling the phrase of another poet, Wallace Stevens... She had taught me how to free my own feelings, taking whatever route was required, regardless of how others might think or whatever they thought they required of me.

And in case this sounds solemn (it's surely serious), I could still step back from the book's 'failure' – in purely or impurely financial terms – to laugh at myself. I envisaged some suave Freudian reading 'castration complex' into much of the above. Here, Herr Doktor, we have a male author living out through the voice of his female narrator the bitter fate of The Book itself! The latter phrase refers to a *text,* a bastard production, an object already rendered androgynous or of neuter gender. Its presumptuous creator/progenitor is powerless/impotent to prevent such an anomalous artefact from further dissection by the butchers of Lit. Crit. Do I hear a cry of Hands Off? Save your breath: sooner or later every author's for the chop...

The foregoing analysis is perhaps only a fanciful interpretation, after all. Some may see it (and they can skip it) as a playful or surreal intrusion, the stump of a pointless digression. But there's no such thing as pure digression; ultimately, in every book the lines meet, everything links up and writer and reader become one. As for my method here, it's in any case rather associative than digressive. I've been examining both my 'public' life, my writing or written life, and – stories behind stories behind stories – my private or 'secret' life. Here, since the time is ripe for it, is some of that secret life as described by Salvador Dali: "All poets have sought one single thing: the angel. But their vice of congenital negativism has confused and perverted their taste and turned them to evil angels, and if it is true that it is always the spirit of evil that animates the Rimbaudian and Maldororian angels this is due to the sole and unique fact of the inadaptation to reality that is consubstantial with poets". Poets in his view were far inferior to painters of course, and I'd been rash enough, I realised, to risk delivering one of that malnourished, much-maligned species 'the poet's novel'.

Woe unto me, whose agent confessed that with *The Stump* he "could not see where I was going"! Mercifully, I couldn't either, though I guessed that agents and angels on certain important levels don't mix, and also that I'd be changing agent and publisher alike in the not too distant future. What should I have done? (I took temporary jobs unconnected with writing, to try to live, to buy myself writing time...) Certainly I didn't make the right career moves. For one thing I'd moved out of London, and for another, I regarded writing as a vocation. It was a process to be accomplished with love, for love. Perhaps I exemplified the Dalinian view and, as poet, could not adapt to reality. But Jean, who also loved and wrote poetry, was an example to me through her own dedication to her art. I think she sympathised with my stubborn youthful idealism, because she had never lost hers: that was why, against the odds, she endured so long.

I was pleased *The Stump* pleased her. Jean understood what I was attempting, and could discern that the novel was, despite its faults, neither too 'literal' nor too 'literary'. There are in it symbols/emblems (of other kinds of reality), yet it's not all style and stylisation: another level of reality is also lived through, whose pattern is naturalistic enough. She didn't read it simplistically – as some kind of early 1970s, early Women's Liberation tract, nor as a young man's *hommage,* a sort of imitation or emulation of her own matchlessly vivid portraits of female victims. She told me after having read *The Stump* that she was now also keen to read Lautréamont, but had searched in vain for my translation when last in London. I can't recall whether I sent her a copy, nor what she thought of it, but I've found her letter of thanks for *The Stump.* She's "just finished reading it & will certainly read it again. For it's that sort of book". I knew that when we next met her comments would be more detailed – always acute intuitions, encouraging me to persevere. She adds: "I do wish you & it the best of luck". That was good enough for me, although I could certainly have used more of the luck. Every novel needed a generous slice of that, as we both knew to our cost.

Jean Rhys was and still is that 'ideal' reader at my shoulder for whom I wrote *The Stump*, the reason why it's dedicated to her. *The Stump* was more than a token of my esteem and thanks: it was a kind of vocational milestone – rather than career landmark! Henceforth I would become more exacting in the writing of novels. They were to sell less, of course, as I experimented more. The road ahead promised to get rougher... But I was pointed firmly in the direction of no compromise, of pleasing myself, saying only what was vital to be said.

This for me has meant a return home. Not to Greece, where I was born and where I found myself the year Jean died in England. Back rather to a starting-place, to that innermost spiritual home to which I belonged in the beginning. It's meant a return to my true beginnings, while acknowledging that first, best smile of fortune. Through accidents of circumstance – the travails of mid-century European history – I'd come to adopt a friendly and to me most hospitable mother tongue. I knew I should never forget that my greatest happiness lay in having learnt such an incomparably rich new language. You are given luck, and must then make more of your own. I'd already led a charmed life: I'd survived some unusual circumstances and a troubled childhood, and was struggling to survive as a writer. Through everything, I could now see, my luck had held. I'd been lucky in meeting Jean.

Once upon a time I wandered into a bookshop. There amid a myriad distractions, among innumerable words waiting to be read, I made my mundane choice. Then I met the unwritten, impossibly serene gaze of the muse. Years passed before I recognized her existence and accepted her story – whatever might be told. I did the best I could, with awe. And having looked into my heart to write, I vowed I would never again not do so. That was the point at which I felt able to continue along the road, for just as long as it took. Gradually I became aware of the direction in which that road might lead. And, luckiest of men and most grateful, I found myself returning home. Towards poetry.

Enthusing

The Glory and the Nothing of a Name.
    – Byron: *Churchill's Grave*, 1816

Years of silence. Personal reticence. Physical frailty. Singular integrity. Gregarious yet wary. Elusively never effusively lyrical. Cruelly sensitive. Deft (and deaf) conversationalist. Cat-lover – therefore a patient observer. And thus too the fatalistic humour. Surviving in melancholy, self-chosen social isolation...

All these phrases applied to Jean, but were also true of another outstanding twentieth century novelist. Apart from the letter of appreciation written to Jean, as earlier described, I'd never felt prompted to approach any other great artist, preferring to admire their work from a distance. I was always too detached to want to be anyone's acolyte, although perhaps I mightn't have spurned the role of apprentice. As far as other writers went I remained reluctant to intrude upon their privacy. This was especially true of those of my elders I didn't personally know. One's motives might be misunderstood, and all via the vulgar intrusion of a fan letter.

Jean's response, however, proved no disappointment, and during the next four years we had become friends. So by mid-1973, when I eventually wrote to a longtime literary hero of mine (whom Jean, incidentally, knew of and mentioned with respect, but said she hadn't read), I was less worried about the possibility of presumptuous interruption. Certainly I was quite sanguine as to whether or not my letter received an answer. By that time I'd published several more books, and Jean herself had encouraged me. I wasn't angling for a reaction from this particular writer; nor did I require a putative father-figure or mentor. The circumstances were very different from my own in 1969 when I first wrote to Jean... No, this was purely a gesture of affectionate admiration towards someone whose books I loved. He was free to bin the letter of course, and doubtless did. But I was glad I'd bothered writing to an old man over twice my age. His own books were mostly out of print or hard to obtain. He himself had published nothing for over twenty years. Nor would he again. He was to die only a few months later.

As a novelist in my early thirties I didn't readily make contact with elderly, reclusive and alcoholic authors. This, the second and last occasion I ever did so, dated back in a sense to the autumn of the preceding year, 1972... Then I had written to a director of the Hogarth Press, pointing out a curious and unfortunate situation. This superb author – 'theirs' as Hogarth must have considered, since the firm put out his other books! – made his début with a novel which the Press never originally published. That novel, *Blindness*, first appeared in 1926 and had been decades out of print. I urged it be reissued, along with a volume of their author's hitherto uncollected work – some short stories, a *Paris Review* interview of 1958, and various other pieces which I listed. There was a deafening silence from Hogarth until August 1973, so I sent them another letter. This time I made sure I also wrote to Henry Green himself.

Like Jean, Henry Green (yet another literary name- and sea-change) was at first praised. Later, he too was unjustly neglected and then, if more widely read, largely misread. By a paradox that might have amused him, it was his own inimitable style and sheer originality which made him (true again of Jean) such an example to and influence on younger writers. Among the Americans, for instance, two very unlike authors – Terry Southern and John Updike – have gladly admitted to their admiration for Green. For this always experimental but unusually enjoyable novelist was the most 'English', and hence perhaps most international, of writers.

But in August 1973, Green gave probably the last and saddest of his anyway rare interviews: "I'm forgotten now. It's disappointing, but there it is. Nothing to be done about it." Why the long silence, though? Why at the height of his powers had he stopped writing? "It was making me so tired it made me ill. Which I still am. Novel writing is frightfully difficult when you are putting everything you have into it." I couldn't help thinking of Jean, fifteen years his senior, who had not given up, and who, though there would be no more novels from her either, persisted in rural solitude to struggle on with her writing. Whereas Jean had been rediscovered, 'rescued' from the limbo in which she'd been marooned, and still wrote daily – longhand, with laborious arthritic determination – Green seemed to be waiting for the end.

I wrote to assure him that *The Guardian* article had given, like his own books, pleasure. I was saddened to read his comment about being forgotten, adding "this is very far from being the case". "For years," I continued, "I have admired and enjoyed your books, all of which I have, excluding *Blindness*. I agree with the interviewer that this novel should be in print, and in fact wrote to a director of the Hogarth Press last year urging him to reprint it if possible, together with your uncollected shorter pieces, so that all your work could then be available to your decidedly not indifferent readers. Unfortunately I received no reply from the publishers and have just written to them again. I would not have persevered with the correspondence had I not felt that many younger writers like myself owed you a debt: books like yours, though inimitable, can and do inspire, and certainly won't be forgotten".

At the end of that month I heard from Ian Parsons, the Hogarth director to whom I'd initially written the previous year. Now semi-retired, he thanked me for my recent letter. He'd not received my earlier one which "must have gone astray in the post". Parsons said he hadn't been aware of the newspaper piece either, until I'd brought it to his notice. But now, "encouraged" by it and my letter, he was writing to Henry Green with a view to republishing *Blindness*. Parsons hoped there would be no objection to their publishing it in "our Landmark Library series devoted to reprints of distinguished novels of the past".

I replied enclosing a copy of my strayed earlier screed with its detailed suggestions. Come September, Ian Parsons told me Hogarth had written to Green as promised, but so far there'd been no answer: "Not surprisingly, since alas he is a very sick man and seldom answers letters". Someone from Hogarth would shortly try phoning him...

Henry Green died soon afterwards. *Blindness* – "a remarkable allegory of awareness", as the interviewer had correctly signalled – was published by Hogarth only towards the end of the decade, late in 1977. Green's uncollected writings, edited by his grandson and with a short memoir by his son (also including an introduction by Updike and the *Paris Review* interview with Southern) were eventually published – by Chatto & Windus. But this was not until 1992, and under the by then ironic title *Surviving*.

For the rest of the 1970s, via the Arts Council's Literature Panel, I tried without success to get Green's complete works back into print – now, alas, having to argue the case for a posthumous tribute. In 1980 I sent details of what had happened (and not happened) to a fashionable English novelist, someone supposedly preparing "the authorized biography of Henry Green". This man neither replied nor produced the biography. The latter omission at least may be regretted. As recently as 1996 I saw mention of a forthcoming 'study' of Green by an academic, Jeremy Treglown. At the time of writing however (mid-1997), this has not appeared, and there's still no proper biography of Henry Green available.

For the moment, and maybe into the millennium, we must be content with his own partial, all too concisely autobiographical *Pack My Bag* from 1940 – a teasing, elegant but in the end enigmatic fragment. Henry Green seems to have been a complex charmer and a lovable man. He shared with Jean a truly painstaking care for language, and both worked their words so aptly as to inhabit an area in which the commonplace became extraordinary. There, sights and sounds might shift and shimmer with all sorts of suggestive magic, while a controlled, expressive prose remained always lucid, exquisitely precise. This was seldom if ever the functional prose of everyday currency: at best it remains miraculously economical, forming graceful patterns that speak of joy. Reading it, you are rescued for a while from sadness and the inescapable dark. Such prose has transmuted whatever struggles it required to create: the result is direct yet oblique, simplicity with ambiguity, giving rise to an almost tactile and curious beauty, an eerie perfection.

As with Jean's work, whose hard-earned, evocative insights I've learned to love, so too I value Green's. He has an equally steely yet suggestive precision, and in both are glimmers of sly, often rueful humour. Maybe this pair of rare birds possessed, in addition to all the novelistic gifts – such as storytelling flair, for instance – something few prose-writers have, or can develop. V.S.Pritchett, in his commemorative address after the death of his old friend Henry Yorke/ Green, defined it as "poetic impulse".

More Greenery

Set against the 1930s writing of Graham Greene, George Orwell and
nearly every other English prose writer of the period, with the exception
in a very different way of Henry Green, her work continued to rest on
the power of style...
    – Thomas F. Staley: *Jean Rhys – A Critical Study*, 1979

I don't know if Jean ever enjoyed or even read the work of Graham Greene. I
somehow doubt that it would have been to her taste, for its general grimness
and glum, functional prose can seem dauntingly drab. I'd guess that Greene's
literary territory did not appeal to her although in certain respects they shared
some common ground. The raffishness of his exiled or displaced characters,
with their bleak addictions and often fatal weaknesses of one kind or another
– that restless self-questioning... The loneliness and botched relationships and
frustrated ambitions, all the myriad morbid traps into which the soul may
fall... Given all that possible area of shared preoccupations though, the
likelihood is that Greene was too copious, too calculating, not poetic enough.

Nor would the politics and religion have appealed to her: novels shouldn't
preach, and she didn't feel there was any hope of salvation, just that death in
itself was our only sure absolution and kindest release from pain. Jean herself
throughout her life was drawn towards rather decent-seeming if not perfect
English gentlemen stereotypes – who then unfortunately often revealed hidden
flaws of one sort or another. She might however have found intriguing Greene's
own personality: the sociable if worldweary traveller, at times seemingly so
suave and cosmopolitan, yet intensely private and receptive-passive. He was
always someone with an 'unrespectable' streak, an edge of the disreputable in
his writerly independence; someone who never quite belonged in any clearly
defined class or milieu, but whose observation remained nonetheless accurate.
An exotic outsider also, an opium-smoker always "half in love with easeful
death". Yet Greene too was absolutely consistent, preserving a keen unillusioned
eye and an unsentimental fascination with the marginal – be it some form of
eccentricity, betrayal, criminality – or with the varieties of indecision and the
failures of love.

I find not a single mention of him in Jean's letters nor in the voluminous Angier biography of her. And I can't recall our mentioning Greene on any occasion. It may be that Jean, herself depressive enough, did not seek out nor indeed wish to explore, writing that might depress her even more! But by an odd coincidence, when I began writing about Jean, my copy of Greene's Mexican travel book, *The Lawless Roads*, fell off its shelf and opened at Chapter 5, which is entitled "Voyage in the Dark". Jean's novel of that title, her personal favourite among all her books, was published in 1934. Greene's book appeared in 1939. Had he perhaps read *her*?

The only solid thing

Six years before her death Jean told a Sunday newspaper journalist: "Looking back on my life, I see that the only solid thing has been my writing." But she also knew how strangely fluid the processes of writing are – what weird coincidences, ghosts, dreams, portents and visions, can all combine to prove of use and encouragement to the writer. For the latter operates often in a sort of trance: routine becoming ritual, then unstoppable rhythm, as page follows page and the book flows into being. Each narrative exacts its own inexorable pace and gains too a surprising, sometimes subliminal, logic. Then every linked detail simply becomes part of the pattern and falls into its place, that special space created for it. The work when it has found its way towards its true end engenders a sensation of hardwon joy like no other, heady yet humbling, if alas all too rare.

Books must have magic – as for example, Jean thought *Esther Waters* had – the inherent individuality within our common fate. We're aware that the books we love best have this vital essence; they cast a spell on us. We say we cannot put them down, we read on oblivious of time. We're taken out of ourselves, transported: thus we live in others and they in us. These works possess hypnotic power it seems, drawing us to reread them, without such familiarity ever weakening their force. On the contrary, new marvels are revealed to us there, further enchantment as we return and revisit their worlds.

Twenty years before that conversation, Jean wrote to an author friend: "I do think there is something very mysterious about books don't you?" And years before that, but not long after Jean Rhys was born, George MacDonald wrote in *Lilith* : "Now and then, when I look round on my books, they seem to waver as if a wind rippled their solid mass, and another world were about to break through."

Rhetorical questions, fanciful statements, maybe. But they answer us, and often do, the books. The books survive. They outlive us. They are legacies. Jean, had she lived, would have loved to read those words of Czeslaw Milosz: "And yet the books will be there on the shelves, separate beings.../ So much more durable/ Than we are, whose frail warmth/ Cools down with memory, disperses, perishes." The poet imagines the strangeness and wonder of the world, moving on, continuing after he is gone. He concludes: "Yet the books will be there on the shelves, well born, / Derived from people, but also from radiance, heights."

Milosz in 1986 might have been addressing her. Jean would have known what he was saying – valuing the aristocratic knowledge generally, the democratic message most particularly. Like every fine poet, she took her responsibilities toward the mysterious energy of language with all due seriousness. As another Nobel-winning poet, Derek Walcott, recognized when addressing her more directly in a poem. Walcott's poem has her name for title. Walcott wrote of "an old woman / who wrote with a fine courtesy to that world" – the Caribbean, past and future, the book of life to come... Time shifts to and fro, it seems, until line by line the poem itself flows movingly to its end, with "her right hand married to *Jane Eyre*, / foreseeing that her own white wedding dress / will be white paper."

Beauty and taboo

Et la beauté devient toujours plus difficile,
c'était d'abord le geste quotidien...
— Rilke: *Fragments*, written in French

Apart from Jean, there were other distinctive and original women writers
living in 1920s Paris. Exceptional in any gathering of literary expatriates at
that time must have been two of my own special favourites – the British poet
Mina Loy and the American prose writer Djuna Barnes. As far as I know, this
particular trio of talents was never brought together in any group context, but
it's a fantasy of mine that three such graces might once have sat drinking at the
same table or that their paths crossed elsewhere, at least in the street if not at
some convivial nightspot or party.

What a Judgement of Paris, in the topographical as well as mythological
sense, that might have provided! For all three, as their contemporaries attested,
were extraordinarily beautiful. And all three used the English language with
such exquisite power and precision... But it's the question of beauty that's
paramount here. The physical beauty, naturally, is what is first apparent – plain
to see, as it were. Yet how great an obstacle rather than an advantage this must
have been. We (and that includes especially men, male writers, and most
literate persons alive at the end of this twentieth century) tend to forget, we
cannot even imagine, how harsh the prospects facing her would have seemed
then to any serious woman writer.

To endure via one's imagination on an elevated level of artistic endeavour is,
and has always been – personally, socially, economically, and of course,
creatively – daunting enough. Few societies have truly valued their creative
artists, especially while those artists were alive and most needed support or
encouragement. As for women, long before the comparatively recent rise of
feminism, their roles were restricted and very clearly defined. Even among
more relaxed, unconventional or Bohemian circles, the combination of brains
and beauty in a woman was by either sex invariably distrusted and resented.
Attractive women also intelligent enough to resist being collected and used by

men – whether for purposes domestic, sexual or purely ornamental – were obliged to adopt survival tactics.

Advances – physical, rather than those offered and offset 'against royalties' – must have been two a *sou*… Jean's pre-war books are full of seedy encounters. In them a whole gallery of stupid or sordid pursuers initiate unwarranted and mostly unwanted chases and chat-ups; like their women protagonists, current readers will soon grow aware of the relentless, plentiful shooting of male lines. What a tiresomely perpetual struggle I think now, secure in my own sex and times, what purgatory to be compelled to share! And from the female point of view what a constantly intrusive and exhausting hunt. A risky pursuit, moreover, that might begin or end anywhere, nowhere – often only culminating with an exasperated submission. That last surrender might in itself be casual, passive, fearful, impulsive, or just the weary by-product of despair, frustration or annoyance. The terrible petty skirmishing of the sexes, which a writer like Jean recognized and so keenly described, would always provoke – if not a great nor decisive engagement – minor conflicts and campaigns forming part of a equally fatal war of attrition. This mortal strife between men and women seems inherent in the human condition, and there is no more rigorous twentieth century presentation of it than the unflinching, angrily lucid conclusion to *Good Morning Midnight*.

To evade or deal with such time-consuming, self-defeating transactions, themselves the outcome of frequently pointless or unpleasurable advances, these artistic women took refuge in outbursts of wit or displays of eccentricity (deeply offputting to most males then and now), lesbianism, alcohol, loneliness, or – best of all, when possible – their own work. The beauty of what they themselves might knowingly make, rather than what others might ignorantly make of their own beauty, could always absorb them. There alone was the best obsession and sole escape. Relationships might come and go and looks fade, but books stayed, art remained.

You might flirt or fight or yield, yet words would not let you down: they were allies that never changed, turned tail or proved false. Winning independence, sustaining it, or making the most modest living within (not: *out of*) the arts proved and still does impossible for many. The novelist 'Bryher' (Winifred Ellerman), Jean's exact contemporary, had to contract a marriage of convenience to one of the well known expatriate Americans-in-Paris in the 1920s, the writer-editor Robert McAlmon. Bride and bridegroom were both homosexual, but Bryher – a shipping-line heiress then involved with the poet H.D. (Hilda Doolittle) – needed the continuance of financial rather than moral support from her family. By keeping up an assumed front of respectability everybody benefited, not least 'Robber McAlimony' as someone enviously nicknamed him. But even Bryher could still write in her 1963 memoirs, *The Heart To Artemis*: "Social taboos have cut me off from much of the material that I should have liked to use. They are also the reason for the greater concentration of women writers upon landscape and mood".

It was to Jean's credit that she did not feel so constrained, and that constant lack of money, along with various not-so-fortunate liaisons could not sink her. Admittedly, Jean was lucky to become involved in the Twenties and her own thirties with *her* particular influential author-editor, Ford Madox Ford. Ford, one of those apparently more-English-than-the-English, rather gentlemanly types to whom she seems to have been attracted, helped her – for several years, be it remembered – without too many strings and in so many vital ways. He proved to be a stalwart protector, provider, mentor, father-figure, friend and agent as well as lover – indeed, more or less everything but a husband. Till the end of her days Jean would remember Ford with affection. For whatever their relationship might have lacked, both of them continued to gain in stature as writers. Finally, both in their individual ways were writerly equals.

Moore style

Where these days are the enthusiasts for George Moore? It seems as though
Moore (1852-1933) has been consigned to a sort of literary-critical limbo from
where, as ever hard to place, he occasionally drifts in and out of the consciousness
of a handful of readers. A strange kind of half-life, to be mentioned more than
read, allowed grudging respect yet dismissed either as too elusive or too direct.
Too 'French', too Irish – or at any rate not 'English' enough. Praised for
experimenting, damned for being out of date. The work is mostly out of print
now, its author becoming even harder to assess. He can be conveniently avoided
or dismissed, labelled 'extra-canonical' and shunted outside whatever current
Tradition is being promoted. A ghostly existence indeed for one who lived for
his work and lived so long trying to perfect it.

    Although there are innumerable Moore anecdotes, few of his contemporaries
remained consistent in their view of him: *vis-à-vis* Moore, they were frequently
revising their opinions, valuations and friendships almost as much as he
himself obsessively revised his own work. Perhaps as Max Beerbohm described,
"There was something blurred about him; his outlines seemed to merge into
the air around him. He never seemed to enter or leave a room. Rather did he
appear there, and in due time fade thence." "Intensely self-conscious", Beerbohm
called him, and Moore may only have been real (or have felt most real) to himself
alone. It's as if he existed in curious detachment, centred and focussed only in
his role as maker of literature. Indeed, he told one young wouldbe writer:
"Should I ever have a tombstone, I should like this written on it – let us phrase

it correctly... HERE LIES GEORGE MOORE, WHO LOOKED UPON CORRECTIONS AS THE ONE MORALITY."

It was this perpetually dissatisfied Moore who "set an example to all artists of absolute devotion to his art". Moore who, putting his whole personality into his work, *becoming* his books, wrote one of Jean Rhys's favourite novels. "A great artist", Moore also remarked to his youthful admirer, "is always before his time or behind it." "I belong to a past age really or a future one. Not now", writes Jean in a 1950 letter. In the next line she is telling her friend about the "relief" of "reading *Esther Waters* – why *Esther Waters*? I don't know. It's beautifully done and doesn't date a bit. I suppose reading about someone strong, quiet and simple helps me."

Three years later, to a different correspondent, Jean writes: "...day before yesterday I read 'Esther Waters' for the 60th time. It is a book I keep for very bad days, and it never fails me. It was published in 1894 and that's near enough to the date of my birth – I'm older a bit. So very old". Jean was actually not quite sixty-three, with a long way still to go, but she must have been experiencing *le cafard*. After all, she dwelt then not in Arcadia but Upper Norwood. (A depressing enough part of London, whatever your age: I lived there too on my return to England in 1979.) "I don't know why 'Esther Waters' has this magic effect on me", Jean continues: "Still there it is. Magic for me. Every time." Strangely enough, Beerbohm thought that "Vital magic, which was just what his [Moore's] novels lacked, was just what his criticisms had." But I'd agree with Jean here and can recall at least two separate occasions during the 1970s when she was rereading this, Moore's best novel.

In fact it was after she first mentioned the book to me that I followed her advice as I usually did and read it eventually myself. Moore once told his young acolyte of long ago, with some amusement, that *Esther Waters* "was, as you must have heard, regarded in certain circles as the most pornographic of books". Not entirely a playful remark, for Moore enjoyed shocking people and confounding expectations. But he'd got the bourgeois-baiting out of his own system with the teasingly-titled *Confessions Of A Young Man* (1886). That was the only Moore I'd read, as an undergraduate, well before I'd lived enough to rate or write any confessions of my own... I learned then that Moore's own hero was Flaubert; Moore even categorised the inspiration for the novel as "pure Flaubert". In fact one of the Cambridge lecturers I actually listened to called

Esther Waters "a great French novel rather than a great English novel" (Graham Hough, *Image And Experience*, 1960).

Perhaps it was the unlikely yet logical 'Frenchness' of *Esther Waters* – what Hough termed "a severe artistic ideal" – and the quietly poetic exactitude of the language with its "delicate rightness of diction and rhythm", that Jean valued so highly on a formal, technical level. Moore had found a way of focussing sympathetically but sharply as Jean later did, on a single main character. He thus eliminated padding and rough edges alike, avoiding the Victorian devices (often vices) of digression, facetious contrast, alternations in point-of-view and so on. Endless revisions went into forging that style which another critic thought "serious, honest, humane, and restrained." (*A Literary History Of England*, ed. Baugh, vol. 4, 1967). "Telling the truth about experience", as Hough appreciated, "instead of merely devising an agreeable story". All this Moore managed to do – for the time very frankly – while ensuring simultaneously that his imaginative freedom was balanced by humour and a scrupulous realism.

"George Moore was by no means a saint," wrote Havelock Ellis immediately after the novelist's death: "But he will live as a saint of art." If some of Moore's achievement has since been questioned, his impressive dedication has not. As for *Esther Waters*, I could see why Jean valued this story. A young woman fights adversity and social prejudice. Faced with every form of dismal exploitation and discrimination, she manages nonetheless to win through to a relatively happy end... And Jean must also have considered it a minor miracle that a middleaged male writer like Moore, from his comfortable background, could achieve a work so touching, fresh and perceptive, quite free from condescension.

Not of course that the lesser writers or more doctrinaire feminists shared Jean's views. That egregious snob Virginia Woolf, herself so irksome a novelist, patronised both author and book: the latter, she declared, lacked a heroine. Thus "its virtues collapse and fall about it like a tent without a pole". Woolf was indeed keen on metaphor (and who can tell how many tents she herself successfully put up?), yet she berated dated, un-Modern Moore for being over-literary: "Literature has wound itself about him like a veil, forbidding him the free use of his limbs". How the privileged do write... But how the poor did live, in those bad old days, Moore described rather better than his genteel critic.

Esther may have been in one sense a heroine of Jean's because while apparently meek and always impoverished, faced with dismal exploitation and discrimination, she beats the cruel odds against her, surviving to bring up a much-loved son. Jean's infant son had not survived: in later years she never discussed this great loss in her life – how could she and why should she? While it's scarcely possible to come to terms with the past, the fictions of the past can sometimes offer alternative worlds, intimately personal words whose consoling messages seem intended for the present. You can lose or find yourself too within words. Comfort can be drawn from books and by being in contact with other minds distinct from your own, not bound narrowly by mortality. The wisest of voices are always audible, generously, uncannily addressing your best self.

Jean cherished Esther Waters as I now do. As Moore must have in imagination, to have answered the call of that unassuming spirit and brought her to life... Looking up to someone, looking down on them: what do such phrases mean or matter, in the long run? Language, communication itself, is democratic yet individual. You cannot care about words without caring equally about people. If great minds are alike in thinking that the search for one's true style is where the meaning of life is hidden, it's also true that nothing is given, all needs to be worked for...

Max Beerbohm thought no one "ever wrote worse than young Moore wrote", but it was "the fine things inside him" and Moore's dedicated singlemindedness that made the difference. Beerbohm, deadly satirist, was serious enough when it came to listing those fine things: "[Moore's] matchless honesty of mind; his very real modesty about his own work; his utter freedom from jealousy; his loving reverence of all that in all arts was nobly done; and, above all, that inexhaustible patience of his, and courage, whereby he made the very most of the gifts he had, and earned for himself a gift which Nature had not bestowed on him: the specific gift of *writing*."

Those things applied to Jean too, and are worth remembrance. Genuine writers do seem to have an innate generosity. It's hard to define, but this may be the core of what's implied by the ancient phrase "a born writer". For surely writers are made: they make themselves, by themselves, learning from and through loneliness. That's not to say they don't need advice and encouragement, nor the influence of mentors of various kinds, living or dead. (Jean knowing

Ford for instance and, on the page at least, Moore.) No writer is or remains completely isolated: that thought must be consolatory.

Writers are mysteriously linked in any case, often by innumerable small codes and ironies, a liking for playful hints and wild coincidences. These familial links seem evidence, within each usually embattled consciousness, of an unusual feel for engaging impossibilities. Such signals and signatures, sympathetic greetings, quirky connections, can come to unite us; they encourage a kindred appreciative humility toward whatever's creative, allied to implicit respect for that very discipline required in order to create. As well as a general sense of commonality and continued indebtedness, it's these smaller goodhumoured particularities which can show us we all persist and exist together in our related concerns – remaining lively human company for one another, on whatever lowly or exalted level we seek to function.

How fine and cheering anyway to be surrounded by true friends and their works! And how curious also to reflect that H.G. Wells, in his own *Experiment In Autobiography*, found Ford "oddly resembling George Moore the novelist in pose and person". I wonder if Jean was ever aware of that reference or resemblance? But then again Wells, like Ford and Moore, was another who realised there was much to learn from women, however his own very different stories might be told.

Surviving

I have full respect for the popular arts but the function of the artist is vision. He must be in advance of his time and as to know is to be outcast from the world, why should he expect recognition? Fame is merely the badge of long service... there can be no reward but the vision itself. It is natural that we should be both disliked and ignored.
— Bryher: *The Heart To Artemis*, 1963

D.H. Lawrence — one who died all too early, scarcely reaching middle-age — somewhat sentimentally began one poem, 'Beautiful Old Age': "It ought to be lovely to be old"... Jean, his contemporary, knew it was not; old age was a trial that often seemed meaningless. Something in general to be endured, horribly particular yet arbitrary too in its cumulative and inevitable humiliations. Old age of course also angered her as another form of injustice, an ordeal with only one possible outcome.

At least Jean's mind retained its keenness throughout her unusually long journey. Although she may have thought that even that sharp gift of observation was a mixed blessing, an ironic double-edged dagger which of its essence could neither excise nor blunt the pain of life. She drew no comfort from it; for her it could provide no easy conclusions.

At the close of a *Paris Review* interview published soon after she died in 1979, Jean remarks "I've thought about death a great deal" and adds "Oh yes, I used to try to imagine death, but I always come up against a wall". The interviewer suggests that for Jean to continue work on her autobiography is "the reason to go on now, no?" But Jean hardly surprisingly is reluctant to concede this rather simplistic point. She sounds sad and tired, at bay almost, as if her back is to the wall (*that* wall... so close!)

I remember how belated fame brought her weariness as well as gratification. She was a daily prey to intrusions of every kind but did not consider turning anyone away. You felt for her and wanted to protect her. In some ways though and perhaps selfishly — with hindsight at any rate — I regret my own reticence. For even when warmly invited to visit I would be concerned not to tire her, never to take up too much of her time, no matter how enjoyable the occasion.

Consequently there were many things I wish I'd asked her and many conversations I had to forego. It saddens me still to think that there were other callers not so scrupulous, parasites eager to drain her declining energy.

Like so many writers solitary yet gregarious, she could not really reconcile necessary (meditative) solitude with unwanted (self-consuming) loneliness. Demands on her time came to mean 'being in demand', not forgotten, no longer meeting a premature oblivion. Far from oblivion, she'd already been resurrected, had extended her life and turned into a legend. It's an extraordinary way to survive.

But Jean was a rare and independent spirit increasingly helpless when faced with her own material needs and others' demands. Had it all been worth it? "I've had rather a rum life, but I was thinking the other day, would I go through it all again. I think not." There's a bleak note adding that "Jean Rhys died following an operation to insert a pin in a broken hip. She was eighty-four." She wasn't, she was going on ninety. She'd seen enough, written enough, talked enough. That interview had ended with a statement I'd heard her make before: "I guess I write about myself because that's all I really know."

Despite that, Jean was always objective and could be sardonic. She might by then have agreed with D.H.Lawrence, allowing him the last bitter word:

Elderly discontented women ask for intimate companionship,
by which they mean more talk, talk, talk
especially about themselves and their own feelings.

Where one ends up

Like her sensual and stylish poetic counterpart over three centuries ago, Jean too was holed up in a tiny rural corner of this large, attractive yet exasperating and often rainsoaked county. "Worlds of ice", Robert Herrick thought, were preferable to "lothed *Devonshire*". But while another poem, glumly entitled 'Discontents In Devon', begins:

More discontents I never had
     Since I was born, than here;
  Where I have been, and still am sad,
     In this dull Devon-shire

– Herrick concludes by admitting that he never in fact wrote better "Than where I loath'd so much".

Here it was, after all, that Jean wrote *Wide Sargasso Sea* and her later stories. A slowpaced place, that nondescript village tucked away between Crediton and Exeter. Back of beyond, in inglorious Devon – how alien both spiritually and physically it seemed to her! I remember the vehemence with which she'd criticize that shabby, leaky little cottage. So damp, 'Landboat Bungalows', and small, small as the average villager's mind. She must have felt, at her husband's death, quite marooned.

Cheriton Fitzpaine by the late 1990s has even lost its name: the signpost that pointed sharp right towards a smaller B-road, as one drove out of Exeter in the direction of Crediton, has been replaced by another with different locations indicated. Cheriton Fitz, as she referred to it (or Cheriton Fitz Paine, as she persisted in writing it), appears to have disappeared or at least to have lost whatever modest status it might once have had.

Jean Rhys lived there from 1960 until her death in 1979. She continued to feel it was a cold, wet, lonely spot to which she could never adapt. In a letter from spring 1971, she wrote: "Do come & see me soon & bring Diane. It would be a charitable act for I'm finding it difficult to settle down in C. Fitz". And she added (somewhat unconvincingly, we thought) – "though it has many good points I know." In other, later letters, she seemed almost to be coming to terms with the village's isolation: "I'm rather glad that Cheriton Fitz is so dull that tourists give it a miss." Yet if neither quite hideyhole nor hellhole, it always did feel and look like a dead-end hole. Somewhere anyhow worth visiting only in order to see Jean. These days that extinct burrow is trickier to find. "And who'd want to?" I hear her say, wryly. "I'm sure I can't imagine."

But her personalised rewrite of its name does seem to me to fit the place, as if stressing or echoing her own Cheriton fits – of *le cafard*, that old enemy always lying in wait. "The place's fault", its dispirited air, doubtless contributed to Jean's restlessness in her latter years: those increasingly frequent trips, the eager escapes despite her frail health, to London. Her visits, usually during the coldest, wettest part of each winter, sometimes made sense; occasionally they seemed to spell desperation and exhausted her more than ever. They might extend for months: hotels, friends' houses, rented accommodation. By then she could finally afford some luxuries, and anything she regarded as 'treats' helped keep her going.

London of course changed greatly throughout the seventy years or so she had known it, yet it retained its glamour. She'd first lived there not long after leaving Dominica, when young, beautiful, naive, and broke. In the 1970s none of these adjectives still applied, although because of her late fame Jean had a different, unexpected sort of glamour of her own, and was 'in demand' again – which must in some measure have gratified her.

The Herrick poem entitled 'His Returne To London' opens with a rueful line that puts me in mind always of Jean and her forays to the metropolis, for she too fled "From the dull confines of the drooping West"… I remember receiving invitations to various drinks parties in London which had been organized here and there for her. Also how I usually, if with occasional regret, declined them. Ironically, I myself was 'stuck' in Devon by then, isolated, young and broke: I couldn't afford London trips at that time, and was struggling – misguidedly, as it turned out – to make some money by writing novels. But I took pleasure in thinking from time to time of Jean enjoying her social whirl. It never occurred to me (it doesn't when you're young) that any one of these trips might prove her last fling, nor that Jean was staving off loneliness and decrepitude the only way she knew how. In a newspaper article after she died, George Melly recalled Jean jazzing at Ronnie Scott's, and toking on a joint – two pleasurable experiences I really wish I could have shared with her.

If Herrick confessed that, rather than return to the West Country, he would beg London itself to have his "Urn", he also knew very well what Jean knew (and I am nearer knowing) – that "Weak I am grown, and must in short time fall". In the end Jean came back west, winding up (or more precisely, down) in the Royal Devon & Exeter Hospital, further along the road from where I live now. In that place several of my friends have died. And there too other friends have worked, or still do. Life goes on, and as for Jean's own "sacred Reliques", I don't think she bothered overmuch about those, or any blue plaques at Cheriton Fitz... Jean's final Devon harbour took her to its heart, ablaze more fiercely than any West Indies sun. At the city crematorium she completed and began her long cherished voyage out of dark, into silence and the bright wide sea.

Beckoning Fair

Dear dead women, with such hair, too – what's become of all the gold
Used to hang and brush their bosoms? I feel chilly and grown old.
 – Browning: *A Toccata Of Galuppi's*, 1855

Perhaps it is just *The Beckoning Fair One* singing her faint irresistible
'very oald tune'. Well, let us be discontented then; it has never hurt art.
 – Christina Stead: essay, 1970

Hauntings have happened throughout history; macabre manifestations are constantly recorded in most cultures and circumstances, everywhere. They can't be written off for they occur and are witnessed with surprising frequency, seemingly bound by neither time nor place. It's impossibly hard finding words to express, even suggest, our own sceptical but curious involuntary glimpses into such unknown territory. While there have been plenty of helpful travellers' tales, literal maps are lacking. And yet the objective is objectivity itself: the distant destination reached at last, absolute proof provided and arrived at. As for these variously disconcerting, very different worlds – unfamiliar and so called supernatural or inexplicable – such worlds may well possess their own patterns and time-zones which on occasion overlap with our own. Nothing is fixed or solid: everything interpenetrates, all is fluid and in motion.

Grasp that elusive concept, or simply imagine it and there's no reason why we shouldn't also allow the simultaneity and multiplicity of all kinds of alternative existences – believe in fact in ghosts. Ghosts too may be made of atoms, although of a subtler sort so far invisible to scientists, and with substance and composition continuingly elusive. However we the living try to record, photograph, define them, these apparitions or presences resemble stars in broad daylight: they may be detected only sporadically, perceived not necessarily at any expected or appropriate times. Which is not to say of course that they entirely disappear, are extinct, or ever quite cease to exist...

Oliver Onions, a master of the macabre who ought to be more widely regarded, has written of "densities" and "texture" of ghostliness, of upsets of equilibrium in "this secondary zone" of spirits. In the twilight world, the shadowland he intimates, nothing is certain or fixed. Wandering within it are those "hardly known to have been ghosts till they have passed". From it they may briefly make themselves – perhaps via more than one of the human senses – manifest. As for the still corporeal inhabitants of what he terms "happy unhaunted earth", they seldom wittingly and willingly discern the other presences. The latter eventually fade, occasionally accumulate, but for some unfathomable reasons may persist. They continue circumambient if generally imperceptible; meanwhile their lack of clearly palpable form causes these entities lingering anguish or frustration. Although we can rarely apprehend or recognize their traces, the idea that they are *there*, more often than not – or than we know, is a universal, ancient, almost inescapable one. It lends singular presence to the twist-in-the-tail of Jean's last story, placed at the end of her final collection.

This succinct farewell to life and letters, 'I Used To Live Here Once', was called by William Trevor "one of the neatest of all ghost stories". When I asked Jean Rhys for her choice of the best ghost story ever written she showed no hesitation. Jean believed the most frightening to be in addition the best-written and therefore for her it remained the finest, most profoundly thought-provoking. Her verdict went to *The Beckoning Fair One.*

As she mentioned tale and teller, I recalled both: an evocatively-titled piece by an oddly-named author. I still possessed the anthology where it had pride of place, an omnibus of the macabre which I'd first read as a schoolboy. I'd not read this particular story in twenty years, although then it succeeded in scaring me right enough. I doubt that I fully understood the narrative – not at fourteen, with scant awareness of mortality. It had seemed for a short story dauntingly *long*, nearer a novella... So, somewhat bemused, but bearing in mind Jean's own stylistic conciseness, I went away and resolved to reread it. Since then, over twenty years have intervened, along with several further readings of this work. As a result I feel I've learned, albeit mysteriously, a little more about myself, Jean, writing in general and poetry in particular.

•

Before venturing closer towards that strangely fascinating text, or risking any analysis of its persuasive magic, here are some additional views and voices from both the living and the dead. These I include by way of whetting the general reader's appetite, to make new converts to the story's cause. Writers, critics, anthologists specialising in the supernatural, have anyhow been quicker than my youthful self ever was to recognize the vivid merits of *The Beckoning Fair One*.

The story took pride of place in a wonderful collection entitled *Widdershins* (1911). Its author George Oliver Onions (1873-1961) was an artist from Yorkshire who'd studied art in London and Paris. He had changed his name to George Oliver and, marrying a writer, Berta Ruck, became one himself, using his original surname (pronounced O-nigh-ons). 'Oliver Onions' in the course of a long and productive life knew both popular and literary success – as author of crime and historical novels alongside several fine books of ghost stories. Many of his macabre tales have a poetic, even decadent flavour, as might be expected of a young man with both visual and verbal ambition, seeing out the *fin de siècle.* They are often therefore concerned with inner turmoil and survival. Onions paints precise yet expressive portraits of obsessed creative types being driven to psychological extremes, or even out of their wits. Careers and lives blighted, haunted, in other words... Such themes – explored with pragmatic, painterly eye as well as poetic phrase – surely attracted Jean, who had come of age herself during the ghost story's greatest era, the thirty-odd years preceding World War One.

Other contemporaries of Onions, themselves noted practitioners in the macabre fiction field, were quick to spot the exceptional merits of his finest story. Algernon Blackwood thought it "the most horrible and beautiful ever written". H.P. Lovecraft agreed: at least that overripe overwriter could himself recognize more convincingly concise, effective prose... The same goes for Hugh Walpole, who rated Onions "one of the most talented writers on uncanny themes". But it took Thomas Burke to emphasise the emotional impact of this fable, its power to touch readers: "I have never yet heard or read a ghost story that could move me. The one that came nearest to doing it was that little masterpiece of Oliver Onions – *The Beckoning Fair One* – a story I have never forgotten." Style and content cohere, or at any rate are perfectly balanced, which has meant too, that the story is timeless. While very much *of* its time, it nonetheless escapes being 'dated', by taking off boldly, rising clear of any such temporal constraint and thus attaining the elusive realm, the purer aether of art. The best British stylists of post-World War Two weirdness praised its quality also. Robert Aickman considered it "one of the (possibly) six great masterpieces in the field" and L.T.C. Rolt too opined that with it Onions "has earned his place among the masters" (*The Passing Of The Ghost Story*, 1956).

Pre-eminent literary historians, critics and anthologists of the weird fiction genre haven't disputed such favourable verdicts from creative writers, as pronounced above. This implies an unusual consensus within a narrow if fiercely partisan sector of literature. The distinguished American critic E.F. Bleiler thought it laid claim to being "the best classical ghost story" while, for his compatriot Jack Sullivan (in *Elegant Nightmares*, 1978), it is "visionary" and "marvellously conceived". Sullivan goes further, in fact, and finds a parallel between Onions and the poet-occultist W.B.Yeats, since both identify "ghostly experience with the world of art, a world both ecstatic and demonic. The Beckoning Fair One represents the final triumph of the imagination, the subjective fusion of 'joy' and 'terror'; neither can be separated from the other, for both belong to the unified 'category of absolute things'". I suspect that the mysterious nature of poetry itself – its incantatory secrets, ritualistic quality and entrancing aspect, which may all bring about truly unforgettable revelations – is wrapped within words supremely well-worked. The poetic aim is awesomely focussed, inviting a direct confrontation with feelings, through sensuous yet endlessly suggestive precision. This is quite consistent with what Aickman was suggesting by his remark "that the successful ghost story is akin to poetry and seems to emerge from the same strata of the unconscious".

The method of the best ghost stories then, is ideally, archetypally poetic. Onions has adapted and shaped such an evocative method to explore creative madness: he seeks, as if through some strange poetic theorem, to demonstrate how imagination-in-action = inspiration. Further, his theme is to show how creativity – in this instance the transmutation of experience into literature – is not merely a risky business but a vexingly fraught vocation. You may find you sell your soul, give up your life, surrendering instead to phantoms: that's the steep price paid for the addictive, elusive pursuit of an impossible perfection. Different forms of creative death lie in wait: here, the writer-protagonist is well aware of them but cannot avoid these traps, so dazzled is he by the mirage, so besotted with his own most personal and intimate chimera. We don't want him to fail of course, but he does, ending like Faustus in fearful disaster. The alembic of his mind is shattered and the Great Work will never be; that alchemy art can achieve at best requires love, selflessness and humbly unremitting labour. Instead of fulfilling his talent as love obliges him to do, the would-be creator is seen to play a dangerous role, falling into a pattern of delusion and sterile indolence that only violence then death alone can disrupt. It's a cautionary tale of the creative urge turning destructive, of inspiration souring to nothingness, starved of all save horrid fancy. Onions is soberly reminding himself, as well as any potential writers (those ideal, always wished-for readers), of the snares riddling the way of Art... His startling story is a 'poetic' parable of imagination destroyed by extremes and thus fragmented, betrayed, lost. The wrong sort of attentiveness results in time wasted not recaptured, in nothing of substance – in ghosts, indeed.

Everybody presumptuously seeking to *create*, will anyhow be required to battle against demons. Be sceptical as you wish, but these malevolent, freakish presences taunt and haunt the mind in danger of losing its balance. They may have deceptively harmless, abstract names, even as they regroup in deadly viral collectives: the author shows us how their seductive combinations can dissipate the vital creative essence. Numbered among such enemies of the intellect, for instance, are *inaction* (blockage, lonely stagnation, melancholic entropy); *hyperactivity* (fruitless distractions, wild dreams feeding a misplaced obsession); *arrogance* (disappointed pride, thwarted ambition, lack of recognition, sense, humour and perspective). All of them familiarly bedevil artists everywhere...

No wonder Jean responded to this grim fable of the author literally wasting away, addicted to romance, obsessed – hence ever more reclusive and 'peculiar' until the final bewildering explosion of violence. That horror comes as no release, being but the desperate soul's abandonment, expressing only the nightmare nihilism of creativity irrevocably denied. Very much like Jean herself, the elderly Oliver Onions was described as "a slow, careful writer [who] works over his material again and again until he has set it down to his own satisfaction". The reading public had largely forgotten the 74-year-old author when the editors of my schoolboy's anthology thus described his writing routine. (*Great Tales Of Terror And The Supernatural*, eds. Herbert A. Wise & Phyllis Fraser, 1947). They also noted the "particularly sinister atmosphere" and deemed *The Beckoning Fair One* "certainly one of the finest and most terrifying ghost stories ever written. Many people consider it the *very* best."

If Onions had sunk from view, out of sight and mind and fashion, his insightful story went beyond fashion altogether: *The Beckoning Fair One* possessed depth, true vision and, especially for writers, a multilayered and abiding significance. It may be interpreted validly enough in a variety of ways as I am hoping to hint. Some of these interpretations and echoes have considerable resonance in, and relevance to, Jean's own literary theory and practice. The Jean who confessed to a *Sunday Times* interviewer in 1973 (the centenary both of Onions's birth and Ford's), "Looking back on my life, I see that the only solid thing has been my writing" had much in common with the story's central character – writer Paul Oleron, who "had chosen his path, and was committed to it beyond possibility of withdrawal." Both the real and the fictional artist's shared seriousness of approach to their art is here taken as read. The vexed question remains: To be or not to be an artist? Adopting such an irrevocable course means giving up one's more 'natural' life in order to embark upon an unreal, artificial, impossible quest. The writer commits to paper sheer impossibilities, spawning thin ghosts, and in the end commits too a form of slow but unsure suicide.

We all need luck, as Jean recognized, just to survive and try to accomplish that art as best we can. Knowing or unknowing versions of selfishness, asceticism, indulgence, duplicity, retreat, escape from the world – these may serve as help or hindrance for a time. But ultimately we must face up to ourselves and our choices, right or wrong. For Oleron in *The Beckoning Fair One*, things fall apart and the centre does *not* hold. The literary man proves not good enough, not true enough to himself nor to the real, live woman who loves him. He lacks the strength to resist the dreamworld and its alluring spirit; he mistakes vampire-creature for Muse, confusing coldness and cruelty with love. There is a somewhat Jamesian failure here, both of perception and of passion, as Oleron loses everything en route to his doom.

A writer moves into an empty house. Inside the house, or in his own mind, or infiltrating both, there exists a presence which will not be denied a habitation and a name. Revealed to be jealous, exacting and malign, this wayward force eventually drives the writer and his lover to distraction then destruction… (As with every complex fiction however, one doesn't want to give away the beautifully paced and frightening plot twists.) Even the surface 'story', while absolutely coherent, seems to resist plain summary. "Onions created a story that, of its kind, cannot be bettered", writes critic and bibliographer Mike Ashley. Ashley continues: "With no overt spectral manifestations, but with mere hints and suggestions, he portrays the accelerated mental disintegration of the protagonist... whilst establishing an almost suffocating atmosphere of ghostly gloom... a portrayal of madness that leaves the reader uncomfortably unsure about the state of reality and sanity". Jack Sullivan refers to "a novelist who falls in love with his unfinished, ultimately murderous female creation", adding that "When the narrator [sic] submits to The Beckoning Fair One, he also, unfortunately, submits to the loss of his sanity, becoming, as much as the expected other ghost, a deranged spectre who lowers all the blinds and haunts his own house". Another commentator, Gary Crawford, has Oleron "haunted by his own heroine". None of these paraphrases and summaries are actually quite correct, but they perhaps unwittingly make the point that the prose itself contains a clutch of haunting ambiguities.

To be fully appreciated, *The Beckoning Fair One* – a far from facile, by no means escapist piece – must be carefully read. In his own lifetime Onions, like Jean, knew the satisfaction of having scaled a creative peak, achieving an undoubted classic. Barely a generation after first appearance it was hailed as "certainly among the best modern works in the genre" (Harrison Dale, ed., *More Great Ghost Stories,* 1932), and has remained 'modern' right through to our particular *fin de siècle.* How has this happened, especially when so many uncanny stories fail to convince and date so badly as to nullify their primary *raison d'être,* the arousal of atmosphere and emotion? Rooted, moreover, so much in its time – a posturing period, within a rather narrow, *passé* world of decadent aesthetes and self-conscious advocacy of 'art for art's sake' – the text miraculously rises above its age and moves far beyond it. The feat is not managed by cunning psychological intimations alone (Freudianism itself has badly dated, after all) but by a fine balance of feeling, vision and literary skill. We are shown a species of psychic vampirism at work, but there is further subtlety in the mounting frustration and mental deterioration described. Negativity accelerates into agoraphobia, anorexia and a near-psychotic murderous rage: then the downward slide is sadly but unflinchingly portrayed.

Sensibly enough though, the author's concern and craft resides not so much in describing symptoms as enlisting sympathies. Onions manages to write simply yet beguilingly about decay and gloom. Always with exquisite economy he allows the horrific inner drama to unfold. Via such disciplined narration, the maniacally self-absorbed protagonist's own dilemma is accentuated. However confused, eccentric or dislikeable his characters, the author makes us care about them. To depict sympathetically and without self-pity an artistic temperament thwarted – love itself frustrated and misdirected, failure spiralling into mental and physical collapse – might seem a tall order. But all this Onions successfully does, with a seamless, timeless skill that surely impressed Jean Rhys.

•

Indeed I rather think Jean recommended the story to me knowing that it would strike a chord: I could learn from it as she had done. Because it was very much for real, this most ghostly of stories… What it boldly told me – of mind at the end of its tether, violent relationships, breakdown; life in death's shadow and thus very much *in extremis* – was personally, most intimately valuable. I'd been at least some of the way there, as Jean herself undoubtedly had. Learning to become a writer means agreeing to live dangerously, precariously to some degree. This must be accepted as part of the deal, the cards fate has dealt… There's no spiritual or material safety in it: expect nothing, work hard for nothing, for no reward. Only then if you are lucky the Muse may visit. And if you're still luckier, you may survive to tell the tale…

For the writer IN *The Beckoning Fair One,* everything goes horribly adrift, since his objectivity and love alike (hence too his dedication) are misplaced; lost talent, lost soul. For the writer OF *The Beckoning Fair One,* everything went superbly well: he got the matter and the manner absolutely right. To start with, Onions settled on a third-person narrative which naturally 'distances' or objectifies, while nonetheless effecting an impression of low-key intimacy customarily only achieved through first-person narration. Just as happens in Jean's own work, this quietly attentive viewpoint elicits a combination of empathy and detachment from the reader who, in turn, won't be tempted glibly to 'identify' with the characters: understanding is what author requires of reader. Even when communicating the worst, whatever negative elements are found necessary, the author still keeps hoping for the best – and in that hope finds inspiration.

The raised voice of the authorial "I", whereby the protagonist is clearly an author's alter ego or self-regarding hero is not here in evidence. But the strange name might offer a clue: Oleron. Oléron is a small island off Rochefort, on France's Atlantic coastline. It's not especially distinguished, nor known for anything in particular. The same goes for Oleron, anti-hero incarnate: no man is an island, but he tries hard to become one, cutting himself off from all humanity, killing the thing he loves, and falling prey to his demon... It seems likely too that by frenziedly playing out an inner scenario of obsession Oleron is doomed, turned to *nothing*. He has wilfully abdicated his own powers and responsibility to darker forces, and is condemned to loveless sterility, a crazed reduction to his own nihilist anagram – *no role*. Or, what's in a name anyhow? as Onions himself might be inquiring... Every writer experiences some love for his or her creations, even the negative, hate-filled characters, because these imaginings are secreted within themselves, contained and secret: **OLivER ON**ions.

Like the painter he was, and like every real artist, Onions has personalised his artefact, stamped it with his individual style, his signature. The exalted notion of the creative role – the maker of art not only simple artisan but also complex Artist – was very much part of 1890s aestheticism. Jean, herself a child of the Nineties, shared this belief in creativity *per se*: your life might be wrecked, yet you could still be saved. If art was your talent, your life's work, the struggle for creative self-justification became literally a saving grace: through art should be found meaning and redemption. This risky new religion might console by bringing at best true vision and revelation. If however you were unlucky enough to fall from grace, if you proved not good enough, the danger of damnation awaited you – oblivion or limbo, but never immortality. In the end everything might have been in vain, vainglory and waste.

The signs and omens are there though for all to read as they wish. Oleron in *The Beckoning Fair One*, becomes a parody of the committed artist, turning his back on life and love in order to embrace death. The necessarily solitary creative mind, the singular, single individual 'wedded only to the Muse' cannot cope with real life and a real, longsuffering fiancée. The latter gives Oleron the clue to what he has found in the new house which so enticingly invites him: "I think I know what it is... It's been used to wrap up a harp before putting it into its case". The Muse, that fair one with her siren song, playing the imagination's Aeolian harp, is an impossible adversary of course and the contest will not be fair at all... The forbearing fiancée, a down to earth, thirty-four year old journalist, does her best to help and support Oleron, but both are doomed. The harp's wrapper, "an old faded square of reddish frieze" will find its final, fatal use, while Oleron's oddly nonchalant answer (six lines later) to her curious question – "who lives in the rest of the house?" is as follows: "I daresay a tramp sleeps in the cellar occasionally. Nobody else." The Id (as Freudians and ghost-story aficionados alike will suspect) lurks and, if too long hidden, may burst forth in shocking disguise, turning love to hate, inspiration to sheer madness…

The story's brilliance resides not only in surprise; *The Beckoning Fair One* also retains its force after repeated readings, perennial proof that the author doesn't rely on shock alone. The prose is exquisitely detailed, while rapid and compact, demanding and meriting close textual analysis: *The Beckoning Fair One* logically, amply justifies its unusual length. In conclusion, the four sentences of its final paragraph are stoically moving, eloquently stark. Here the cadenced prose touches perfection, sounding a chord of bleak poetry. It's a spine-chilling representation, poised where the mystical and the mundane meet – precursor perhaps of a Hemingway at his all too rare best. But more eerily still it puts me in mind of certain other subtle yet unerringly vivid scenes. To recall them however, means being free in my reader's way to relive, try to apprehend these disturbing moments. They were effected through an obstinately female, persistently controlled artistry, the singular visions Jean Rhys herself later brought to life.

•

Haunted in this context once again, by Jean, her life and works – I recalled the novel in which she appears, where her ex-lover and mentor Ford Madox Ford cast her as a vengeful, destructive Muse. Recent commentary on that weirdly fascinating book *When The Wicked Man* (see Max Saunders's *Ford Madox Ford – A Dual Life*, vol. 2, 1996), bears an uncanny relevance also to *The Beckoning Fair One*. Such relevance indeed, that on finding among my notes one quotation about the Fordian *roman à clef*, I almost mistook this for a specific opinion on Onions's own masterpiece…

A novel such as Ford's, writes his biographer, "indeed produces an apparition – the illusion of a character – by processes of refraction… the experiences of character, reader, author, and earlier characters, readers and authors are all refracted through and reflected in each other, to create a virtuoso impression of the hallucinatory discourse of the not-quite-conscious..." Ford's alter ego, Notterdam, indeed resembles Onions's Oleron. Both are depressive types, sexually vulnerable yet rather repressed literary men laid low; both are duly led into hallucination and frightening violence by the machinations of a spellbinding (if false) Muse, a destructive female principle, real or imagined.

A poetic enchantment, a delirious romantic obsession sets in and overwhelms these poor susceptible men... They aren't tough enough on any level to handle and tame their creative urge, their 'inspiration', so they fear what they cannot control: that way madness lies, with escape their sole thought – a last desperate, drastic exit. Madness and death, or both, are what the frustrated Muse will bring if the soul does not admit and fulfil her – without even the possibility of "the lineaments of gratified desire". When Onions heard by the bedside his wife Berta Ruck combing her long hair, he gleaned the idea, or found inspiration for, the heart of the fable, the central image of *The Beckoning Fair One*. What if you heard that fascinating static, that metrical rhythmic crackle, but it proved an electricity of absent beauty – none being there! *What if?*

So it all starts, the haunting, the possession... Yet the answer to the next inevitable question, *How?* is the crucial one beckoning, beginning to unfold. It is a secret, naturally, kept by every individual artist – a grace of language, an idiom so pure and personal it can only be called 'poetic'. The writer is explorer of experiences at their dangerous extremes; writers live on the edge of the most difficult, inexplicable or 'visionary' aspects of reality. To recapture or recreate these states, they must marry attractive (if sometimes enigmatic) form to elusive (if often shapeless) content. This it seems to me is what Robert Aickman implied when formulating a theory of the ghost story: "The ghost story... can include ingredients from the totality of experience, as can poetry; mainly, once more, experience which is neither fully conscious nor a field for deliberate and prudent selection. Only poetry and the ghost story draw on a world so wide."

When Aickman goes on to praise "the author's disconcerting blend of worldly knowledge with unworldly lyricism" he might have been referring to Jean Rhys, just as much as Oliver Onions. *The Beckoning Fair One*, Aickman thought, "brings great power to the Nintiesish theme of the quest for perfection and the ruin to which the quest so regularly leads", but when gifted imaginative writers like these – Aickman too, go in search of the(ir) imagination and its workings, the results will always be extraordinary. A very appropriate phrase, one adopted from the 17th century French philosopher Nicolas de Malebranche, has come to serve as epithet for the imagination and sometimes also poetry itself. (*Herself*, in French, both words being feminine.) This is *la folle du logis,* meaning literally 'the madwoman of the house / the weird creature within the building'. Which of course is the spiritual link, the very theme connecting both *The Beckoning Fair One* and *Wide Sargasso Sea.*

There like the ghost in an older story now newly inhabiting Jean's last novel – her own timeless book – it's time for the wild Muse to walk abroad, recovering strength and pride. The various, newest names of this madwoman in the attic are Antoinette/Bertha Cosway/Mason, and she is not content to be subjugated or subdued, a weak enslaved creature seeking identity. She walks towards her fierce, transcendent triumph – that deceptive wraith wanting poetic form, who had haunted Jean herself for so many long years. Jean told a 1970s interviewer: "She seemed such a poor ghost, I thought I'd like to write her a life." Jean did, and we are the richer. She wrote herself a life too, affirming always the value of the imagination. After Jean's death one notoriously macho British critic, who during the process of her 'rediscovery' had praised her to the skies, broadcast a superficially strange comment on her. In some ways though, the man was as percipient as flippant, when summing up Jean – "in the Muse business".

Her life had risked just such an impossible pursuit, following the Muse's way, finding a personal voice. (This, Mr Critic, is business more than serious and never *as usual.* It's a vocation, the call of a voice you rarely hear...) The process requires sacrifice, a search for meaningful style, grace under *any* pressure. It might even involve acting as a smaller-scale, lowercase muse, to and for others; even becoming muse-to-oneself, in the sense of reinventing one's Self, always writing and rewriting one's own life. Jean by example slowly but surely let them know. The books continue to speak for her, beyond death. They contain a wealth of surprises. In them, among so much else, she seems to warn lovers, husbands, mentors, peers, Lenglet, Ford and all whom it may concern: "I am my true self, neither *femme fatale* nor object. No longer the object of your writings, attentions or affections. But fully able to be *me,* my own subject, obedient to none in order to fulfill my individual fate." What mattered was to learn and complete her own lonely truth, earning a world of unforgettable ghosts now given new life. To enter that final, perfectly real life of words lived on the page.

Coda to the fair one

If artists are always haunted by the unattainable and grieve for impossibilities – phantoms, abortions, outcast creatures, beings whose breath has been cut short, themes undeveloped, books unwritten – where rests their hope? Each is conscious too of the danger of killing the thing loved, of how destructive the so-called creative urge may be. What kind of 'normality' remains available to those possessed by art who nevertheless cannot realise their particular dream?

No one can survive on or with sterile imaginings, yet how shall we rid ourselves of these? A ghost is paradox personified, the presence of an absence, an awareness of what's beyond us. Dead to our frail logic, some ghosts live on and continue to walk, in daylight not broad enough to contain them, in air not thin enough to constrict them. Gone but not forgotten. Lingering somewhere within reach, they play haunting themes composed only of grace notes: thus perhaps are created illusions of actual sounds.

When should we attend to them, listening for how long? Is it advisable or possible to shut off any of our senses, turn our backs to what may disturb? The elusive music of what happens, the musicality within this and every story, may chance to reside in the mundane: Oleron hears it first through the drip of a tap. Then with the onset of the Mystery is discerned a sensuous rhythm and, since nothing is new under the sun, that "very o-ald tune" once "sung to a harp". Oleron hums it without knowing what it is or what he does. It hardly concerns him to be told that this ancient air is called 'The Beckoning Fair One': he comes to believe in its existence. (The reader, matching music to story-title, may find different implications as to whether such an air 'really' exists.) But for Oleron, "The phrase he had hummed had been that which he had associated with the falling from the tap": its 'originality', ownership and composition are mysteries beyond words, given to him alone. Tragically, he fails the test; words fail him. Denying both lyricism and love, abandoning all former dedication, he burns his book as prelude to oblivion.

The Muse has led Oleron on, only to disappear; her fatally teasing music fades for ever and leaves him with the devastating echo of a scream… This extraordinary fable, so full of original verbal music (poetry, that is) and curious harmonies, might itself have taken on a new form in 1946. Apparently an

American producer, Lester Cowan – married to Ann Ronell, writer of one sublimely, suicidally melancholy jazz classic, *Willow Weep For Me* – wished to film *The Beckoning Fair One*. Oleron, recast as conductor-pianist, would be played by none other than Leonard Bernstein! It might have made a tantalisingly offbeat music-drama but the project remained Hollywooden velleity, not even the ghost of a film.

Come to think of it, such a delicate yet durable masterpiece can't easily be transposed into another medium. First-rate verbal artefacts are only ever approximated on film: this seems a true axiom. Just look at or avoid the deadly, unimaginative adaptations of Jean's books for films and TV. No screen versions so far have approached her elusive, very particular lyricism, let alone told a story with skill and wit. These were demanding creations demanding proper respect. These her phantoms were alive once like Jean, and like her continue to haunt the living.

A forgotten man

Beside the few known details of his life and the clues to be gleaned from
his fictions, John Metcalfe remains a mystery. Apart from his work, the
man cast no shadow.

> – D.A.Callard: *Pretty Good For A Woman –*
> *The Enigmas Of Evelyn Scott*, 1985

Had I heard of Jack Metcalfe? When Jean once asked me, the name rang only
a distant bell. But after she went on to call him "a rather good writer of ghostly
stories", I realised this must be the same elusive John Metcalfe whose work I'd
in fact read here and there. My familiarity with Metcalfe then amounted to a
scattering of memorably odd and elliptical stories ('Mortmain'; 'The Bad
Lands'; 'The Double Admiral' and two or three others) buried in a few old
anthologies. The latter had been edited by certain shrewd anthologists of the
macabre – Hugh Walpole, Dorothy Sayers, Dennis Wheatley – themselves
lesser practitioners whose writings by 1970 or so were decreasingly read.
Metcalfe appeared to have published between 1925 and 1956 five novels, a
couple of novellas and two collections of short stories. None of these books were
in print at the time of my conversation with Jean. (Nor were they at the time
of writing, 1997.)

John Metcalfe had died in 1965 I later learned, in miserable poverty. For
most of his life – he was born the year after Jean, in 1891 – he was the victim
of ill-health (epilepsy and recurrent mental breakdown) compounded by
alcoholism and the pressures of a peripatetic, Bohemian life-style. Readers of
Jean's *Letters 1931-1966* know that most of the correspondence up to 1936 is
addressed to the American novelist Evelyn Scott (1893-1963), who'd married
Metcalfe in 1930. Fascinating letters they are too, for as the editors point out:
"The Metcalfes were perhaps the most enthusiastic and generous of all Jean's
early admirers and Evelyn was tireless in her attempts to promote Jean's work
in America." Evelyn Scott was an attractive woman and a prolific, if none too
talented and indeed neurotic writer. Scott, a Southerner, seemed to know
everybody on a variety of American literary scenes. She'd had an affair with
William Carlos Williams, and invited Thomas Wolfe to a New York party she

gave for Jean and Leslie Tilden-Smith on their return from Dominica in 1936. The latter gathering occasioned a spectacular Rhysian scene, chronicled in both the biographies of both women, after which friendships ended, correspondence fizzled out.

D. A. Callard, Scott's biographer, quotes a memorable retort of Jean's: "It was Jack, who is a writer, who told me that my hatred for England was thwarted love. I said disappointed love maybe." He then points out: "Outside the correspondence, this reference to Jack Metcalfe is the only allusion in Jean's published or unpublished writing to this friendship." But she could still remember him with evident respect and affection years after his death. Metcalfe was in some ways so very English, the old-style gentlemanly type Jean liked. This Norfolk-born but much-travelled writer had a naval and RAF background. He'd taught both at public school and for a year in Paris. He'd even captained a barge that had been run down and sunk on the East River. Yet he was insecure and introverted, the clubbable type only on the surface.

As Angier suggests: "Jack Metcalfe's style was more like Jean's. He wrote tight, macabre tales of psychic horror, and novels of failure in love, set in grey English towns. He was given to drink and ill-health, extremely reticent, withdrawn and lonely." The poet and most rigorous of critics Geoffrey Grigson, who admired Jean's work, seems to have liked Evelyn Scott ("a darling") rather more than her husband. "Metcalfe was vaguely sinister", Grigson recalled in 1981, while acknowledging that "his book of short stories *The Smoking Leg*" was "perhaps unfairly forgotten". Metcalfe has also drawn praise for his tales of "lonely misfits out of step with their times" from other distinctive specialists in the macabre, including Thomas Burke, Robert Aickman, H.P.Lovecraft and August Derleth.

The sparse details of this singular author's sad decline are as grim and affecting as anything he himself wrote. Widowed and virtually helpless, he collapsed, was committed to a New York mental hospital and, through friends' efforts, finally discharged and repatriated to England. Alcohol, tranquillizers and a fall down the stairs of a shabby London boarding-house saw him out. It was not long before Metcalfe's books and papers too were disposed of piecemeal. This occurred when his drinking crony and alas, literary executor, John Gawsworth met an even more destitute alcoholic end.

Metcalfe at least does not deserve the oblivion he seems to have courted or found hard to avert. As with Jean – albeit not in terms of such innate talent or eventual achievement – a sometimes unsettled, often painfully squalid life didn't prevent his crafting a body of beautifully stylish work. There are a very few autobiographical paragraphs in a 1942 American authors' directory, followed by some brief comments by the editors (Kunitz & Hayward). Their first sentence might have been describing Jean, a Jean by then sunk in her own alcoholic limbo and mercifully temporary oblivion: "His work is characterized by a rather grim, bizarre, and sinister humour, and is markedly individual and *sui generis.*" The editors go on to warn or further bemuse would-be readers: "He should not be confused with John Metcalfe, an Australian librarian who writes frequently on his special subject, or with John J. Metcalfe, a writer on India and the British Empire."

These days, the distinctive, distinctly un-jolly Jack Metcalfe is confused with none other. Connoisseurs of the macabre appreciate him, but the man who wrote so well of unease is difficult even to collect. Out of print. Two or three short stories only, anthologized here and there, to be discovered if you search hard, but these tend not always to be the best. Out of sight, out of mind, Metcalfe has become one of the literary missing. Almost, but not exactly a ghost...

Which reminds me – in another collector's item, Sir Andrew Caldecott's *Not Exactly Ghosts* (1947) occurs the following exchange:

'Have you by any chance got a book called *The Bad Lands?*' he replied.

'I'm afraid not: but I remember reading a short story under that name: by John Metcalfe, I think.'

Frent seemed quite excited.

'Was it about a fellow being in two places at the same time, and doing something criminal in one of them while he thought he was doing something good in the other?'

'I don't think', I protested, 'that the author would appreciate such a crude summary! The tale was extraordinarily well and carefully written.'

It was indeed. The author wrote there of what he knew, a Norfolk and Suffolk background, depression and disquiet. And the tone of voice of this deeply troubled writer does not date: it's a 1920s story, but both bleak and oblique, suggesting so much and so imaginatively. By indirection find direction out...

Wandering timeless in broad daylight, in that all too level landscape of agoraphobia, facing the fear of one's own fears... H.P. Lovecraft – who wrote his own version of 'Dunwich' very much via those blank, eroded flat lands which might just as well be bad ones – allowed Metcalfe his "rare pitch of potency, the tale entitled 'The Bad Lands' containing graduations of horror that strongly savour of genius."

How sad then that the fine writers are forgotten, while coarser visions prevail. Not even nightmares nor exactly ghosts – but the crudest, most predictable grand guignol rules. It's odd too that while both M.R. and Henry James are admired and still read, Metcalfe, who had learned from both masters in finding his own originality, has momentarily disappeared. "My craft foundered", wrote Metcalfe, but he did manage to escape from the freezing East River in January, and I am sure Jean's old friend – the "rather good writer of ghostly stories" she rightly commended to me – will resurface once again. He didn't really receive his due. Is due for revival, is charming, diffident, sinister Jack Metcalfe.

JR and TR, youth and age

When all that story's finished, what's the news?
In luck or out the toil has left its mark...
            – W.B.Yeats: *The Choice, 1933*

In 1970 Jean was interviewed for the remarkable (and remarkably long-lived – it ran from the Fifties through to the late Seventies) international literary magazine, *Transatlantic Review*. The result was a brief but rather relaxed and revealing little piece.

The interviewer finds the eighty year old Jean "still beautiful", also "very frail" and "possibly a little sad". He correctly observes, vis-à-vis Jean, that publishers always seem to need prodding before they look for "books to reclaim from obscurity". He mentions Jean's "very modern collection" of books noting among others on her shelves my own books. Gratifyingly, these are set beside *Nightwood*, that ageless, superb novel – or extended prose-poem – by another former Parisian beauty and ancient experimentalist. Its author, the undaunted seventy-eight year old Djuna Barnes, is living obscurely in New York. Barnes, something of a recluse, has experienced neither the benefits nor the drawbacks of 'rediscovery' and alas, never really will. Jean herself is wary of her own fame since 1966 and *Wide Sargasso Sea*. But if it is her fate now to receive a constant stream of visitors, it's better than being forgotten or growing lonely. So, graciously, she gives up her time.

Increasingly in her latter years the result is that the far-flung visitors take up too much of it. They tire her and, she comes to feel, exploit her. Her writing time and energies are limited. She becomes resentful and suspicious, yet she's too weak to send them packing! (I've heard her complain about intrusions: every genuine writer young or old is hypersensitive about hoarding their time allocated to work...) But the young man is attentive and knowledgeable and Jean likes young men. Always self-conscious about her voice, she gets him to put away the tape-recorder and thereafter all goes well.

The interviewer is duly charmed and comments that Jean "has something about her which positively makes one fall in love with her on sight". They discuss her admiration for Hemingway and Colette (neither of whom she'd known in that distant Twenties Paris, except by sight), and of how and when she started to write. She began writing she says, at the age of about thirteen, and with poetry, which she showed nobody…

After I'd seen the magazine interview I told Jean that by a nice coincidence my first fiction published on leaving Cambridge in 1962 had appeared in *Transatlantic Review*. (Come to think of it, she herself had been educated at Cambridge, at the famous Perse School, 1907-9.) Also, of course, there had been an earlier, more celebrated, if lower-case, incarnation of *TR*. This was during the 1920s, when Jean's first work was published in the *transatlantic review*, then edited by… none other than Ford Madox Ford.

So it's possible that she agreed to the interview with, or prompted by, a certain sense of nostalgia. Jean was anyhow just as kindly as Ford her mentor had been towards *les jeunes*. She told the young fellow from the magazine (as she'd also admitted to me) that she was "always very shy". She was indeed extremely sensitive, and only alcohol helped make her more 'outgoing'. The problem was, while lessening the shyness and rendering her for a while spryer and, as she felt, more sociable, drink would also deepen her depressions and make her aggressive and somewhat maudlin. Generally however, I remember her in very good and yet mischievous humour. A mood which her own generation once called 'gay' before a later age annexed and changed the meaning of the word. And I now recall the further mischievous tale she told me, smiling. This young fellow, nervous as herself, had worn an extravagant shirt and hat, the latter putting her in mind of a cavalier. She thought him quite sweet, if a bit affected and very probably… She knew the word's newer significance and sought to avoid it. More suitably, considering her background in the chorus of musical comedies, she giggled slightly, fluttered her eyelashes, and finally opted for "rather camp".

Jean herself had an old-world courtesy which she invariably extended to others whether they merited it or not. Straight or gay, young or old, people warmed to her singular charm. I still remember how delighted Jean was to meet Diane's thirteen year old daughter, how delightful the old lady's mood that afternoon. And that young girl's bright excitement. Jean's charm was of a quality touchingly rare, like her talent. A sweet gift you would never forget.

High horses and low blows

Que ton absence soit une nouvelle figure
de ton être à jamais senti;
ton ineffable départ, sûre amie, inaugure
tout un art de survie...

— Rilke: *Fragments*, written in French

Jean never played the *grande dame*. She was quite often querulous – and from time to time had cause – yet she was disinclined to be either lofty or petty about others. You sensed, as she must have, that life was too short for all that posturing nonsense. Besides, those whose health and finances have been, to put it mildly, uncertain, do not bother to indulge in such empty snap(ped) judgements.

Contrary to any current, revisionist views of her, she was no feminist icon. That typecasting she would have resisted as unwarranted and unwanted, insulting flattery with an insinuated whisper of limitation.

To be sure she liked women generally and, in her latter days at least, liked beauty in other women too. But feminism of the distorted and aggressive contemporary variety appalled her, especially when deployed simplistically to denigrate men. Again: whatever was its point? Life was too short, and that applied even to a life as long as hers. Sisterhood remains as much of an illusion as the so-called brotherhood of man – one is out there in the harsh world on one's own. And the true writer works alone, in inevitable isolation, fearless, genderless, asking for no favours or preferential treatment. That was understood, that much I understood from her. Luck was what was required thereafter and luck she invariably wished me on parting.

Quality was Jean's sole aim, and that is always unique and does not seek or need solidarity. It is doubtful whether the plaudits of any narrow claque – in this instance, a vulvarchy or vaginocracy – could set even a belatedly correct value on such quality. Proper, informed appreciation she herself valued. Jean was priceless though – a gem and a laugh. She herself would have laughed off some of these earnest journalists' jargon-riddled misinterpretations of her own admirably clear prose.

You cannot write well without integrity and a measure of spiritual independence. This was recognised by Jean's equally attractive and admirable contemporary, Mina Loy (1882-1966). Ford Madox Ford, editing *transatlantic review* in 1929, published a letter in which this poet and artist alliteratively and authoritatively criticises "our public inured to the unnecessary nuisances of journalism..."

Loy duly became a recluse herself and published little yet she's an important modernist whose stock, inevitably, is still rising. (Whether or not she in turn will be adopted as a posthumous feminist legend remains to be seen.) Jean didn't have Loy's self-evident toughness and she found it hard to turn away interviewers for example, especially if they were women and persistent. Her own manners were impeccable: I never knew her to be rude or even brusque. It may be that I only saw Jean when she was relaxed, sober and friendly, but that was always fine with me. We enjoyed each other's company – and besides, who is not partial towards one's friends? Thus I had nothing to criticise her for, nothing I wanted from her, and she knew it. I could learn things of course, but quite incidentally and on my part without calculation. I wasn't about to unearth painful episodes from her past nor did I see her as an anachronism suddenly fashionable, some unlikely and lurid survival who therefore merited media attention.

Jean deserved her late acclaim but soon came to realise that with the revived interest in her work, intrusions and interviews and criticism in every sense unsettling would result. Various more hurtful or *ad feminam* comments – misguided or sensationalised perceptions originating from those she regarded as helpers and friends – would have enraged or depressed her had she lived to read them. She might even have been amused, on a good day. However, despite the likes of Messrs. Melly and Plante, she cannot be partially caricatured, and hence patronised, as grand old trouper, camp relic of days beyond recall, literary fag-hag. She was at least spared that overripeness-is-all stuff. But it's sticks and stones now, anyway.

Making up

The charm of rouge on fragile cheeks,
Pearl-powder, and, about the eyes,
The dark and lustrous eastern dyes...
    – Arthur Symons: *Maquillage*, 1892

Jean in her latter years attracted a variety of devotees of camp and fashionable nostalgia, or retro-chic – or whatever the latest term the media next coin to express their sentimentalised promotions of times past.

Jean was seen as a legendary survivor of that 'Lost Generation' she'd never been any part of. But the misplaced zeal and literary-historical revisionism of certain wellmeaning if ill-informed journalists irritated far more than flattered. It was curious how this elderly woman's unsettling personality and work could retain – for a motley crew of cranks, wouldbe littérateurs of both sexes, and homosexuals (ditto) – its mysterious and magnetic allure. The Rhys spell seemed to work even at some distance.

For example the wealthy, incestuous American, Barbara Baekeland – stabbed to death by her own gay, drug-addicted son in London in 1972 – had towards the end, "a look of old furs and feathers – like a Jean Rhys character", as one friend of hers recalled. Baekeland herself wrote to a lover in 1970: "Read Jean Rhys's *Good Morning, Midnight*, which profoundly depressed me. She is so much of my skin that I am alarmed – like suddenly seeing oneself in a harsh unlovely light – all those many flaws and her despair honed by that extraordinary sensibility – I hope I am saved – " But it's ironic that the idle rich, snobbish yet louche Yankee socialites included, could ever identify with Jean Rhys's financially embarrassed outsiders. The Rhys woman, perpetually embattled, without visible means of support, staggers along life's tricky tightrope; her very honesty is an additional burden threatening to unbalance any of that precious grace and beauty, however much admired.

Always with Jean's protagonists – not heroines: they are unheroic, hoping somehow to do their best simply by enduring the worst – a necessary tension is maintained between narcissism and detachment, self-pity and ruthless scrutiny. Her books fascinate because of her own fascination with surfaces, and with what lies behind or beneath: she was unsparing, obsessed with those discrepancies between image and word, the glamorous look and the plainer reality.

Jean's last words as reported may have been apocryphal, but as a final statement they were most dramatically apt: "Please, my eye-shadow". Face to face with the unknown you are politely anxious, stoical yet self-aware; you are conscious or you kid yourself that you are not ultimately alone, that someone is there to provide what you need... You may be facing the great void, but your life's last reflex sums you up. It reflects the need to look your best, be it for St Peter or some jealous Medusa of nothingness. Right until the end, you lived up to that motto of yours you so often wryly quoted, *Dum Spiro Spero.* Stylish and brave, to the last breath, bonny Jean.

•

Some years after her death one critic, Peter Kemp, wrote a very shrewd short analysis of Jean's obsession with facial appearances. Entitled 'Deep Beneath The Cosmetics', his article was primarily and ironically a book review. Kemp's reviewing target, hit with wit and despatch, was the transatlantic epitome of such a 'critical study' of her novels as Jean herself might have sadly predicted and shuddered at. This laboured effort from an American female academic who duly travels (and travails) "through shadowy mazes of Freudian symbols and into the Jungian world of mythic archetype", was brought forth by a grim outfit calling itself 'Eden Press Women's Publications'. A highly serious work indeed, and one which therefore displays in grindingly ungrammatical language the dottiest of pretensions: it may some day be rediscovered by connoisseurs of unintentional humour and of the absurd. Rarely though, do we learn much from these overblown 'in-depth' critiques, whereas an intelligent reviewer like Kemp, focussed by deadline and word-count, makes various perceptive observations, full of insight into Rhys's women.

One such is praised in her first novel, *Quartet* (1929), for her "astonishingly accurate make-up", while a Montparnasse homosexual too is "beautifully made up". Here, as Kemp notes, artful aids to beauty are by no means simply decorative. As for Marya, the focus of the book, caught up in an awkward *ménage* (based on Jean's own relationship with Ford Madox Ford and Stella

Bowen), she feels desperately unsure of herself: is she some spiritually lame duck, fair game to be exploited for her physical beauty? How shall Marya deal with her new circumstances and what words (and kisses) must her mouth frame? Hence her lips at one point are "hastily and inadequately rouged", while a deceptively brief alliance with Lois Heidler, her lover's wife, takes the form of a 'girls together' make-up session. Vanity and self-esteem, survival and disguises, make-up envisaged as a form of protective mask...

Certainly references abound throughout her work, especially the prewar novels and stories, to face-painting, coloration, enhancing of appearance. It's as if the detailed criticism of outward style were the corollary of a more general inner dissatisfaction or distress. When does one in any case show one's true colours? *Who Are You?* And just what is *My Face For The World To See?*

Those italicized phrases seem to sum up her own and indeed every novelist's dilemma. They were the evocative book titles used by a pair of fine, almost forgotten writers, Anna Kavan and Alfred Hayes. I remember talking to Jean enthusiastically about them both.

The former – Helen Woods aka Helen Ferguson aka Helen Edmonds, who finally and triumphantly metamorphosed into 'Anna Kavan' (1901-1968) – was that rather rare paradox, an elegant, comparatively longlived and compulsively creative drug addict. Jean knew and liked Kavan's stories. In 1964, writing to author Francis Wyndham (who twenty years later would edit her own *Letters 1931-1966*) Jean comments: "I have her novel *Who Are You?* Very short but what a splendid title. If only I'd thought of it". Jean adds regretfully, since *Wide Sargasso Sea* on which she had toiled for so long was then still unfinished and untitled: "but it would have been too late in any case".

The two women never met, but each in her particular and isolated mode admired the other's writing. They had much in common: a ruthlessly detached, disabused vision of mankind; drug dependence, and literary reputations like admirers, that waxed and waned with curious and bewildering frequency. In their general demeanour both were women of singular charm and immaculate appearance, whose life-styles in their latter days could combine a feeling for traditional courtesies with outbursts of eccentric or 'disreputable' behaviour. By a nice coincidence, both authors were 'profiled' more or less side by side between the pages of a smart monthly magazine in autumn, 1967. Without conscious irony links were made as I recall, between the strange, perplexing survival of that endangered species – the elderly female writer – and the subsequent, impressively hardwon storehouse of Sibylline wisdom it was assumed each such survivor thus acquired. Mere perseverance alone merited some sort of revival. And of course, our glossy magazine was duly 'reviving' these anomalous, demonic angels, giving them space and image – the legends-in-their-own-lifetime, the icon-painting clichés. Such an accolade made them no longer dangerous nor inspirational but cosy rather and, for a while, fashion-worthy.

As for Alfred Hayes, he like Kavan and like Jean herself had gone through many changes of country and literary style before developing the very pared-down, 'poetic' (i.e. crystalline rather than purple) prose for which discerning readers will surely continue to cherish him. Hayes (1911-1985) was born in London but raised and schooled in New York where he later worked on newspapers and radio. He wrote leftish poems for the likes of *New Masses* and other magazines and, as Malcolm Cowley noted, established a modest literary reputation during the Thirties. He then served with the US forces in Italy during the war, afterwards working with Roberto Rossellini on *Paisa*. On his return to the USA, Hayes published his first novel, and was employed by Warner Brothers in Hollywood. Apart from his novels, Hayes was the author of various collections of poetry and short stories. He wrote also for cinema, TV, and the theatre – including a Broadway adaptation and a musical.

He was clearly a versatile and skilful professional, that much must be conceded. By 1997 however his books were out of print: eight or nine of them are on my shelves but there are other titles I've never managed to find. Hayes in any case doesn't deserve to be forgotten. During his writing life he was for the most part both commercially and critically successful – which often means work will be consigned to a period of oblivion after its author's death. This process of forgetting and being forgotten is just as often a temporary cycle, or perhaps an inevitable negative reaction. An echo of silence and absence, it may well be followed by rescue and reassessment. Hayes at this time of writing is certainly ripe for rediscovery.

Hemingway's opinion must initially have helped. For it was Hemingway himself (the goodlooking fellow Jean had seen in Parisian bars and cafés in the Twenties although, she told me a little wistfully, they'd never actually met) who had found "first rate" the début novel by Hayes, *All Thy Conquests* (1945). This story of soldiers and civilians during World War Two in Italy was poignant and perceptive, and merited Papa's pat on the head. Hayes's second novel, *The Girl On The Via Flaminia* (1949) also drew praise – from John Hersey, among other writers and critics. Indeed, though its background was similar, the book itself was even better. A third novel was published by the end of the Forties, but always Alfred Hayes – "whose feeling for people" Malcolm Cowley had earlier recognized to be indeed "his own" – would continue to refine and discipline his style.

This meant – it had also been Jean's and every other young writer's problem in the Twenties and Thirties – escaping the seductive literary grip exerted by Hemingway. And what a great style-pincher and hand-biter Hemingway himself proved, as Sherwood Anderson and Gertrude Stein had finally discovered! Yet the clammily earnest clasp of Clan Hemingway still endures... Such posthumous machismo is still drunk up eagerly by the average, jovial literary jock. It can be hard to shake off even decades later, even among that bullyboy's paler-faced academic aficionados. A professor at North Carolina State University, Michael Reynolds, in his *Hemingway: The Paris Years* (1989), gives us this illuminating critical gem, which seems to catch the required adolescent tone: "Having spent a good bit of time coaching young Jean Rhys in the finer points of creative writing, [Ford Madox] Ford apparently was equally successful in coaxing her out of her underwear".

The grace, style and insight all too many critics lack, both Rhys and Hayes abundantly had. I heard from Jean at the start of 1970 that "the Hayes novel arrived safely & I was grateful for it & liked it". The book I'd sent her was one of my particular favourites. I'd guessed it would appeal to her as an unsparing, unsentimental, very bleak and very concise love story, told with an elliptical elegance that contains and distills its passion. Again, the title of this 1953 novel was simply and inevitably apt – *In Love.* There would be years in between each clearsighted and unadorned Hayes novel, but each usually proved worth the wait. Writers and readers alike seemed to agree on that. And his work appealed to both men and women – as if they recognized that its sharp truths, its focus on feelings and intimate relationships seldom blurred towards sentimentality. Hence the Hayes-praise from so many estimable British literary figures of the Fifties and Sixties: Antonia White, Stevie Smith and Penelope Mortimer, Elizabeth Bowen, J. Maclaren-Ross, John Lehmann, Peter Quennell, Walter Allen, Angus Wilson and, once again showing his customary discernment and generosity, from Jean's own 'rediscoverer' and staunch friend, Francis Wyndham.

Hayes at his very best reminds me – I'm never quite sure whether it's the perceptions given and the chances taken, or an occasional similarity of tone or some poetically-charged stylistic compression – of a male counterpart of Jean Rhys herself. Like Jean he was aware of those Faustian pacts and lures, the baits of glamour and success that never do actually assuage the writer's perceived and experienced isolation. In fact, in one poignant poem 'The Imitation Of Faust', Hayes sees himself and every artist as ultimately "uncertain of the world where I belong." In the end it is the tension behind that shared hunt for certainties which helps forge a writer's style: we're all made or broken by it. Most of us just get by, trying to cope with the struggle, while hoping somehow to establish enough credit for the day of reckoning… But I no longer recall giving her to read what in my view was the last really successful novel Hayes published, *The End Of Me* (1968). This sharp narrative in its bitter brevity reads simultaneously like an anatomy of and an elegy for the Sixties. It's both love story turned sour and aching analysis of the generation gap, and my guess is Jean must have relished that book too.

Certainly, come 1973 and *The Stockbroker, The Bitter Young Man, And The Beautiful Girl*, Hayes had somewhat lost his edge, as one might infer from the resoundingly Saroyan-ish title. Although one reviewer considered "the extravaganza is highly stylish and brutally funny", 'extravaganza' is the giveaway: how could such a word apply to that hitherto scrupulously precise and understated author, Alfred Hayes? It was sad, but every writer who gets past sixty must dread that dubious milestone with its attendant twinge of decline. You can't and don't 'retire', you go on writing, because that's what you know and it's taken so long to learn this little or this much… And yet you dread drying up, just as the alcoholic will dread drying out… Jean managed it, she didn't do either, but went on drinking and writing into extreme old age. I admire that feline endurance against the odds – and almost wrote 'against the gods', which might have made a nicely Promethean typo. Towards the end then, in stylistic terms, Jean soldiered on stoically if not heroically, while Hayes grew tired sooner and seems to have capitulated, resorting to artifice and winsome vanities. In their later prose it shows.

•

Yes, Jean herself at times seemed vain; even as octogenarian she was sensitive to any kind of attention – be it mere politeness, routine gallantry or fulsome homage. I remember when I happened to admire a particularly fine photograph of her, circa 1915. I must have murmured some or other appreciation: it was not mere flattery from me. The lighting was right, the pose was right. And she had been extraordinarily beautiful. And knew it still, seeing no reason not to flirt a little with someone then in his thirties... I remember her ancient smile, and how she fluttered the false eyelashes that used to give her so much trouble to fix. (More of them, later.) And yet she could write to me in 1970: "I'm longing to see the photographs. I've just seen a perfectly hideous one (of myself) and it made my 'flu *much* worse – I'm just not photogenic I'm afraid." Jean was, however, not coy nor a narcissist. Vanity when she showed it or permitted it to show was like a little treat she occasionally allowed herself, a minor self-indulgence to help her keep going.

That was harmless and understandable enough. She'd earned the right to it, although quite often it could lead to doleful mockery at her own expense. On a deeper level of self-awareness she was properly unsparing – honest, humorous and objective. She was indeed obsessed as all good writers surely must be with the discrepancy between external or 'simple' *appearance* and its more complex, usually unglamorous, frequently harsh, substratum of *reality*. Here Jean might have also have found herself in agreement with a very different writer, another from whom much may be learned. This was the rivetingly bleak and alcoholic American crime writer Jim Thompson. Thompson – as heterosexual as he was misogynist – became too a somewhat black humourist, turning himself into an expert craftsman. Though experimenting ceaselessly with the novel form, he would always maintain "there is only one plot – things are not as they seem".

In any case nothing is ever simple – not situations and especially not style. Style only seems so: it's been worked on of course, until the desired effect is produced. Now you seem to see it, where really you don't. Or shouldn't... Making up a story has much in common with making up a face. It's an act of recreation and creation, both. The plainer, most fascinating truth is there and always is, behind and beneath the mask of semblance if you look harder, deeper. No plastic surgeon, no sophisticated or simplistic critic can change that... But the version of the self presented to the world – that face for the world to see – must, if it cannot be beautiful, at least be brave.

My first view of Jean I shall never forget. I never dreamed of telling her about it, and am glad I never did. She would have been mortified with embarrassment to know of that 1969 impression. Sighting is perhaps a better word, under the circumstances... Jean and I had corresponded over some months, but I can't recall if by then we'd actually fixed on a particular time for me to visit – indeed, for us finally if initially to meet. It was an overcast, clouded afternoon, though (for once!) dry. Diane, my loving companion of the time, sat beside me as I drove our aged and rusting Mini slowly, very carefully down the narrow country lane, looking for any sign of 'Landboat Bungalows'. Or, failing that, for some villager we could ask.

Then we suddenly, simultaneously caught sight of an old woman, frail and hunched, wearing a headscarf and a long beige overcoat which may have been a mackintosh. She was moving with utmost slowness or perhaps deliberation away from us and up the slight slope towards what we later found was the main street, such as it is, of Cheriton Fitzpaine. She had the rickety gait of some pantomime crone, half-hobbling, half-reeling, but all caught in an extreme and dreadful slow-motion. One hand held a carrier bag bulging with empty bottles, the other gripped a walking-stick deployed it seemed with greater exasperation than effect.

Diane and I were both struck by the same wretched thought. No – we ourselves felt veritably stricken. Neither of us needed to say a word, as I restarted the car. I had at once stopped, appalled, in order to let this hopelessly vulnerable, painfully caricatural figure go doddering up the lane and out of sight... We held our breath a while, relieved she had not looked back and noticed us. In our minds, however, continued to seep the one abiding, absolute and awful conclusion: this was none other than my heroine, our cynosure, Jean Rhys.

Still in silence and after a considerable pause, I turned the car round, turned back for home, turned tail. And am I now a turncoat for telling this tale? I don't feel so. I think my concern and friendship for Jean was not diminished. Having caught her off guard in the first place, Diane and I thereafter became more protective towards her, ever more scrupulous about making arrangements to see her. Jean's remaining time allotted – as with human beings in general, not just the exceptionally creative – needed to be respected. It had mysterious yet necessary value, however lonely or sociable she herself might maintain she was. Her privacy was not to be casually invaded; nor, we determined, would we tire her or overstay our welcomes.

Many years later, as I write here and invoke the guidance of that friendly shade, I notice among my papers a postcard from Diane, dated 1993. "Guess JR always knew you would write about her one day, and that she trusted you." Well, we never did try to push or steer Jean around nor make demands of her, as too many others did in her latter days. Her strength and resilience were remarkable yet by no means unfailing: so with her we'd always be cheerful and look out for every situation's bright side, trusting to that luck Jean herself invariably invoked...

•

Lucky indeed for Jean when on another, later occasion, in London this time, Diane accompanied me. It was in the mid-1970s and Jean, on one of her periodic escapes from Devon, had decided to stay for a while at Blake's Hotel. She'd invited us round to her room for a quiet drink. Some press interview was arranged for earlier that afternoon but Jean said she would be delighted to see us afterwards. There was plenty of time for her to recover and rest she assured us, adding that she felt well and was looking forward to our visit.

In the event we found her lying exhausted on her bed, crying tears of annoyance and frustration. What she'd thought was to be a properly conducted or at least intelligent interview with a sympathetic woman journalist turned into a prolonged, grotesque parody of a fashion-shoot. The reporter, photographer, stylist, dresser and a couple of others had all crowded into Jean's modest room. They'd taken over. Jean couldn't back out by then and wasn't strong enough to send the motley crew packing. She knew too that her own vanity had caused her to make an embarrassing mistake. Flattered, coerced and conned, she'd next been tricked out in unsuitable finery – courtesy of the newspaper in question! – and so caught by the camera. She clearly feared the end-product of such exposure, of being held up to possible ridicule. The misrepresentation that might result... The mindless, helpless, bewildered postures they'd made her adopt, which might in turn suggest some geriatric doll...

She should have foreseen what lay ahead, she muttered, and she blamed herself. The worst problem for the moment, and to her utter mortification, was "the damn eyelashes, I just can't get 'em off". A preliminary drink or two hadn't helped either, but no one could blame her for that after or during her ordeal with the hacks... On to this octogenarian's eyelids long false lashes had been affixed and no one had bothered to help her, finally, remove them. Her painfully misshapen, arthritic fingers proved no match for the minuscule tenacity of these foolish 'accessories' dictated by fashion. She'd peered – "oh, for ages" – into the small mirror, and tried with no success to tug away the offending obstacles stuck fast above and below each smarting, tear-filled eye. Accordingly, she had now reached a state of apologetic panic and maudlin desperation.

Jean was in luck because Diane was with me that evening and Jean trusted her. "Just as well I'd had experience as a model", Diane wrote to me years later and recalled that, in order to prise off the eyelashes, "the only way was to start picking off with finger nail on the inner edge. As you pulled it off by peeling slowly away, you had to press firmly with other hand on skin of eyelid, to ease the pain from the glue. I really don't think Jean could have done it herself." And Diane quoted the 1990 autobiography of another Jean, who adorned the fashion world during the Sixties and Seventies – Shrimpton: "... make-up was the model girl's own problem. It was the era of false eyelashes. We bought them in long strips, cut off a length and stuck the strip above our own lashes. If you were not careful there was a nasty, gummy line of white glue showing on the eyelid, which was torture to get off... Some models had eyelashes stuck on one by one at beauty salons with something that acted like super-glue."

At any rate, all I now remember of that strange occasion resides in a single image whose main components are henceforth inevitably juxtaposed. Everything falls into place, as once again I watch the willowy figure of my young blonde love lean across the frail, hunched shoulders of our old, our most elderly, friend – Jean. Diane is firmly and tenderly unpeeling the blackness, to help unseal those ancient eyes which had seen so much but flinched from nothing that might still remain for them to observe.

Years on, the shutter of memory clicks again, or the mind's eye reassembles its vision; there are various further pictures to rearrange. I find copies of letters I have mislaid... In one, Diane writes: "I know you have said, on reading what others have said since, that that was not the Jean you knew. You never saw her like that. Could it be that that incident in the hotel with the eyelashes was a kind of turning point? She gave up resisting those who were putting pressure on her, even though her instincts told her otherwise. Although the Mellys were undeniably kind to her it may be that what could have been interpreted as selfish and ungrateful behaviour from Jean was perhaps an anger against her situation, against herself for being too old, against dying... but obviously her relationship with you did not contain that anger. She knew you before it really took off. You never put pressure on her then, and didn't after, and she knew that. Looking back I think you did well with Jean, were the right chemistry". Now I'm reading what I wrote to Jean, even longer ago: "The enclosed is from Diane. She was looking for lipsticks recently in London & thought you might like this one". She replies "Please thank Diane for the lipstick – just my colour".

And there we were, the way we were, the way most are – concerned, if not to be or act our age, then to ignore it or conspire together against the ravages of time. Life may be brighter, bolder, more gallant, if we value and celebrate our friends and never relinquish the search. The search itself (for that eidolon) is difficult if not impossible, since beauty in that sense – in the classical term – is an insubstantial, ghostly image. A mere idea of something, yet it erases cliché and takes on so many concealed or unexpected forms. But the consolation is, it exists, and may be created, enhanced, increased – or simply found, if you learn how and where to look. As Donne, for one, did. He discovered he was describing "The Idea of a Womanne, and not as Shee was".

•

Colour was what was important: a vital force in the fight against greyness. And the greyness could be everywhere, worst of all within. The displaced Petronella lonely in North London, "hated those streets, which were like a grey nightmare in the sun". There, even the rare and longed-for sun offered no easy solace, no proper warmth: it might contribute to a fleeting, surface sensation of wellbeing, but that too would be deceptive. Even between victims, among women themselves, there existed precious little sense of solidarity or common humanity. "You saw so many old women, or women who seemed old, peering at the vegetables in the Camden Town market, looking at you with hatred, or blankly, as though they had forgotten your language, and talked another one". In Petronella's next rueful thoughts I hear Jean herself, so exactly that the words make me smile: "I hope I never live to be old. Anyway, however old I get I'll never let my hair go grey. I'll dye it black, red, any colour you like, but I'll never let it go grey. I hate grey too much".

In her Paris days, Jean told Diane and me, she had been a blonde; in Vienna she became a redhead. In her old age, she wore a variety of wigs. Looking good was of course important, in that (and if) it made you feel good... But you aren't usually pushed, like her character Petronella, as far as thinking of suicide; get to that stage, know the worst, and things look up. There *is* a brighter side: "After that I put a better face on things".

But when she was not fully involved in writing, not populating her own unique world, Jean just like most writers did not care to be alone too much. Unfortunately for her, physical circumstances – age, shaky health, alcohol, geographical distance – all combined to accentuate her isolation. She had to face up to that, as to her mirror. The paradox was that Jean felt she needed the buzz of cities, those restlessly active, often hostile, hives of energy; until very late in her long life, however, and even through sourly alienating experiences of exhaustion or disappointment, she would manage to bring back some form of narrative honey.

It was, though (as Peter Kemp has recognized) the "polarities", "the interplay of opposing types" that Jean sought in cities, sited often in those "blurred impressionistic streetscapes Rhys so potently evokes". In her books, "the well-heeled are set against the penniless; the cosmopolitan clashes with the suburban; the chilly greyness of European cities is intercut with technicolor memories of the West Indies and their hot luxuriance". It wasn't simply a matter of flight from a small backwater in the west country, where it's all too easy to float on a slow, cosy current of acceptable deprivation, sensing oneself – in cultural terms at least – both retired and retarded. Nor was it that she couldn't help herself. In fact, Jean knew what she still needed: occasional change and stimulus, and hence variations on and supplements to her accumulated store of memories. So Jean continued to yearn for company and city delights.

"I've just got back after a long visit to London," she writes in spring 1971. "I did enjoy it so much & it was such fun. Escapist of course – but why not?" Immediately she realises what her life will continue to be like. And goes on:

> Do come & see me soon & bring Diane. It would be a charitable act for I'm finding it difficult to settle down in C. Fitz though it has many good points I know. If anyone had told me I'd be homesick for <u>London</u> I'd have laughed. But I am! So mind you come & if you know of a restaurant in or near Exeter couldn't we meet there & won't you have lunch with me?

I don't remember why we settled for a hotel none of us had ever been to. Maybe it was simply that the location was central and the hotel itself, while old-established, looked neither too grand nor too antiquated. It had at that time a hint of faded elegance: Diane and I might have been swayed by the Gallic name with its faint suggestion too of cosmetics. Anyhow, we had the capacious diningroom to ourselves – yet sweltered all too stoically against a boiling wall-radiator. Even Jean, who so loved warmth, shed her appropriate red hat and matching coat before the furnace-like heat finally forced us to change tables. Alas, almost all else I can recall of that occasion at the Rougemont is that the lunch was indifferent. And that the talk at one point touched upon lipstick and perfume, those two singular women reaching enthusiastic agreement on their favourite scent – Guerlain's peerless and ever sophisticated L'Heure Bleue…

In December 1996, aged 91, Jean-Pierre Guerlain died, and an obituarist noted how, among the products of this famous family business (founded by Jean-Pierre's chemist grandfather in 1828), scientific rigour provided the essential complement to a rare sense of glamour. With L'Heure Bleue, first produced in 1912, had thus been born a delicate strength, a most feminine subtlety, and it was pleasing that such qualities could cohere and endure so long. There had also been some intriguing literary connections: the house had created specially for Balzac his own cologne, while Vol de Nuit had been dedicated to Saint-Exupéry… Only a month or so before Guerlain's death, I'd visited Barcelona and chanced upon the extraordinary Museum of Perfume on Passeig de Gràcia. On display are fragile survivals, the perfect artefacts from another era. Bright-coloured, haunting souvenirs of sentiment, in scintillant flasks and bottles mostly empty now, their elaborate, exquisitely-crafted glass once held all these magical and fragrant substances!

To dream and invent what gives perennial pleasure. To work with an alchemical flair, combining patience, continual insight, and utter refinement. To arrive finally at the mysterious heart of the matter, achieving that unique blend – true artistry and hard sagacity. To present to the world a memorable creation, ripe enchantment.

Guerlain did it his style, Jean in hers. I thought of her then in Barcelona (a city she'd like, these days) as I think of her in Exeter. And for an instant that scent of the past pervades the present... L'Heure Bleue, how it lifts the heart and lightens the mood! Dusk, it suggests to us perhaps – that sentimental time of early evening, crepuscular hour of promise, romantic lull or interlude, an interim moment of flirtation. Just the time for intimate drinks in some sidewalk café, making the most of any evanescent glow. Our twilit hour that seems to soften and anoint everything as it passes, on its own way to becoming inevitable dark.

Jean and the journalists

Today I understand that taking someone's portrait can be interpreted as a sort of theft. That fine writer, Jean Rhys, was reluctant to be photographed when I visited her home near Exeter, and I respected her wishes – to my lasting regret.

– Daniel Farson: *Henry – An Appreciation Of Henry Williamson*, 1982

Isn't it remarkable to write so well and be so old? Such questions they really wanted to harass and embarrass her with... (And what an original angle, thinks the average hack, endorsed by some equally blasé or earnest editor.) So go forth, dig out a geriatric, a mythical oldster to set in opposition to or contrast with the Kulchur of Youth. Longevity versus fashion. The greatest Age against the latest Ephemera.

Instead, they intruded on what time she had left, to waste it in platitudes, tiring her out with their foot-in-the-door stupidity and insensitive persistence. They never knew enough, never read enough to ask the right questions. Those questions, that is, neither exclusively literary nor pointlessly personal – but which *illuminate*.

Illumination can't be expected from parasites, however. Shedding light is not their grubby function: they feed off the dead and, when they can, batten on the living.

This brings to mind the late John Osborne who whatever his merits as a playwright more often than not got it right as a polemicist. His war with those he perceived as hate-filled hacks and jealous journos was wittily unremitting. "Youth has become, like death, almost a taboo subject", he wrote for his 1973 adaptation of *The Picture Of Dorian Gray*. "Everyone is not merely afraid of losing it but of even admitting that such a possibility exists. Again, youth is all-important, all-reaching, all-powerful. It is obligatory to be trim, slim, careless."

Which in turn makes me recall one horribly unnecessary, poignantly gruesome occasion. It required Jean to be bedizened in various outlandish outfits, made up, and made to pose – an awkward model of media-manipulated senescence. This absurd photo-call seemed senseless, something dreamed up just to fill space, amid the arid acres of one 'quality' Sunday newspaper's fashion columns. The result for Jean was exhaustion accentuated by embarrassment; for me, and surely for many others of her devoted readers, anger at her humiliation. The misbegotten idea had not been hers or her publisher's, I gathered. She later complained to Diane and myself – complained bitterly, and she was right. But it takes a lot of strength, more strength than Jean then possessed, to turn away importunate persons from the press, particularly when some trimmer and timeserver pleads, wheedles, misleads or appeals to one's vanity.

Any space is better than none, will insist the press agents and PR people. Project an image, any image, no matter how undignified. That way (they reckon) you occupy space, you exist. You're somebody, you at least possess an image and a reflection; you are not one of the Undead... Nor do you belong to the nameless masses, a mere dot amid those myriad unimportant page-skimmers out yonder! It's also true though that the moment needs to be seized. So you too must dwell there if only for a single day, a mayfly trapped and allowed brief breath in a trivial world. Thinking it will soon be over, you agree... Does it matter in the end? Well, yes – any space better than none, it seems.

What a tempting maxim, especially to survivors like Jean who have been forgotten or disregarded for so long. You do not want to risk falling back into limbo once again. And yet life, even a long life, is so short! To seize the day is all that counts, no matter how you are portrayed tomorrow. But she must have known that that particular game was not worth the candle: her own stubbornly flickering flame was what she had to remain true to. Ah Jean: artists, and age, and artists in old age, should all be respected – not made to posture nor held up to ill-mannered, ill-informed ridicule in such crass yet devious ways!

Four years of photographs

Faces are fixed on paper, seem all set to stay,
yet fade infinitesimally, by the day...

1970:

I'm glad about the prints. Are they really any good? I've just been looking at some newspaper photographs (French) & gosh they did depress me! So if there is a nice one it would cheer me up like anything.//

Thank you so much for the photographs. Such a relief to have some that aren't caricatures. If you saw the one in the German papers I believe you'd agree. It wasn't even a caricature – it was fiction.//

Thanks again for the photographs & please thank Diane.//

About the photographs – Yes, I do like them & am going to ask you if you could let me have a duplicate set. I sent all my available photographs to Denoel in Paris who asked for them – And very forbidding they were especially when reproduced – So it would please me so much to distribute some pleasant ones if they're wanted or even if they aren't. I know that it doesn't matter a damn really – or so they say – but it would please me. I'm not at all sure 'they' are right either. You should have seen the German one. I'm sure they made it up!//

Thanks so much for the photographs. I like them... Do let me know if I owe you anything for the photographs.//

I'm looking forward to the photographs. They may come in very useful.//

Thank you so much for the photographs which I like very much.//

I'm longing to see the photographs. I've just seen a perfectly hideous one (of myself) and it made my flu much worse – I'm just not photogenic I'm afraid//

I haven't heard from John Smith but I suppose he had the photograph. Thanks for that.//

1971:

As a matter of fact I'm feeling a bit weary. I had sessions of being photographed three days running at Whitsun & I was so hollow-eyed at the end. I expect the result will be awful. Diane's photographs were such a success and taken without any fuss at all!//

1972:

Thanks – for the photograph though oh dear how bent & ancient I look! I must see what can be done about it & live up to my motto 'Spiro spero'.//

1973:

Several photographs from the Sunday Times have arrived – nicer than the published ones I think. But more like me – I don't know. However if you'd like one, I can get a smaller copy & then you'll tear up that quite awful thing you have I hope.//
Do bring the photos when you have them – one fine day soon I hope.//
The photographs arrived yesterday. Very well done I think. I have sent Mr King a cheque… Thanks for arranging the photographs.//

Lost illusions

The difficulty about all this dying is, that you can't tell a fellow anything about it ~~after it has happened~~, so where does the fun come in?

– Alice James: *Journal*, Dec.1891

Her obsessive concern with appearances and surfaces did not derive from any banal habit of self-deception. The look of things – and *her* look *at* things – revealed, with eyes honest and undeluded, no smug narcissism nor even its ghostly traces. Making up a face as best one could was an act that resembled making up a story: both were then presented to the world as versions of the self, acts of recreation and creation. Art was always artifice, of course. You created the illusion that everything was natural and easy; authors had to accept that books which took years of difficult pain to deliver would give strangers pleasure or provide an 'easy read'. What was yours and once lived inside you could not remain yours: abortion or adoption lay in wait. Failure or success. What you'd brought to life, to book, had never really belonged to you and would next exist independently. How precarious anyway was life!

And if your brainchild was beautiful, the shapely product of your best thought dressed in your finest words, you might briefly be happy. There was a certain understandable pride for a while before the relief, the release, the emptiness. Humility, not vanity, was what the true creators felt. Too many, who should have known better, never even came close to understanding these fitful revelations of the spirit.

Jean told me and Diane one day with a wry smile that the vicar of Cheriton Fitzpaine, which she dubbed "really one of the dullest places under heaven", had given her the benefit of his advice. "Now Miss Rhys", he told her on one occasion when he called by, "the time has come for you to lay down your pen". This to the woman whose fingers were twisted out of shape with arthritis and who still wrote draft upon draft, always with care and love and in laborious slow longhand. This to the woman who'd said that when writing, she felt like "a pen in someone else's hand" and who left us some of the finest work of the century. This to the woman who even after the triumph of *Wide Sargasso Sea* never thought to rest on her hardwon laurels nor relinquish her vocation.

We tried none too convincingly to laugh with her. That she should be patronised by doubtless wellmeaning if not godly folk who did not know her quality struck us as painful. Famous, but properly sceptical of that belated fame, she could yet write in all humility and isolation to a young author like myself: "Of course I'm struggling against a fit of depression & can't write anything escapist or otherwise. I suppose one gets used to it but I never have". It was a time when, just turned thirty, I was tasting a sort of success with the four or five novels I'd published: my name was printed in far larger type than the titles of the books, and I'd received some excellent reviews. But every book seemed a battleground; I had experienced numerous problems with publishers and agents; it was becoming clear that I could scarcely scrape a living. Jean's doubts about her own writing, and her remarks about the setbacks she continued to encounter, opened my eyes. It was a privilege to compare notes with her. To be able, every now and then, freely to complain to one another, felt (for me at least) like a companionable reassurance. I learned that as a writer I should expect nothing from the world, and that the greatest joy lay in good work. So much Jean taught me; visiting her was a joy, too.

Likely stories and light blue relief

It appeared that nobody who mattered was capable of being explained.
Thus was inculcated a feeling for the dark horse.
— Elizabeth Bowen: *Out Of A Book*, 1946

Jean by her dogged example proved a great source of encouragement to me
during my own youthful struggles to survive as a writer. I was impressed by the
determination she had shown and still did, and by the amount of drafts and
redrafts required to produce even a few paragraphs. She was devoted to her craft,
and over the years it had grown part of her and into an art. All this took solitude,
long intense hours of application and hard work. By then, of course, she could
not do otherwise. Writing had been and still was her raison d'être; she knew
nothing else, but in her final decade at least she must have had a comfortable
if not actually substantial literary income. There were subsidiary rights —
adaptations, options, translations, and reprints of all her books, although she
always seemed to be getting into muddles and disputes with agents, or those
representing or trying in different ways to organize her. She was old and tired:
she wasn't used to the attention and zeal of such types which, while gratifying,
could exhaust or confuse her.

Sometimes she needed quite simple, practical assistance. I remember how
Diane and I spent much of one afternoon with Jean, early in 1970, discussing
music. We talked of how even a short fragment of something one liked could
lift the spirit and brighten a wintry day. Soon afterwards Diane had a letter from
Jean: "It was so kind of you to tell me about the record player. I thought about
it — then decided that as I've never had one and am a perfect donkey about
everything mechanical I'd better buy one that can be *explained* to me carefully
and lengthily. Yes I have a what's itsname socket? point? I'd better wait till my
daughter [Maryvonne, domiciled in Holland] arrives — it's wiser." A month or
so later, Diane heard from Jean again on a more plaintive note, remarking that
she's "had rather a crowded time, my record player's gone wrong — this and
that."

Practicalities of a technical nature seemed indeed to defeat her, but she could
always laugh at herself. Wordprocessing would have scared and paralysed her

utterly: longhand, however laborious, was the only way to write. Slow, leisurely deliberation and revision would get one there in the end… Yes, I would think to myself after paying her a visit: that was true and all very well, yet I couldn't *afford* that much time. Somehow or other I was obliged to *buy* mine, and I had very little money then. We were clearly on divergent time-scales, she and I, both of us having reached very different stages in our lives.

Jean Rhys had become respected, securely 'established', with editors scurrying to publish anything she cared to offer them. Whereas I felt – after ill-advised moves around several publishing houses – that I still had to prove myself. And not only to prove myself as a writer, but also to justify my existence as commercial prospect to the latest of these publishers. Editors in that booming paperback era were quick to play wellpaid musical chairs: there was little or no continuity as far as even 'their' authors were concerned. Ambitious editorial career moves were the order of the day; author-insecurity increased, while loyalties were not so much divided as abandoned. Difficulties arose if the younger writer were neither English, Northern, proletarian, patrician nor otherwise easily classifiable. Novels of mine might duly be described as 'eagerly anticipated' by the blurb-writers, yet they always provoked arguments over their message and merit. For a while, 'saleability' saved them, until the magic charm of that word faded or fell also into dispute. It didn't occur to me then to try being noisier, less professional, and more pugnacious or perversely difficult – pushing your personality alongside and beyond your books. Some writers are skilled at self-promotion by any means necessary, but for what it was worth, I knew I wasn't one of that particular breed. Consequently I never looked forward to having to fight my corner with agents, publishers and critics, however unrepresentative of lasting literature they themselves might really be.

Whether my own books required weeks or years to write, they generally took an inordinate length of time to be accepted for publication: nothing, ever, seemed straightforward. When it came to the publishing process itself, that often proved more fraught or prolonged than the actual writing. How satisfying eventually to be shown good reviews and good sales figures – but as for good money I was always short. I seemed to be paid too little for work that took too long. This last may be a perennial literary dilemma, and perhaps also I was naive, intemperate or impractical. In the publishing sense, I too (echoing Jean) might have resembled "a perfect donkey", whose toil enriched his masters as long as the poor beast revolved in their circumscribed circles. Apparently doomed to hack it, the earnest littérateur like myself could somehow make shift to keep going – going the rounds, going round and through the mill of prose.

•

In order to survive, of course, it was important not to take oneself or others too seriously. The work was what mattered – doing the best you could, whatever the project, trying to salvage or learn something from difficulty and routine alike. Because nothing, really, was run of the mill; every book in the actual writing was of absorbing fascination, whatever its special obsessions and anxieties. You tried to entertain, or to unburden yourself, to make money or literature or both or neither, for the love of words and life, with some laughs along the way. The laughter was important, a *sine qua non*. Without it, Grub Street could grind you down; with it, craft could escape the dullness of graft.

Jean enjoyed funny books, books which might at least amuse her and dispel fits of *le cafard*. While her own books tended toward the grim, she herself didn't lack a sense of humour. Admittedly her wit wasn't gentle or whimsical, but her humour was rather more sardonic than Rabelaisian. I think she felt the world was too dismal to be taken straight, without a shot of satire, or anyhow a smile.

Jean told me she thought I could "do dialogue", and that I should develop a satirical streak she detected in my novels. Encouraged by this, I showed her in 1971 the manuscript of a book I'd written the year before. The publisher who'd originally suggested the novel had, when presented with my MS., developed a sudden chill of the pedal extremities immortalised by Fats Waller. The book this publisher now reckoned too hot for his firm was intended as a satire on pornography, a narrative to be read also as an 'exercise in style', *au* Queneau, simply an erotic comedy. Zazie and Candy were, I thought, wittily imagined heroines in the genre. (Which itself went back centuries, beyond Cleland, Defoe & co, and had more to do with society and language itself than sex.)

My own variation of the female-innocent-abroad theme was called *Instrument Of Pleasure*. I dictated the novel to Diane in a fortnight, punctuated with bouts of laughter, making very few changes after she'd deciphered and transcribed her shorthand. I'd hoped it would provide a passport out of London, at least temporarily, but the novel on its way to eventual publication was destined for a series of misadventures quite as curious or hilarious as any its heroine experienced. Strangely, everything in this fiction is indeed 'drawn from life': it's the most documentary, uninvented, or truly autobiographical of all my novels. What happens *did* happen. The anecdotes and events were related by or they related to, particular friends (e.g. Diane, some previous flames, jazz drummer Philly Joe Jones, and a whole host of acquaintances) – but all are ascribed to a single, somewhat naive narrator-heroine, Celeste Piano.

The book proved too explicit for Jean, who wrote to me during June 1971: "I am dutifully reading Celeste's adventures. A good title." She told me later that she'd laughed "quite a bit", however; she'd liked its use of place and its pace, and could appreciate the novel as a 'lighthearted' fiction that had probably been written quickly. When I told her just how quickly, and how and why, there was further laughter. But I mightn't have found the situation so amusing had I known what lay in store. It wasn't until 1974 that *Instrument Of Pleasure* at last saw publication. The comic novel that almost wrote itself in two uproarious weeks took nearly five years to appear in print. My harmless period-piece about growing up in the 1950s and 1960s managed to create new problems and enemies: I began to realise just how subversive humour might seem to those who lacked it.

The publishing history is a cautionary tale and a laugh in itself. My highpowered agent, a gent at one of the largest and oldest firms, encountered a mere five rejections then huffily abandoned ship. "You missed the boat on this," he wrote. "Had I known you were embarking on this book I'd probably have tried to dissuade you". Prior to this, he'd found the book "really difficult to sell", adding to my disbelief that he had "become absolutely satisfied it wasn't going to be a runner". Served me right, he implied, for not toiling over *le mot juste*. (But I had.) Served me right for not being a serious writer. (But I was.) All I wanted was a halfway decent income: that too I was serious about, and I didn't need moral lectures. So I countered his disapproval of my supposedly indecent book by persevering without him.

I continued to be cheered, and amazed, by the fact that one of the rejecters considered the novel "too strong" for his well known house, even invoking "the chill wind of the reactionary backlash whistling through our corridors"! History did seem to be repeating itself however, when the buccaneering

Olympia Press (who almost published my first novel in 1959), informed me – after their move from Paris to New York, and a considerable consideration period of two years – that *Instrument Of Pleasure* was "unfortunately not suitable for our list". Back in London, a bold new American-founded firm turned it down next "for the obvious reasons". (I think they meant S&S – Sex & Satire: to them perhaps a more unsettling mixture than S&M.) One rejection later, to my relief and pleasure, *Instrument* was welcomed aboard. The publisher's enthusiasm seemed ironically appropriate, for the book had found a home with my customary paperback publishers, Panther – the first to have rejected it when my erstwhile agent originally tried them five years earlier.

Seriously published – the only time a novel of mine ever appeared with a plain rather than lurid cover – *Instrument Of Pleasure* sold well enough in this original format, if never reprinted in its pristine white first edition. However, two different British publishers subsequently bought and reissued it also; there followed two American editions and a Polish translation, and the book is still in print today. What was intended as just a *jeu d'esprit*, an episodic, parodic bit of baroque bawdry, has proved more successful than my most serious work. And after one of its reprints in 1984, a large-circulation men's magazine *Club International* dubbed the book "extraordinarily erotic".

Ought I to have heeded that doubt-filled agent and been more mindful of literary 'reputation'? But I needed to eat, to ease my financial worries somehow! Meanwhile, proving pundits wrong may often afford a modest pleasure... As for this immodest work, which itself has enjoyed something of an underground reputation over the years, I'm never quite sure whether the joke, obscurely, has been on me, or if in fact I've had the last laugh. I feel rather like the young fellow in the famous story by Somerset Maugham, who does everything his elders advise him against, and in the end comes not to grief but laughter.

•

There's a sort of freewheeling footnote (or possibly a pedal note) to the adventures of Celeste Piano. Years after Jean's death, Angier's biography enlightens me: Jean didn't learn to ride a bicycle until her late teens. She had gone from her bikeless little island Dominica to the imposing capital of academe, Cambridge – cycle city itself, even then. Evidently it was the classics mistress at the Perse School who taught her selfconscious foreign 'charge' to ride... Jean mentioned how she would follow in the young teacher's wake, "wobbling dangerously from side to side". This reminded me of an early scene in *Instrument Of Pleasure* – with cyclist Celeste crashing into a jaywalker, an upperclass undergraduate and 'Blue' who introduces her to the university's gilded youth. I don't know whether Jean did or didn't smile at this: perhaps it was too near the knuckle! I remember her saying she enjoyed best the book's descriptions of Dublin, London and Paris. The Cambridge part was never mentioned; I'm sure Jean could not have looked back happily on her time there. But I like to think that lonely girl had a laugh or two on her bike, by way of lightening her homesickness, and that she met with some bright spark of warmth even in the cold unfriendly fenland of ninety years ago.

Voices

I've never had a long period of being happy... D'you think anybody has?
If I had to choose, I'd rather be happy than write.
  – Jean Rhys: BBC R4 interview, 1974

The spools revolved and the tape at once unwound its spell. Here was an eerie sensation, hearing her voice again after twenty years. I'd always liked that unique melodic lilt, softly croaky yet cadenced, at times almost approaching a mew. To me it had a tune, hints of plaintive rhythm which suited her well; its tone seemed indeed to have Welshness and the West Indies in it. The rarest notes sounded felt neither young nor old, yet were perfectly placed and somehow timeless. The voice was so un-English, but although low and not in the least powerful, attractively wise. I admit I never heard it raised or raging, but in that exotic timbre there was feline subtlety, along with a suggestion of distant singing and dancing, a moving and bruised grace amid words which cost so much.

About Jean's voice, her instantly distinctive and special sound, she herself was always self-conscious. It was not just shyness nor that she felt she could not easily 'project' among or towards other people. True, her stage career had ended in humiliation – as described in stories and letters – but then she was too introspective and sensitive a character ever to have made a success of impersonating others. It was all she could do to cope with the incessant dramas of her own life, while only within the intense privacy of literary creation could she fully exist, exploring and eventually finding herself. Anyone who believed and declared as Jean Rhys did, that people were "a pack of damned hyenas" could scarcely wish to give her all in pursuit of public approval and appreciation! Throughout her life anyway she seems to have aroused extreme personal reactions in whoever she met, however reclusive or gregarious she tried to be, however well or badly, conventionally or disreputably she behaved. The voice might calm or charm, cajole or enrage, yet it remains unforgettable.

Jean's voice in 1929, according to her second husband's daughter, was "not strong" and "rather high" and there were discernible traces of a Caribbean accent. These 1970s recollections – from a newlywed twenty-one year old, about the thirty-nine year old Jean who as yet was still her 'unofficial' stepmother – refer to a time just after Jean had published *The Left Bank* and *Quartet*. It's interesting to compare the young woman's comments with some that soon followed, from the partial but always acutely observant Ford Madox Ford. The score-settling, vengeful descriptions of Jean's vocal mannerisms in Ford's *roman à clef When The Wicked Man* must surely have hurt. There one learns, for instance, that "her voice was extraordinarily soft and stealthy" and this insistence on "her soft stealthy voice" is continued through the book. The passive, desperately determined masochist – as Ford portrays her – uses this sly attribute in order to beg and persuade. That languid yet insidious tropical eloquence creeps in to possess the portly Ford-figure's ear, deceptively soliciting favour as 'Lola' worms her lowkey way towards his bed and (in another manner of speaking) into the upright publisher's good books. When crossed, she will scream, swear and threaten like some grotesque creature of voodoo... Verily, hell hath no fury like a wordman suborned.

•

> And the sigh of that child
> ...the white hush between two sentences.
> – Derek Walcott: *Jean Rhys*

If disappointment in love seemed to Jean to be her own personal fate, she later admitted that her feelings towards England too were of "disappointed love". But what could the seventeen year old Jean expect, after convent school on a Caribbean island? It seems she was apprehensive and felt she was being sent packing, as in some ways indeed she was. By exchanging a tiny island for a larger one she could scarcely fulfil any cherished adolescent dream, nor would she necessarily manoeuvre herself towards a better, more independent life of her own. Going to England, where Jean was concerned, was no romantic embarkation for the Promised Land. After all, as Jean's contemporary, the Trinidad-born author Yseult Bridges (1888-1971) wrote: "it was considered essential that a girl, before being launched on Society, should spend at least a year in England, preferably three or four, being 'finished'".

"There only would she have a chance to eradicate the insidious singsong Creole accent and acquire that poise and complexion, that *cachet,* which would enhance her chances of making a 'good match': which, if she failed to do, would mean that she had failed in the whole object of a woman's existence, and after a season or two would be relegated to the background of the home, there to live parasitically or to eke out a genteel existence in some ladylike way." Such prospects, home or away, must have seemed unfair gambles with fate, only certain to fill intelligent and articulate young women like Rhys or Bridges with dread. Bridges, at the end of her posthumously published memoir *Child Of The Tropics* (Collins Harvill, 1980), has set sail for Southampton lamenting her departure as Jean must have done: "I knew with a clear, nostalgic certainty that now, in that very instant, I was bidding farewell to my childhood; that though I should see these familiar scenes again, and see them with a happy heart, yet never should I see them with quite the same untrammelled rapture, the same pure, unsullied joy."

Jean was to see those "familiar scenes" again only once, and then in middle-age, with a far from happy heart: time had brought changes, wrought ruin that was visible, tangible. This is why her story of the 'revenant', 'I Used To Live Here Once', is so unsettlingly poignant. Certainly Jean's own raw awareness of rejection and displacement persisted, alongside her keen selfconsciousness about her voice. By the time Jean wrote the book she said she liked best, *Voyage In The Dark* (1934), she was looking back at herself as the young Dominican Anna Morgan, exiled in London. And Anna in turn looks back at her white family and her aunt 'Hester'. "Impossible to get you away from the servants", she is chided: "That awful singsong voice you had! Exactly like a nigger you talked – and still do. Exactly like that dreadful girl Francine." 'Francine', black and a servant, is envied by the privileged white girl for that very sexual maturity and a knowing kind of freedom which Anna despairs of finding. Perhaps by this time, however, Ford's critical strictures and Francine's carefree independence had been subsumed into Jean's own fearless literary voice.

Even in Jean's later years though, the matter of the voice seems to have rankled. 'Let Them Call It Jazz' – one of her finest stories, first published in 1962 – has her black heroine Selina Davis fall foul of the law and, as was the case with Jean herself, it is the quiet tone of the hypocrite that she most distrusts. Policemen and officials all of course have "low voices". "The magistrate is a little gentleman with a quiet voice, but I'm very suspicious of these quiet voices now", observes Selina, who then becomes tongue-tied and cannot even plead her case adequately. "I want to tell him" (she thinks) "the woman next door provoke me since long time and call me bad names but she have a soft sugar voice and nobody hear – that's why I broke her window, but I'm ready to buy another after all. I want to say all I do is sing in that old garden, and I want to say this in decent quiet voice. But I hear myself talking loud, and I see my hands wave in the air." In exasperation, the immigrant who can never fit in merely weeps. Her accusers and judges whisper and nod and she ends up in Holloway. There and thereafter (I shan't even try to summarize or do justice to this tough but tender tale), she is saved by a song.

It's as if Jean Rhys constantly needed to ask of life and the world at large: Can't they *hear* what I'm really like, what I really have to say? While Jean wanted people to play fair, she felt they seldom did. She knew of course that quiet voices do not necessarily imply dissembling or deceit. In another marvellous late story, 'Till September Petronella', the first-person narrator and Rhys-projection is specifically given her own stage-name [Petron]Ella Gray, and finds herself cast by a friendly stranger as a sort of siren:

"Well," he said as we got into the car, "you've got to tell me where to drive to. And you don't happen to know a little song, do you?"

"That was very pretty," he said when I stopped. "You've got a very pretty voice indeed. Give us some more."

But we were getting near the cottage and I didn't finish the next song because I was nervous and worried that I wouldn't be able to tell him the right turning.

At the foot of the path I thought, "The champagne worked all right."

"When slightly tight I can relax", wrote elsewhere the elderly Jean, ever consistent and unsparing about herself. As Petronella in the above story, she is rejoining a quartet of people paired off for a fortnight's country vacation. After various qualms about the whole set-up, which lead to her temporary flight, chorus girl Petronella has more or less regained her confidence in the company of an affable farmer who's just given her a lift back. She pauses with him a moment outside the cottage, only to overhear herself being discussed. By a telling touch, not so much paranoid as documentary, the voice she hears belongs to the charming – and of course dangerously unstable and unsuitable Julian. Julian, the lover of the other young woman present, is scathingly if casually patronising:

> Julian said, "I think, I rather think, Marston, that I hear a female pipe down there. You can lay your fears away. She's not the sort to kill herself. I told you that."

'Julian' for whom she feels both attraction and repulsion, was the composer Philip Heseltine – himself, ironically, a suicide and better known under his *nom de guerre* 'Peter Warlock'. For such a fascinating and gifted reprobate – occultist, drunk, practical joker and proto-Bohemian that he was – to assume Petronella-Jean was just another flighty piece represented a cruel wound, beyond invention. That Heseltine, a genuinely exciting musical talent, perhaps even a potential new love, should dismiss her very *voice*, was equivalent to writing her off altogether, whether as woman or artist. It says much for Jean that she could tell the story so soberly and sombrely, frank without glib hindsight, and facing up as she always did to her deepest insecurities and disappointments. Unmusical, unsociable, unattractive: the aged Jean stared hard at that worst image of a bygone self, helplessly adrift in England before the Great War...

The story that began with a barrel organ playing (tunes she liked) ends in tears, with loneliness, a ticking clock. Times have changed and time itself has changed Petronella, the young woman Jean so truthfully describes as she looks forward only to an inevitable autumn, the bitter-sweet September song she will soon enough learn to sing. Dan Davin, the New Zealand writer and chronicler of a later London Bohemia itself long vanished, voiced it well: "... we were now in that time when we must take life not as it comes but as it goes". Jean would have recognised the sharp wisdom of that.

Lost loves, lost opportunities, lost weekends, years... Yet if as Jean said people did live "beastly lives", that was no reason to lose your head or your voice. She kept going, through abortions and pregnancies, alcoholism, breakdown and detox, sickness, poverty, deaths and a whole catalogue of disasters. Diana Athill, her publisher at Deutsch, believed that Jean wrote not out of "need for money" but rather as "a therapeutic exercise". If so, hers is an even more remarkable achievement, since she makes the reader also care, listening with rapt attention to an exceptionally honest voice. This most personal of writers always involves us in variations on her own predicament, but what might initially seem narrow invariably runs deep.

Jean Rhys herself survived miraculously and long; logically enough, survival is her main theme. Not money or sex, nor the fate of women, not sexual dependency and betrayal – although the nexus between them all exists and is examined in her work. One of Jean's finest critics, her friend Francis Wyndham, has pointed out that while her books might seem "about a passive person" (one to whom things happen, things more often than not unpleasant), there is always an active energy in the writing itself. Her other best critic Carole Angier underlines this, stressing Jean's utter perfectionism – draft upon draft after draft, until she got right what she wanted to say. Feelings, not explanations, are shown in action, happening right there on the page. This is rare, an unsettling, even frightening experience. You aren't just being entertained or talked *at*. No, you as reader now live in and through the book: the writer preceded you, lived it out and leads you back as you read, through the dark labyrinth of feeling. What you hear is indeed intimate, a vulnerable and thus most human voice: neither powerful nor strident, only just loud enough to come over clear.

The effort, persistence and sheer hard work these exemplary modulations cost did not show. *Ars est celare artem*. No writer can afford to let that inner struggle show. The art and strain alike should always be well concealed; it's part of the magical process, and writers must absorb and transmute the difficulty whatever form it takes, sweating it out as a matter of course. The reality of *Wide Sargasso Sea* for instance, which as she said "began with a dream and ended with a dream", was that it took at least a decade. No wonder she dubbed it a "devil" and a "demon"! After which, prizes and money must have seemed as it were immaterial, unreal pleasures. All that ever truly matters is for the work to feel right, to read easy – not the same as an easy read. Or being easily read...

The result may appear puny yet we all live in hope, trusting Dr Johnson: "What is written without effort is in general read without pleasure". The book becomes and is your gift and part of life – the best part of a special life. It's you and no longer you – something like a child, the child in Jean's 1966 dream, new life delivered to the world, hers and no longer hers, the debt paid back, her own death continuing to be earned.

Without wishing to sound too solemn, I celebrate here the fact that Jean's voice has not dated, but seems timeless. ("Ahead of her time", Angier called her.) In one letter of 1934 however, Jean speculated on time itself being an illusion: "I mean that the past exists – side by side with the present, not behind it; that what was – is." In another, from 1950, she says: "I belong to a past age really or a future one. Not now." Meanwhile (1997) I relish listening again to her actual, instantly distinctive voice. It's a change from simply hearing her in my head or via that imaginative music her words still make on the page.

●

A coincidence-coda. Coda to this theme of the immediately recognisable voice, also to those variant ideas of fame and continuance I've discussed. A joke for Jean to have enjoyed. First though here's the connection, jazzrap of sorts... *Two Creoles he black she white, spikily lyrical souls, flying high above the poles of lies & mediocrity, impatient with hypocrisy. You know them at once, you'll never forget, vibrant phrases echoing yet. Strong reactions the two inspired – fear & desire & love were fired. Boozers both, they put it about, neither afraid to fight it out. Both might get sore, but sure could they soar! Singers in flight in finest style from jails of flesh that held them a while. Self-taught perfectionists driven to rage, foes of racism, smugness, old age. Never content with secondbest they put everyone through their bullshit test.*

In 1897 the younger of this passionate pair was born. (Cue, as I write, for centenary programmes etc.) Bland standard voices of the BBC radio announcers, their received pronunciation soothing and smooth as ever, had done the double, getting both sublimely wrong. 1974: the male R4 announcer called *her* Jean Rice. 1997: the female R3 announcer calls *him* Sidney Becket.

Did I hear that aright? Who else out there was laughing? But they speak to me still, this unholy pair, these fiercely emotional voices. Lifting the spirit with something akin to love. They live on, on and in the air, the timeless voices of the past. Our lilting lively contemporaries, neither correct, conventional nor decent. So shout it out for them – "Bechet as in UNASHAMED, Rhys as in RECENT!"

The place of poetry

In this world (the *Isle of Dreames*)
While we sit by sorrowes streames,
Teares and terrors are our theames...
  – Herrick: *The White Island: Or Place Of The Blest,* 1647

That autumn, 1969, I was still living in London. The first of September brought a letter from Jean. "This place is completely deserted – even more so than most days. Not a farm cart passes. Or a car. I envy you in Soho – I only know the restaurants there. Chelsea & Bloomsbury were my places. I expect I'd find them very much changed though. I've never resigned myself to living here really, & am always making plans to come to London for a visit. But last time I tried – it was at Christmas – I got terribly tired and rather hated the noise. So it's got to be carefully arranged."

During the next decade, her last, she did get to the city quite often. There were more frequent trips and visits, lengthening stays with friends and acquaintances, prolonged spells of hotel residence or rented accommodation for up to several months at a time. These exhausting changes to Jean's life and her Devon routine might have expressed, even assuaged, an inner restlessness or dissatisfaction. But perhaps too they represented vague, somewhat half-hearted attempts at the 'escape' she mentioned in letters. Seeing her in London, she invariably seemed lonelier still, if anything more isolated among people. Socialising merely accentuated her isolation: among people she appeared smaller, frailer, physically more fragile. I wonder now how much she truly enjoyed herself or how long the fleeting relief of leaving Cheriton Fitzpaine could ever last.

The loneliness surrounding her was no longer linked to poverty nor was it, as with so many artists, evidence of a perennial self-absorbed concern with their work and its proper appreciation. Age isolates one of course, but did Jean remain as wary as in her youth, when anticipating life's real or imagined humiliations? Sometimes I thought her isolation went deeper, approaching some chronic spiritual displacement – she seemed to have become an exile from the world itself, lacking a true home. Her books tell us clearly enough how painful it is not to feel part of the real, material world: those later London binges, city fixes and partytimes must have used up as much adrenalin as they supplied. She was older, richer, better-known and obviously flattered, after so long in various sorts of wilderness, to be welcomed as a fashionable phenomenon in literary circles. Who would not have relished an occasional change from a rural backwater? Yet in other respects she herself cannot have been so "very much changed".

That interwar London she remembered and recaptured so well in her fiction was faithfully corroborated by a male contemporary, the now little read Thomas Burke. "Bloomsbury is still a sort of centre of the lonely hard-up", wrote Burke, noting that while London was "not so rich in oddity as it was, there are still some quarters that hold veins of it, notably the boarding-house quarters." There, he maintained, "you find the lonely, and the lonely are most apt to keep and to sharpen their differences. You see the lonely sitting in the lounges of the cheap hotels; wandering about the shopping-streets; going to the cinema at midday; nibbling sandwiches at all hours in the snack bars and milk bars. These are the hard-up lonely." Burke's book *Living In Bloomsbury* was published in 1939 and amply documents that much-changed world. It confirms that Jean, in keeping with her own characters, observed herself and her circumstances with unflinching accuracy – while simultaneously seeking refuge however temporary within what she later called "her places".

The Rhysian Bloomsbury was very far from snobbish self-congratulation and that tiresomely over-familiar, now diaried-to-death group of privileged aesthetes. According to Burke, it was a cheap and cheerful Bohemia; while he described the area as "mainly literature and art, which are the madness of humans engaged in reproducing the sanity of the gods", he liked the atmosphere of licensed eccentricity. The place might seem precarious yet not hostile – quite the opposite. You could exist, quietly desperate, or go noisily crazy, "and it will not matter. Bloomsbury has seen madder things than you..." Jean would have liked that, the individual's freedom to be left alone, to make the inevitable mistakes without hypocritical condemnation: feeling free, in fact, to find and somehow pay one's own way.

Artists struggle to survive in any case, sensing some pattern to lives often apparently meaningless, but as Burke – an astute and still readable writer – pointed out: "In my youth I had known the poverty of real want, but it had been so urgent a factor that I had not noticed what it 'felt like'". Creative people are all solitaries despite trying nonetheless to fit in as best they can. Where writers are concerned, most must somehow buy their time yet not sell out their lives. Dreams and plans are free however, at least for a while, and more necessary than we care to acknowledge. As for Jean's own dreams of escape, did she in her declining years yearn for Dominica, lost paradise island in the sun?

If Jean's distant birthplace held little magic for her by the time she returned briefly in middle-age, it continued to cast a spell on her creative imagination. "But the magic is particular to the place", wrote an *Observer* journalist, nearly nine years after Jean's death. "It is in the novels of Jean Rhys, the white Dominican whose house in Roseau is now a restaurant (you have to tell the Americans who Jean Rhys was)". And in 1989, readers of *The Independent* were exhorted to "sit in the shady courtyard of The World of Food, once Jean Rhys's garden, and drink a glass of milky sour-sop". By now I expect there are also inexorable guided tours, but many of those tourists, Americans or not, may know a little more about Jean.

Jean *used* to live there once, and she concluded by imagining herself a *revenant* in that bright landscape of dream. It was, naturally, the land of lost content, to which she felt she was forever denied access. But hadn't she after all fully earned her death? Even that might have been too sweet a dream, akin to believing paradise ever existed in the first place… Perhaps one simply wakes up *from* something, *to* something – who knows?

A contemporary of Jean's delivered into the world as many babies as poems. Curiously enough, like Jean's father, he too was Dr Williams. "I tell you the poets are not dreamers", he wrote at seventy to a friend: "they know what they are and what they are talking about is a living hell." Poets are realists, in other words, but what is real anyway? What's real for me of my friend is the poet she once was. The struggle is done: she endures and remains in mere words, words lively, honest and always memorably set in place. Jean will continue to be met and reckoned with upon the page. For there it is she has a home and a place of her own.

True poets may be read many ways. Let's make believe for instance, that what Herrick envisioned was the very stare of freedom itself, the vast, blank but wholly seductive expanse of infinity, contemplated with sure lyricism centuries ago. For now, let it be whatever timeless page awaits us. The paper is pristine:

it's open to everyone who seeks new life through the embrace of words and the endless quest for the chimera of meaning. That distant, spacious zone not only exists but extends. Whether viewed as an elusively pure democracy or a fine and private enough place, it's a location made for the living and the dead alike. There all may meet, communicate, and greet one another,

In that *whiter Island*, where
Things are evermore sincere...

Ghosts in summer light

> It was one of those days when you can see the ghosts of all the other lovely days. You drink a bit and watch the ghosts of all the lovely days that have ever been from behind a glass.
> – *Voyage In The Dark*, 1934

Anna Morgan, nineteen and, as the initials imply, only in the morning of her life, struggles to survive. The original draft of Jean's own preferred novel had the diffident chorus girl die after a botched abortion. Jean reconsidered, and brought this ghostly younger version of herself back to life: the resultant conclusion is if anything harsher than ever. There are no short cuts, no 'easy' ways out: one is sentenced to life, to repeating one's errors, to loneliness and despair...

Much later, in 1964, Jean wrote to Francis Wyndham rather sorely recalling that in her younger days she like Anna had been thought of as decorative, spineless, and brainless all at once. She had good reason to resent the extremes of condescension, even hostility, she'd encountered. (The reactions she prompted were by no means confined to men only.) A young woman of exceptional beauty and intelligence, thereby set apart, but also evidently and materially quite on her own, was in those bygone days something of an anomalous creature. She would have been seen, socially, as a kind of alien, a form of exotic toy – as potential threat or possession. That tension is clear in all Jean's work: she raged against being misread, typecast, treated like some unrealistic puppet. The septuagenarian Jean wearily told Wyndham she was now "no longer a doll, but a kind of ghost".

Placeless and classless, yet unwilling to sink into the exploited ranks of women living through and off men – those whom Gissing had dubbed "the unclassed" – she began her new, teenage life in Edwardian England, as does Anna. "I didn't want to talk to anybody. I felt too much like a ghost." Jean like Anna was a warm-blooded woman who longed to fulfil herself. In the meantime, she needed the time and means to do so: only the former ever seems easily available, but that too can prove illusory. Time to discover and be oneself never comes free, it's dearly bought, and self-knowledge works out expensive. It would have been painful also for the middleaged Jean – starting to be 'successful' as a writer – to voyage back into that darker past and confront that younger self. In the event she naturally, gracefully, shares origin and memories with the youthful Anna, who is "born in a hot place" but finds herself fated to battle against coldness, fighting off what Lawrence Durrell during the Thirties called "the English Death".

Writing again to that staunch ally Wyndham in the mid-1960s, Jean points out how her first husband Lenglet has portrayed her in his novel *Barred*. He (at least as 'Edouard de Nève') "thinks of me as without will power, unable to fight, languid, indolent, a kind of a shadow". Not to know what one is doing in the world, not to have a purpose to existence, being devoid of love or direction: that way despair and madness lie, there the dark voyage leads. The conclusion to *Voyage*, when Anna's fevered visions of a dead past and of the future (the death from which there's only temporary reprieve) meet in a delirious present, a stream of semi-consciousness, is as painstakingly and illuminatingly written as anything in Jean's work. The 'real' world turns into an ever narrower, frightening reduction that may suddenly open out just as dizzyingly onto the unknown: *shadows are ghosts you look at them and you don't see them.* She who has always felt herself somehow to be a ghost – detached from reality, and/or 'unreally' self-aware – is henceforth condemned to a sort of Sartrean continuance, amid the hell of other people. No escape, no exit after all. Starting out, beginning over again, is the cruellest possible ending. As for that doctor with the power of life and death, even he cannot finally afford compassion and so does not offer it. "When their voices stopped the ray of light came in again under the door like the last thrust of remembering before everything is blotted out".

What must be kept in mind in order to keep going? Do we remember that we actually can create, that contained within everybody is something of the creative spark? Perhaps this notion will save or dupe us or induce us to keep on. At any rate, some affirmative personal belief may rescue and console us for a while, for as long as it takes to make something other than emptiness, the opposite of waste. Though tired and ill, Lenglet wrote to Jean from Holland just before his death in 1961. Jean later confided to Wyndham (another who never doubted her talent) that the remarkable and gifted Lenglet, himself such a vital figure in her life, "asked me among other things, never to give up writing."

•

Jean understood however that writers were expendable, dispensable, while in the bookworld as elsewhere fashions came and went. "I don't believe in the individual Writer so much as in Writing", she commented in a 1953 letter. "It uses you and throws you away when you are not useful any longer. But it does not do this until you are useless and quite useless too. Meanwhile there is nothing to do but plod along line upon line." Brave words from a forgotten writer then in her sixties, but she meant them. She had found purpose and determination; when technique, voice and theme cohered, her time would come.

Yet Jean had more than simple dogged commitment: that in itself is never quite enough. See Oleron, the writer in her favourite ghost story *The Beckoning Fair One:* "He had chosen his path, and was committed to it beyond possibility of withdrawal." But Oleron is courting "the succubus" (of 'success', elusive as always and requiring the wrong kind of egocentricity off which to feed). He has entered the shadow-world of vain imaginings, whose ultimately vampiric muse brings neither success nor enlightenment, only darkness and death. Illumination is not to be his – quite the contrary. "Direct sunlight, of which, as the sun passed daily round the house, each of his rooms now had its share, was like a flame in his brain; and even diffused light was a dull and numbing ache." The only revelation for this betrayer of inspiration and abjurer of love is to be damned. And damned, ironically and irrevocably, by that putative public he will now never reach. The last section of this extraordinary novella starts: "In the bright June sunlight a crowd filled the square..."

It's a shocking and superbly judged moment: the surprise that is no surprise and yet retains its own inevitable logic. The light breaks in, bringing even further dread. L.P. Hartley, himself a notable practitioner, wrote of the ghost story: "If not the highest, it is certainly the most exacting form of literary art, and perhaps the only one in which there is almost no immediate step between success and failure." *The Beckoning Fair One* is that rare thing, a successful story about erotic and artistic failure, and one which manages to be both credibly objective and intimately involving. Quite a lot in common there with Jean Rhys, her own preoccupations, work and superstitions.

She also appreciated – and not only through Oleron, of course – how isolated every writer can feel. When I sent her my teenage apprentice novel *The Summer Ghosts,* she wrote in reply of how "the long summer evenings can be ghostly – far more so than winter. Especially if it's hot & one's alone. (This is a very silent place.)" It seemed in accord with what Thomas Burke remarked: "Winter twilight is usually accepted as the apt time for ghost stories, though I think the right story would evoke the shiver more certainly on a summer evening by the river." Illumination, that matter of life and death, comes from how one sees or accepts the light, how the lens of the eye and the darkness of the mind record that sudden realising of the impossible.

It's rarely possible to find and fix the right phrase, to develop the material, the memory, the mindfilm, framing that invisibility, fixing that picture which is more than shadow while definitely not a photograph. What could not move, could not have been, has moved, is moving. There is evidence here, in words. This is where something happened, took place and form. In sunshine, on a summer morning. This is all the substance memory can grasp. And so, years later, something further is remembered. The page remains blank, yet the ghost of something darkens to fill it.

What if – and what else? The hair on the nape of the neck rises as one realises no explanation exists for whatever has been experienced.

•

Ghosts are everywhere in her work – the imprint of the past and all we have as memories. When do they let go; when do we let them go? For that matter, when do they let *us* go: when do we stop being aware of them, believing in them?

I've been haunted by her for so long. In many ways I've been content to be so. Yet in remembering I'm shocked to think how long it's been. It's taken me that long to discover what I owe her. Twenty-six summers gone since she wrote to console that other ghost, my younger self:

My dear Alexis

I wish I could think of exactly the right thing to say.

You can write, don't think of what other people want you to say or do. Think only of what you wish to say (or do).

I've grown to dislike Cheriton Fitz intensely this summer so I'm most sympathetic.

But there is no escape for me – or such a hooha planning it that one's courage fails. There is escape for you & many years & the book you will write one day I am pretty sure.

•

There'd occurred some unexpected and unsettling changes to my life. By early 1979 I'd not been in touch with Jean for a while. I didn't contact her that year before travelling back to Greece. I must have imagined she'd miraculously continue as she had always done. And that on my return to England, after a few months away, she would still be there, a reassuring elder – already a kind of kindly immortal.

It caused me regret not to have seen her, in person, one more time. But how, visiting her on any such occasion ("the ghosts of all the lovely days"), should I have guessed the time of a final goodbye? One never does know.

Hence I came to lament what I perceived as an unfathomable distance between us. In fact I was wrong, for I know the sole farewell to Jean Rhys, the right and proper one as far as I'm concerned, is by means of a book. Something so intimately private, that yet appears public. An irreplaceable paradox. Others may read into it here or there what could not have been said. Let them call it fiction. In words and through them, writers must think how to tell what may have happened, voicing their own forms of truth.

A *change of scene*

The subject was myself, was self, was literature, was writing, was the reader, was experience, was death... but you cannot live without yourself and the purpose of this kind of writing is to beguile you into finding yourself.

— William Saroyan: *Births*, posthumously published, 1983

The time came when I could no longer continue living in that Devon cottage which Jean was never in the end destined to visit. She, Diane and I had often discussed the possibility of her coming to stay there with us for a few days, but nothing definite materialised. Jean once even mentioned that one day, driven by her invaluable chauffeur-helper Mr Greenslade, she had passed by Tillworth, though without knocking on the door. We were probably out, or away, she thought, but how pretty the cottage looked! We took this as a heavy hint that she would indeed like to come and stay sometime, having checked for herself what a quiet and attractive little place it was.

But by the late 1970s the two hundred year old cottage seemed to be collapsing around me, along with my whole rural idyll – if that's what I ever really imagined it to be. A new roof was needed (there was also a colony of bats in the loft), while the entire whole building wanted considerable internal and external repair, not just a cosmetic painting and re-pointing job. I had neither heart nor money to set things to rights. My agent of the time seemed to dislike my work, and even when he did like it, could not sell it. I owed the bank, which had a lien on the house, a large sum, while my job in London as a Writer-in-Residence was for only one year and in any case not well-paid enough to delay the inevitable: I would have to sell up.

You must change your life, the Rilke poem concludes, but it seemed I had no choice in the matter. My seven year relationship with Diane was collapsing too: like the house, it had been crumbling for quite a while. To complicate the issue, I'd met Kate, a young woman with a fiery and wilful temperament that matched her quite striking beauty. She, after leaving her husband and art college in the North of England, wished to share a new life with me. When you are young, impoverished and in love things move faster than usual. Rapidly then the house was sold, debts paid off, books and furniture put into store, and a succession of temporary homes and travels followed. Ambleside, Greece, London, Exeter...

During the six months or so that Kate and I were away in Greece, Jean died in hospital in Exeter. I learned of her death only after our return and was filled with regrets. Our correspondence had inevitably lapsed, due to her increasingly frail health and my own emotional and geographical journeys. Looking up a couple of bland obituaries of her – the world-famous author, much-translated, bestowed with honours, prizes and money, I recalled Jean's rueful comment that it had all come far too late. Not when she was truly struggling and most needed appreciation and encouragement and financial support. But that's the way life always is, and she knew and accepted it, while no less furious at the injustice.

I grieved for her, but the process seemed strangely incomplete. I realise now that in 1979 I was still mourning part of myself that had been lost, something which, following that extended and traumatic return to Greece, could never be regained. There was once a young writer... But Constantinos Lykiardopoulos had been left behind long since, like his distant place of origin... So what's in a name, once again? Returning to this damp, cold island, beset by continuing uncertainties, I was hardly prepared for the struggle ahead. On every level it would be a struggle for survival since during our absence and to our horror, Great Britain had become Little England, opting to follow a nightmare script of shallowness and greed, entitled The Thatcher Era. If the ghost of idealism anywhere remained, it was rarely apparent.

Jean's scrupulousness when it came to writing – her care and fidelity for the art, and the love and determination she brought to it, whatever her personal circumstances – have helped me maintain at least some idealism of my own, an unexpected legacy. Equally unexpected was my last encounter with her. Which is another story.

A *valediction*

That story comes next of course and is, for now, the more or less final one. In May 1985 I was booked to work with an author I knew, John Moat, on W.H.Smith's & The Poetry Society's *Poets in Schools* scheme. Three visits were scheduled, to Braunton School in North Devon, quite near John and Antoinette Moat's home at Hartland. The school was rather far from where I was then living, in a village on the south-eastern edge of Dartmoor. So I'd been invited to stay overnight at the Moats'. That way he and I could start our first day at the school at 9.30 the following morning.

After my arrival at the Mill there was a pleasant and convivial dinner. I went to bed no earlier or later than usual, soberly enough, and enjoyed a good and dreamless sleep. But as sometimes happens after even a short journey, and when one has passed the night in unfamiliar surroundings, I woke with a sudden jolt. To be precise, I found myself quite wide awake, unusually so, and sitting bolt upright, as if given a firm yet abrupt shake out of what felt like a very deep sleep. I had no idea where I was. I was in a strange room whose outlines I scarcely acknowledged. I could remember neither how I came to be there nor what my purpose might be. It seemed very early morning, because diffused light was filtering in past the curtains.

I heard no birdsong, however. I could hear nothing at all. In fact I felt most peculiarly insulated: on one level very alert and receptive. On another and simultaneous level, my own thought processes seemed not to be functioning normally – indeed without any rapidity at all, as if my mind were numb. It was perplexing but in no way unpleasant. I accepted this curious sensation of distanced wakefulness; I dreamed a dream of waking in a strange room while at the same time I knew I was already wide awake. Yet I also understood that my waking, my volition, did not for the moment belong to me. I felt shocked into a weird openness, a condition oddly empty of any logic or emotion. Where or who I was no longer mattered.

This was as I soon discerned a singular or enhanced state of awareness, quite different from those induced by any drugs I'd ever experimented with. I was being somehow gently reproached. We had never said goodbye. I felt the hairs on my neck separate and rise, a sensation that I'd experienced only a few times before in my life. On those rare occasions in the past, that sensation had been unbidden and filled with cold, utter dread. I am a sceptic and an atheist, but one who believes, however reluctantly, in some form of supernatural. The latter area I find increasingly difficult to define.

Now I was sure of nothing. Except that (the time has come to say the unsayable) here had gathered a companionable presence, reminding me of her own long absence. This might be described as a visitation, rather than a vision, for I could not actually *see* anything, although I had a powerful if quite intangible perception of her. She was summoned up, back into a kind of existence. Or else some image very much resembling her had once again drifted into my consciousness. My sense of smell is not especially acute, but I recalled, or gained a sudden impression of, L'Heure Bleue, the Guerlain scent for which she'd always had a predilection. And there was a familiar tone of speech, wordless of course, but like notes of music distantly sounded, that I recognized at once. Nothing more precise, nothing anyway to fear. Something welcome yet disconcerting, fleeting as a smile.

An ending

Oliver Onions, in the *Credo* preceding his masterpiece *The Beckoning Fair One*, writes: "I myself have never been able to understand why the unvarying question should be, 'Have you ever *seen* a ghost?' when, if a ghost cannot exist apart from visibility, his being rests solely on the testimony of one sense, and that in some respects the most fallible one of all. May not his proximity be felt and his nature apprehended in other ways? I have it on excellent authority that such a visitor can in fact be heard breathing in the room, most powerfully smelt, and known for a spirit in travail longing for consolation, all at one and the same time, and yet not be seen by the eye."

The belated thought occurs to me here that it was I myself, in my life then, who needed consolation. Jean had achieved what she was born to do: it had not been easy, it never is. But surely she herself could rest easily? She had always been obsessed by her appearance, constantly remembering, perhaps, the ghost of her own beauty, which I'd admired in the faded old photographs of herself she had shown me. As far as I was concerned, she had achieved and left behind something very substantial. The idea of her that persists with me is as I hope she would have wished it to be: an example of beauty and courage, the twin qualities writing and people should always have and so rarely do.

But she was not finished with me, nor I with her...The author of *The Beckoning Fair One* would have the writer investigate "the varying densities of the ghostliness that is revealed when this surface of life, accepted for everyday purposes as stable, is jarred, and for the time of an experience, does not recover its equilibrium". A mediation is required between the living and the dead. Along with a recovery of balance, a keeping of accounts. We call it memory and sometimes, like Odysseus, but in our individual and separate ways, we must make journeys to the land of shades.

I reached like a somnambulist for the notebook placed by the bedside the night before. I did not remember having placed it there. At home I seldom keep a notebook by my bed, while often reminding myself that I should. But there – then – where I was – *it* was. What was at hand and I wrote or was sent next appeared in one swift draft, in what must only have been a matter of minutes.

The poem possessed a clearly defined form, being in metre and rhyme, with something of a ballad feel. Most poems I write invariably go through many versions and revisions. This did not. It was finished at once. Nothing more needed to be said, and I felt relief rather than sadness. I'd been, apparently, entranced, and now at last the farewell had been said. Better still, the poet she also was might slyly have added, it had been *written*.

Jean Rhys revisited

I drive through that dull place again,
quickly past 'Landboat Bungalows'.
She'd rail at Cheriton Fitzpaine –
no sort of haven, what she chose.

Unhappy simply to be happy, she
hummed sweet paranoia's tune:
Death, she sometimes said to me,
could not come too soon.

Paris is bleakest in the spring,
London always wet and cold,
but worse, far worse than anything,
is being alone and growing old.

Dressed up by the *Sunday Times*,
she played the famous fashion-plate.
Journalists' lies, researchers' crimes
can't rouse her now to flirt with fate.

Nothing further to conceal,
nothing that's not on the page.
What those big blue eyes reveal
seems too disquieting for old age.

A ravaged beauty does remain.
"I never should have settled here...
In the fridge there's some champagne,
shall we drink it now, my dear?"

Our talks were fun. How you adored
your memories, all you had left.
Sex, booze and blues, Ford Madox Ford,
word-magic and much else. Bereft

of sharp-tongued humour you were not,
witch of the village, frail tough friend.
Some – you among them – like it hot:
style, it boils down to, in the end.

Acknowledgements

Thanks are due first and foremost to Diane Leigh, who accompanied me on many visits to Jean Rhys – so freely sharing with me in the 1970s her own life, memories and photographs.

I am very grateful to Francis Wyndham, Jean Rhys's literary executor, for his initial encouragement and permission to quote from Jean's letters and works. When, years later, on completion of this book, I contacted him again, he offered helpful advice and generously and enthusiastically read the MS. All friends of Jean Rhys, and her many readers past and present, owe Francis Wyndham an immeasurable debt. Without him, her rediscovery, continuance and literary triumph might never have happened. Jean Rhys is published in the UK by André Deutsch and Penguin Books.

Various friends, acquaintances, colleagues – all sympathetic readers or writers – have contributed to the making and emergence of this book, in some cases more than they know. Among them: Lindsay Clarke, Alan Dent, Roy Fisher, Peter Graham, Anne Grimes, Suzanne Hodgart, Ted Hughes, Annemarie Macdonald, David Miller M.D., John Moat, Bernard Phillips, George Steiner, Anthony Wood.

Thanks also to those author-editors whose magazines first published extracts, sometimes in slightly different form, from this book: *Artrage* (E.A. Markham); *Books And Company* (Susan Hill); *In Other Words* (Peter Bush); *London Magazine* (Alan Ross); *Palantir* (Jim Burns); *Penniless Press* (Alan Dent).

'A forgotten man' originally appeared as 'Afterword' to *Nightmare Jack & other stories* by John Metcalfe, ed. Richard Dalby (Ash-Tree Press, Canada, 1998). My thanks to Barbara and Christopher Roden of the Ghost Story Society and publishers of Ash-Tree Press.

'Beauty and taboo' first appeared in *A Glass Of New Made Wine*, eds. Glyn Pursglove & Wolfgang Görtschacher (University of Salzburg, 1999).

It was a special pleasure after so many years to meet Jean's daughter, Maryvonne Moerman, and to spend two days with her in the Vaucluse. Her warmth and hospitality were indeed memorable.

Christopher Sinclair-Stevenson was once my publisher and is now my agent: his enthusiasm both for Jean Rhys's writing and my own is particularly appreciated.

Finally, most heartfelt thanks to Maggie Fisher, who since 1990 has offered invaluable suggestions and support, ensuring that at least in process and intention the result would be a labour of love.

Photographs

Reproduced by kind permission of the Estate of Jean Rhys.

Jean Rhys © Pearl Freeman.

Jean Rhys at Landboat Bungalows, Cheriton Fitzpaine, 1970s
© Diane Leigh.

Jean Rhys, late 1960s, and R.C. Dunning, late 1920s
– photographers unknown.

Jean Rhys in Exeter, 1970s © Alexis Lykiard.

Other photographs – Cheriton Fitzpaine, 1998;
Maryvonne Moerman & Alexis Lykiard at Apt, 1999
© Maggie Fisher.

Index of names

Plante, David, 32, 33, 34, 35, 69, 220
Plath, Sylvia, 39
Pound, Ezra, 157, 158
Pritchett, V. S., 180
Putnam, Samuel, 159

Queneau, Raymond, 243
Quennell, Peter, 226

Rabelais, 161, 243
Ramsay, Peggy, 103-104
Reynolds, Michael, 225
Rilke, Rainer Maria, 23, 174, 185, 263
Rimbaud, Arthur, 174
Rolfe, Frederick William, 59
Rolt, L.T.C., 201
Ronell, Ann, 212
Ross, Alan, 88
Rossellini, Roberto, 224
Rotten, Johnny, 71
Ruck, Berta, 200, 208

Sage, Lorna, 69
Saint-Exupéry, Antoine de, 233
Saki, 63
Sansom, William, 34
Saroyan, William, 226, 263
Sartre, Jean-Paul, 259
Saunders, Max, 81, 132, 207
Sayers, Dorothy L., 213
Scott, Evelyn, 125, 213, 214
Scott, Ronnie, 196
Seabrook, William B., 105, 160-163
Seferis, George, 39
Shakespeare, William, 82
Shrimpton, Jean, 230
Simenon, Georges, 26, 115
Siodmak, Curt, 99
Smart, Elizabeth, 88
Smith, John, 237
Smith, Stevie, 226
Southern, Terry, 178, 179
Spender, Stephen, 39
Spurling, Hilary, 69
Staley, Thomas, 67-68, 181

Stead, Christina, 198
Stein, Gertrude, 225
Stevens, Wallace, 174
Stevenson, Robert Louis, 71
Styron, William, 32
Sullivan, Jack, 201
Swinburne, Algernon, 164
Symons, Arthur, 221

Thompson, Jim, 227
Tilden-Smith, Leslie (2nd husband of J.
    R.), 214
Times Literary Supplement, 69
Tomalin, Claire, 69
Tourneur, Jacques, 99
Transatlantic Review, 132, 217-218
Traven, B., 18
Treglown, Jeremy, 180
Trevor, William, 53-54, 102-103, 199
Trilling, Diana, 102

Ungar, 68
Updike, John, 178, 179

Vaz Dias, Selma, 29, 103, 147

Walcott, Derek, 39, 184, 248
Wallace Inez, 99
Waller, Thomas 'Fats', 243
Walpole, Hugh, 200, 213
Warlock, Peter [see also Heseltine,
    Philip], 109, 251
Webster, John, 64
Wells, H. G., 50, 192
West, Rebecca, 82
Wheatley, Dennis, 213
Whistler, Peggy [see also Evans,
    Margiad], 123
White, Antonia, 226
Wilber, Bob, 114
Williams, Ella Gwendoline Rees
    (baptismal names of J. R.), 14
Williams, Martin, 116
Williams, William Carlos, 9, 141, 213,
    256

Index of titles